Moya Aliya Malamusi

Za Using'anga Ndi Ufiti – About Healing Practice and Witchcraft

Studien zur Ethnopsychologie und Ethnopsychoanalyse

herausgegeben von

Werner Egli, Gerhard Kubik, Maya Nadig,
Johannes Reichmayr und Vera Saller

Band 9

LIT

Moya Aliya Malamusi

Za Using'anga Ndi Ufiti – About Healing Practice and Witchcraft

A Culture & Personality Study of Traditional Healers in Southern Malawi

LIT

Cover photo:
Tortoise shell as a magic "aeroplane" operated by Mr. Ncherewatha. At Chipula village, T.A. Njolomole, Ntcheu District, October 6, 1995. Photo no. 95/2/20, by Moya Malamusi.

Bibliographic information published by the Deutsche Nationalbibliothek
The Deutsche Nationalbibliothek lists this publication in the Deutsche Nationalbibliografie; detailed bibliographic data are available on the Internet at http://dnb.d-nb.de.

ISBN 978-3-643-90764-6

A catalogue record for this book is available from the British Library

Klosbachstr. 107
CH-8032 Zürich
Tel. +41 (0) 44-251 75 05 Fax +41 (0) 44-251 75 06
E-Mail: zuerich@lit-verlag.ch http://www.lit-verlag.ch

Distribution:

In the UK: Global Book Marketing, e-mail: mo@centralbooks.com
In North America: International Specialized Book Services, e-mail: orders@isbs.com
In Germany: LIT Verlag Fresnostr. 2, D-48159 Münster
Tel. +49 (0) 2 51-620 32 22, Fax +49 (0) 2 51-922 60 99, e-mail: vertrieb@lit-verlag.de

In Austria: Medienlogistik Pichler-ÖBZ, e-mail: mlo@medien-logistik.at
e-books are available at www.litwebshop.de

Contents

Preface

There is a time in everybody's life when one gets hurt deeply in one's mind by unfortunate events. Such experiences can motivate a person to begin a long search in order to find out the causes of the misfortune. For example, a relative whom you love very much dies without an apparent cause. Such a traumatic experience will linger on in your heart and create a need for you to know exactly what is behind the death of the beloved person.

This is what happened to me when my young brother to whom I was deeply attached, died in January 1982. He died without any apparent cause. It was at that time that I remained with persistent thoughts and the determination to find out what had really killed this young boy aged sixteen years. In my pursuit of the causes I heard about a *sing'anga*, a medical practitioner whose name was Milimo and who was a specialist in helping people to discover what was behind many similar causes of death that had occurred in my home area, Chileka, near Blantyre in southern Malawi.

For a long time I was continuing the investigation about the death of my brother, but I did not find any answer. And yet those thoughts did not go away from my mind, they were continuing and they are still with me. This is not only because of my sadness about the loss, but also because of <u>fear</u> that otherwise what happened to him might also happen to me some time in the future.

If one stays with these kinds of thoughts for a long time, one begins to develop a desire to learn something about the work of those who are concerned with the same sort of questions: the *asing'anga*, The basic issue for me was to find an answer about the death of my brother, but also to find a way to protect myself from similar hazards, just in case there were wizards or witches *(amfiti)* who were planning some kind of insolence *(chipongwe)* against me.

It was at that time that I began to meet with *asing'anga* quite regularly, here and there, to discover something about their work and learn what exactly they were doing. It was because of many conversations I have had with them over the years that I have learned much about their work, and also about the deeds of the *amfiti,* the wizards and witches, and what was in <u>their</u> minds. However, most of what I know about witchcraft (*ufiti*) comes from the side of the *asing'anga*, because it is very difficult for a researcher to know directly about witchcraft, if you are not a wizard yourself. But there are *asing'anga* in southern Malawi who are well informed about witchcraft, because they are in a permanent power struggle with the *amfiti.* Each contest ends with one of them winning; and next time the competition starts all over again. Indeed, certain *asing'anga* were capable of explaining to me in great detail what the wizards and witches do.

In 1989 my sister Lidiya Malamusi and I founded a small research centre in my home village, Singano/ Chileka in Blantyre District. We called it Oral Literature Research Programme, because of the emphasis on the spoken word, the documentation of storytelling, oral traditions, and musical texts. Gradually we began to build up a library, installed an office and constructed a small museum of ethnographic objects. My centre is an independent institution. It is not connected with government or any other organization, but it depends on internationally available research grants and private sponsorship.

The centre is located only 1½ km from the International Airport Chileka (Blantyre) which gives it a strategic position. Its location is suitable as a base for anthropological research trips to any area in Malawi and neighboring countries of south-east Africa, particularly Mozambique, Zimbabwe and Zambia. In the vicinity of the centre, across Likhubula river there are the majestic Michiru mountains, about 1700 m high, with their beautiful scenery.

When we founded the centre, my sister and I were no longer novices to cultural anthropology. In fact, we had both participated in two research projects directed by Gerhard Kubik, University of Vienna: in 1983-84 in Malawi (FWF project no. 4977), and in 1987 in Malawi and Zambia (FWF project no. P 6316), financed by the Fonds zur Förderung der Wissenschaftlichen Forschung, Vienna. The results of these projects have been written up in various publications, among others in our joint booklet: G. Kubik (in cooperation with M.A. Malamusi): *Nyau – Maskenbünde im südlichen Malawi,* Vienna: Austrian Academy of Sciences, 1987.

Then it happened that in the same year when our Oral Literature Research Programme was founded, my sister Lidiya Malamusi also died. Ever since then I have continued to work on my own from the base in Chileka. Since 1989 I have undertaken many field research trips, virtually covering the southern region of Malawi, village by village. This has resulted in a collection of tape recordings of nearly 2.500 items of oral narratives, interviews, song texts, and a large photographic coverage. For my field-work I have used two DAT recorders and one reel-to-reel tape recorder, as well as still cameras and occasionally a video camera. I have had modest transportation from my centre into the field.

All recorded materials have been preserved, and there is comprehensive documentation. My field-notes in Chichewa, my language, are type-written and cover several bound volumes, more than a thousand pages. Security copies of my recordings have been made and stored in various places, notably at the archives of the Institut für Ethnologie und Afrika-Studien, University of Mainz. The collection of ethnographica in my museum contains objects I acquired on various field trips to rural areas, mainly in southern and central Malawi. They give visitors information about the life styles and local technology used by people in our areas. My museum is open to external and local visitors, including schools. Some objects from my museum are currently on exhibit at the Vitra Design Museum, Weil am Rhein, Germany.

I have been able to publish some of the results of my fieldwork since 1989 in various journals. Three volumes of text transcriptions of *nthano* (folk tales) by my sister, the late Lidiya Malamusi in cooperation with Gerhard Kubik, still await publication, and so do several other manuscripts I have completed. My center has cooperated with several international institutions. In 1990, Dr Andrew Tracey, International Library of African Music, Rhodes University, Grahamstown, South Africa, was a visiting scholar. Dr. Mitchel Strumpf, Department of Fine and Performing Arts, University of Malawi, Zomba, has been a frequent visitor. With sponsorship by the cultural-aid-programme of the Ministry of External Affairs, Bonn (Germany) I was able between 1994 and 1996 to carry out substantial recording work in the region. I have also cooperated with the I.U.A.E.S. Commission for Urgent Anthropological Research (Head: Dr. Anna von Hohenwart), Vienna.

In 1993 I was awarded an Andrew W. Mellon Research Fellowship to work at the Metropolitan Museum of Art, New York, and in 1997 I worked with a Rockefeller Research Fellowship at the Center for Back Music Research (Director: Dr Samuel. A. Floyd) Columbia College, Chicago. This has greatly enhanced my field research techniques.

Against this background I have been carrying out the work on *using'anga* and *ufiti* (healing practice and witchcraft) which is the subject of this book. There are many people who have helped me and supported me in this endeavour; I can hardly mention all of them, but let me give the names of some to whom I am particularly indebted:

Donald Kachamba, musician and composer who was with me on most of the research trips;

Akaning'a Gerhard Kubik for his tireless support and encouragement;

Ananjeza Maliya Moya, my wife to whom I am most indebted;

My children, Monika Malamusi and Yohana Malamusi for various forms of help;

My mother Anasoko;

Wolfgang Bender, University of Mainz;

Samuel A. Floyd, CBMR, Columbia College, Chicago;

David Evans, University of Memphis,

Sigrid Paul, University of Salzburg;

Manfred Kremser, University of Vienna;

Watisoni Mtekesa, research assistant in my centre

And Saimoni Kanthambi, mechanic, who always repaired my car after the breakdowns on each fieldtrip!

My work of recording and conversing with *asing'anga* really gained momentum in 1992 during research on various subjects which I was carrying out in the southern part of Malawi. My interest in the medical practitioners was also stimulated when I saw that they were so many. Some were, of course, fake *asing'anga,* but others were taking their profession seriously. I developed a comparative interest in both, those who were trying to tell the truth, and those who were deliberately deceiving their clients. In this way I experienced a wide spectrum of activities during my research (*mukufufuza kwanga*). Some of the results, this is what the present book is all about.

The content of this book is composed of my original research results. All the interviews were conducted by me on the spot; all the photography is mine. In the audio-recordings I myself and Donald Kachamba were sharing the technical task. It is clear, however, that our endeavours would have been futile, had we failed to obtain cooperation from those concerned: the *asing'anga* and their patients.

They are all named in a list, in the central section of this book. Herewith, I would like to express my sincere gratitude to them and acknowledge the good reception we were given.

Moya A. Malamusi — Vienna, September 15, 1999

Fifteen years have past since this book was written for my master's degree. In 2004 I earned a Ph.D. at the University of Vienna, in cultural anthropology with a dissertation on another important subject of culture studies in south-east Africa: the *nyau* masked secret associations.

For historical reasons I have not significantly changed the text of the present work on traditional healers, except a few editorial corrections. Cultures and their personalities disappear fast. Some of the *asing'anga*, so Simon Banda whose personality and work I studied in the 1990s have passed away, some others have stopped their practice. This book therefore is a testimony to their work, and the research I was carrying out in the field during the 1990s could, of course, never be repeated exactly in the same way, not even with the same personnel. In 2001 we also lost my relative and research companion Donald Kachamba, and several relatives, friends and colleagues listed among those who supported my endeavor have died: my mother Anasoko, Dr. Anna von Hohenwart, Professor Dr. Sigrid Paul, and Professor Manfred Kremser.

This work therefore is also a form of commemoration for them and for the many discussions we had about the subject of healing and psychotherapy. Bibliographical references to some of their work have been included, as well as selected publications since 1999, with reference to south-east and central Africa.

Moya A. Malamusi — Vienna, 18 March, 2014

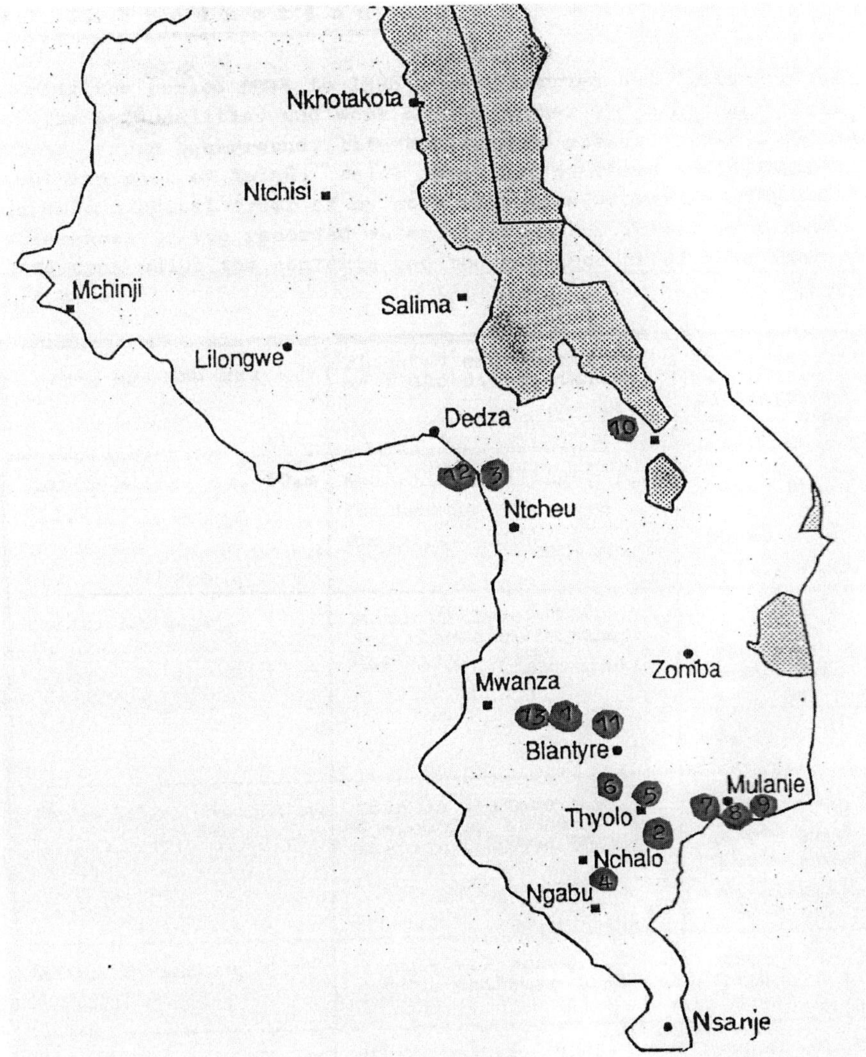

Fig. 1

MAP of southern and central Malawi with the approximate residential places of the thirteen *asing'anga* whose work I have studied

I. Introduction

During the period 1993 to 1996 I carried out field studies of the personalities and work of altogether thirteen *asing'anga*, each with their own background, life history and specialization, in the southern part of Malawi. Below is a list of these individuals in chronological order of my work with them, together with references to the recorded material. This has formed my data-base upon which the contents and the conclusions of this book are based.

Name, age and sex	Place(s) and year(s) of field documentation	Field material (recordings and photographs), tape nos.
Simon Banda, ca. 50, m. (1)	Khumbilina village, T.A. Kunthembwe, Blantyre District, 1993	tape No. 93/13 photo Nos. 93/5,8,6,5,4,15
Jonasi Masangwi, ca. 50, m. (2)	Nzuna village, T.A. Ntchilamwela, Thyolo District, 1994	tape No. 94/5 photo Nos. 94/4/3,30,29,1,26,27, 31, 94/11/ 35,33,31
Paulo Luka, ca,30, m. (3)	Chipula village, T.A. Njolomole, Ntcheu District, 1994/95	tape Nos. 94/3, 95/4 photo Nos. 95/2/8, 12,20,21,23,24,28,26,27,29
Akina Thomas ca. 52, f. (4)	Tizola village, T.A. Rundu, Chikwawa District, 1995	tape Nos. 95/1 photo Nos. 95/2/ 8,7
Milimo Phiri, ca.55, m. (5)	Mdala villge,T.A.Ntchilamwela Thyolo District, 1995	tape No. 95/2, photo Nos. 95/2/12,13,14,15,16,17
Sumbuleta Gustro, ca. 85, m. (6)	Chibwana village, T.A. Nchilamwela, Thyolo District, 1995	tape No. 95/5 photo Nos. 95/3, 7, 3, 5, 2, 8,
Headman Ngolowela, ca.65, m. (7)	Ngolowela village, T.A. Chikumbu, Mulanje District, 1995	tape No. 95/3 photo Nos. 95/3/34,35
S, D. Maloya, ca. 63, m. (8)	Ngolowela village, T.A. Chikumbu, Mulanje District, 1995	tape No. 95/6 photo No. 95/3/ 12,13,14, 17,16,15
Kodyoni Lichapa, ca.67, m. (9)	Chambo village, T.A. Chikumbu, Mulanje District, 1995	tape No. 95/1 photo Nos. 95/3/ 18,19,20,21,22,23,30,31,33
Yesu Samson, ca. 54,m. (10)	Nkungwi village, T.A. Nankumba, Mangochi District, 1995	tape No. 95/2 photo Nos. 95/ ----
B. S. Nyalugwe, ca. 65, m. (11)	Chinkango village, T.A. Kuntaja, Blantyre District, 1995	tape No. 95/3 photo Nos. 95/ ---
Labison Saizi, ca. 45, m. (12)	Kanjonjo village, T.A. Mtengowambalame, Mozambique	tape No. 95/24 photo Nos. 95/--
Eliya, ca. 56, m. (13)	Ngoleka village, T.A. Kunthembwe, Blantyre District,1996	tape No. 96/3 photo Nos. 96/1/ 15,16,17,18,19,20,27,28,29,30,31

In a MAP (fig. 1) preceding this chapter I have marked with numbers from 1 to 13 the approximate locations in Malawi from where those medical practitioners listed were or have been operating. Some are, unfortunately, no longer alive; some others have moved. The list and the map reflect the situation I encountered at the time of my field-work in the mid-1990s.

Due to limitations in the size of the present book (not exceeding 200 pages) I will not be able to present the complete database about all the thirteen individuals I studied in the field. Instead I will discuss (in the book's central section, Chapter II) the personalities and the work of only four of the *asing'anga* I worked with, in extenso, using audio recordings, photographs and my field-notes. The purpose is to give the reader an intimate look at the minds and work practice of at least some of these traditional healers, their individual characters and interests which are highly variable from person to person. In the extensive interviews I have conducted with them and which I have transcribed from the tapes in the original language, mostly Chichewa, with my annotated translations into English, the traditional healers reveal something direct and intimate about their conceptual world. Together with reports about my own field observations as a participant observer, about their actions, the reader will be able to form a picture, case by case, person by person, about these individuals and their work.

To transmit something directly about their lives and their interaction with other people, notably their clients, and the invisible wizards and witches, is the purpose of this book. My way of presentation is also meant to demonstrate my ethnographic field techniques: the way I have organized my travels, the manner I have interacted with the people during my fieldwork, the channels of communication I have used, the way I conducted the interviews or conversations; how I reacted to unexpected events, modifying my programme according to the circumstances, and how I have used my equipment, tape recorders, still cameras and note-book. All my notes were originally written in my own language: Chichewa, including the written documentation of the recordings.

My book should therefore also be useful for students who want to learn some good ways of doing field-work in Africa. However, although I will only discuss at length the material relating to four *asing'anga* in this book, my conclusions have been drawn from the bulk of the material, i.e. from conversations and observations relating to all the thirteen individuals listed above who form my sample. In addition, for the purpose of wide-ranging comparisons, I was able to expand my knowledge between the years 1996 to 1999 by collecting archival materials from little known sources in Malawi, such as the police archives, newspaper archives and little known local publications. Some of this material will be discussed in Chapter III of this book.

I did not only conduct interviews with the various *asing'anga,* but also with their patients and I recorded verbal interactions between the two during sessions. In this way I anticipated to get a more complete picture, alternating between different viewpoints. For example, during my long conversation with the *sing'anga* Paulo Luka (no. 3 in the list), I also had the opportunity of talking to the victims of witchcraft and their relatives, such as the boy João from Mozambique who had been revived, i.e. brought back from death according to local testimonies. I also talked to his mother, Elite. It was important for me in my research to discover psychological realities. Like in the famous film "Rashomon" 1950 by Japanese film-maker Akira Kurosawa, the interactors in the plot between *sing'anga*, patients and wizards/witches have conflicting reports to give; they relate the same stories each from their own viewpoints, their own memories and experiences.

Above all I am trying to show in this book what the various individuals themselves think and how they express their ideas in their own language. For this reason, a major part of this book is transcriptions of the interviews I conducted in the field, giving us a glimpse of how the various highly individualistic *asing'anga* interact with their patients and how they formulate and theorize about their medical practice.

Occasionally, I will relate what I think myself, sometimes expressing criticism, or what I thought under the impact of our involvement at moments during my fieldwork. In no way, however, is this study designed to generalize about medical practice as such by the *asing'anga* in Malawi. The matter is too complex. I prefer the reader to make acquaintance with specific individuals and specific field situations, rather than mere abstractions.

There are certain terms, however, which will come up throughout this book. Although I will always add descriptive translations as a reminder, it will be beneficial if readers familiarize themselves with some of them before reading on. These terms are in Chichewa, as the language is called in Malawi, respectively Cinyanja as it is called in eastern Zambia. It is a Bantu language of Zone N/ Group 30 in Malcolm Guthrie's (1948) classification, and widely spoken in central and southern Malawi, eastern Zambia and central Mozambique. Migrant workers have also carried the language to Zimbabwe, notably to Harare and to the South African mines. The following chart enumerates some of the terms we will encounter throughout this book, followed by an approximate translation into English. These English translations are only to be regarded as tags.

Terminology:

using'anga	=	medical practice, healing practice
sing'anga (p1. *asing'anga*)	=	medical practitioner (s)
ufiti	=	witchcraft, sorcery
mfiti (pl. *amfiti*)	=	wizard or witch
matsenga	=	magic
mankhwala	=	medicines
nsupa (sing. and p1.)	=	phials (s)
nyanga (sing. and p1.)	=	"horns" of witchcraft
nzimu (p. *mizimu*)	=	spirits(s)
chizimba	=	catalyst, code, processor etc. (something that is indispensable to make the magic work)
maula	=	divination, "oracle"
kuombeza ula	=	to cast the lot, to divine

Why do people go to see a *sing'anga*?

There are many reasons why people consult a *sing'anga*, but the common theme is that they expect some kind of treatment and medicines (*mankhwala*). These may be of many different kinds, according to the problems the patients bring along. One motif, however, that pushes people to go and see a *sing'anga*, is the assumption that something is behind their ailments or the death of a relative. And they expect a *sing'anga* to discover and reveal to them who the wizard or witch is, and with which medicines one can be protected.

What occurs to most people is that whenever a funeral has taken place, and there are suspicions about the cause of the death – especially if it is a young person who suddenly died – they will not be content with the diagnosis obtained in hospital reports. They will have doubts and desire to know exactly what killed that person, particulary if the cause of death has not been ascertained. The result is something like a dispute between all the people in this kind of environment and the feeling "that we have not seen this funeral proceed well, because this person died without a clear cause." In that manner, if the dispute goes on for a long time, they usually arrive at a theory that such and such a person might have killed the deceased. At that point, however, there may be considerable disagreement, until the people begin to say "it is better that we go to a *sing'anga*" for verification. If everybody agrees to the idea to go and consult a *sing'anga*, it may happen that crowds of people set out for a journey there. The *sing'anga* Jonasi Masangwi (no.2 in the list) reported to me that from time to time groups of people were coming to him from their clans or extended families, expecting him to reveal to them what had happened in connection with the death of one of their relatives. Because of that, Jonas Masangwi already knew beforehand that when a group of people arrived, he would have to discover the one who was the *mfiti*. Thereafter he would go to his or her house and take away their *nyanga* (horns) which they had used for their witchcraft.

In Malawi there are many kinds of professional healers who treat people who are ill, including those who complain that they were bewitched (*kulodzedwa*) by wizards or witches (*amfiti*). In Chichewa, the language spoken across Malawi, in eastern Zambia and central Mozambique – also often called Chinyanja (= language of the lake, i.e. Lake Malawi) – local medical practitioners are known as *asing'anga*[1] (plural term). The singular is *sing'anga*. In Ciyao, an important language of southeastern Malawi and northern Mozambique, such a person is called *nganga* (cf. Sanderson 1954: 202). The term is sometimes also used in Chichewa/Chinyanja and pronounced *ng'anga.* Medical knowledge and the medical activities of a *sing'anga* are referred to as *using'anga* which can be rendered in English as : medical practice. A *sing'anga* can be a man or a woman. Often in opposition to the *sing'anga* is the *mfiti* (wizard or witch), plural: *amfiti.* A *mfiti* harms and kills the victim through the act of *kulodza* (to bewitch). The practice of a *mfiti* is summarized as *ufiti* (witchcraft, sorcery).

---

1 Pronunciation: *asiŋanga*. The phonetic letter [ŋ] as in English "to sing" is rendered /ng'/ in standard Chichewa orthography.

Different categories of *asing'anga*

Among those professionals who carry out medical practice in the rural communities of southern Malawi there are many different specializations. Prolonged conversations with *asing'anga* in the field and my own observations of their medical practice has led me to a preliminary classification of the *asing'anga* according to how they help people, what medicines they use, whether they practise divination or not, and what their relationship is with local communities, e.g. whether they are famous, respected etc. What follows first is a kind of folk classification elicited from many conversations.

In public perception there are several types of *asing'anga:*

1. Those *asing'anga* who help people with herbal medicines within their own home communities. These medical practitioners are not known by many people, because they only operate in their home villages and nearby. They are considered to be very knowledgeable in medicines that come from leaves, bark and roots of trees and other plants. People with physical ailments such as a wound, or stomach problems or diarrhea – without any witchcraft behind – often get cured very quickly.

2. The second type of *asing'anga* is those who sell medicines in the market or other public places. They, however, buy all those herbal medicines from *asing'anga* in the villages, i.e. from the experts in small-scale communities who would not want to leave their homes and be exposed to the wider public. This type of *asing'anga* assumes an intermediary role in the society.

3. There is a third type of *asing'anga* who learn their trade from a famous *sing'anga* in the area, someone who is well known for his or her knowledge of herbal medicines, and of *matsenga* (which can be roughly translated as "magic"). They learn from the famous person and afterwards pay for the apprenticeship. When they know something about *using'anga* they begin their own practice. But their medical practice does not reach out very far.

4. There is then the famous type of *asing'anga* who combine enormous knowledge in several fields: they know about medical plants; they also know *matsenga*, magic that works automatically, and finally they also know the tricks of *amfiti* (wizards and witches). Those powerful *asing'anga* are able to go to war with the *amfiti* and to defeat them. They are very much feared by the wizards and the witches, and people flock to them in order to obtain advice, because they also perform divination (*maula* in Chichewa) in order to find out what is behind their clients' troubles.

5. A fifth group of *asing'anga* is called *asing'anga amizimu* which means "the medical practitioners of the spirits". Nowadays, in southern Malawi, they have increased very much. They carry out their spiritual work with the bible in their hands, hoping that thebible would help them to see the background of the problems of their patients. This is one way by which many *asing'anga* nowadays persuade people to consult them in thebelief that the basis of their work is their ability to get in touch with things of the spirits.

6. But there is another group of *asing'anga* who work with spirits. It is those that are called *asing'anga amambo* which means "the medical practitioners of the *amambo* spir-

its". They communicate with spirits which were known by the grandparents and great-grandparents. Their work is different from that of the other *asing'anga.* They obtain their messages from the spirits' words and songs which an ordinary person cannot hear.

This is only an outline of the various types of *asing'anga* found in southern Malawi and adjacent areas. It is clear that the categories overlap, and that an individual *sing'anga* can belong to more than one category. Although at a later stage of my work I opted to reduce the six categories to only three major ones (see the revised categorization presented at the end of this book) I would not want here to "improve" on folk taxonomies.

When I realized and understood that there were several, quite distinctive types, I developed an enormous interest to study their individual personalities comparatively, see them at their homes and conduct long conversations most of which I have recorded on tape (see the third column in the list further above). I became interested not only in their work but their personal histories, as well. I first tried to find out what type of *sing'anga* he or she was, according to popular theory, and thereby I gradually came to know from personal observation not only the different types, but also the specific aims of the work of each.

What follows is my own ideas about how the *asing'anga* differ in their personalities, their work and their concepts.

(a) <u>Experts in herbal medicines</u> (group 1, but also 3 and 4)

Perhaps the most frequently encountered small-scale *asing'anga* in the villages are those who obtained their knowledge from older members of the profession, and then begin to practice within their communities. When they become professional healers at the end of their training period, they almost exclusively administer herbal medicines to patients. These medicines are referred to as *mankhwala amitengo* (medicines from trees) or *mankhwala adzitsamba* (medicines from leaves), since they are from roots, bark or leaves of various plants which contain chemical substances of pharmaceutical value. However, quite often this type of *using'anga* is of short duration. Unless they have gathered superior knowledge from their teachers, such herbalists practice for a short time, giving people medicines; but because of a lack of demand, they soon close their practices. Somehow the variety of medical expertise they are able to offer gets "exhausted", dries up. People often see them once and never come again.

However, there are also some more specific reasons why this kind of *using'anga* may come to an end very quickly. At the end of his training period, this type of *sing'anga* is given special medical preparation by his teacher, usually by rubbing substances into scarifications made in his skin (*kuwachekela*) accompanied by powerful verbal instructions (*malangizo okhwima*). The apprentice is subjected to a code of conduct; he is warned about what he should do, how he should behave as a medical practitioner, and what he should never do. This kind of instruction with warnings about certain actions under the threat of punishment is called *chilango.* The associated verb is *kulanga.* For example, the teacher can tell his apprentice to abstain from any extramarital sexual relationships. Literally he is told that he should not sleep with a "woman of the bush" but only choose his wife (*asakagone ndi nkazi wina wapathengo kupatula akazi wawo okha basi*); if he offends against it, his *using'anga* would not go well. *Nkazi wa pathengo* (a woman of the bush) is a common reference to a man's extramarital relationship, a concubine, besides the wife to whom he is married.

Many times it happens to this kind of *asing'anga* that they start their work well, after completing their apprenticeship, but soon their practice deteriorates, because they begin to do precisely what their teacher forbade them to do. In my home area there are many *asing'anga* who learned about herbal medicines from a single elderly man, Bwanali, who at one time operated at Lisungwi, a place near Blantyre on the road to Ntcheu (see map). Bwanali gave his apprentices (*ophunzira aBwanali*) serious instructions. Most of those disciples did not continue for a long time. As soon as they committed a mistake, their practice was spoilt.

It also happens that one of those disciples eventually gets a lot of money from his work, and at the sight of this income, he begins to overrate his power, believing that he has become more powerful than his teacher. In such a case his *using'anga* is finished within a short time, and there is no way that he would ever start it again, and become famous.

What I have explained concerns one type of *using'anga.* It is acquired by processes of practical apprenticeship, but its practice is not durable (*ndi wosalimba aï*).

(b) Middlemen and traders in herbal medicines (group 2)

The second type of *using'anga* involves those who can be considered middlemen and traders. They try to make money out of customers in big markets such as found in the city of Blantyre, or in Lunzu (not far from Chileka). In these places you often find a small house, even a shack with the *sing'anga*'s name written on top; for example in Lunzu market there is a Dr.Seven Days!

This serves as a notice to the public, that customers can find herbal medicines here. Very often, however, those *asing'anga* are merely middlemen or traders, who do not know much about medicines; but what is really behind it is that they buy small roots (*mitsitsi*) from some other people who really are *asing'anga*. They try to squeeze out as much information they can get from those experts who know those roots and leaves (*zitsamba*) and learn about their medical applications. Then they sell those medicines to people who want help. They learn all the tricks of the trade, even cheating and like to tell their customers frightening stories. One type of medicines on their panel is aphrodisiacs (*mankhwala achisomo*), so that someone should be attracted sexually. For example, a woman asks for medicines so that a certain man should love her, so she is given an anointment to rub in (*mankhwala wodzola*) or she is subjected to scarifications (*kumutemela*). One can also obtain medicines for the treatment of syphilis (*chindoko*) and gonorrhea (*chinzonono*) and various other diseases. It is in this way that those traders try to demonstrate that they are herbalists, but in the opinion of others they are "fake doctors" (*asing'anga abodza*), though some customers are grateful to them, if they help them in one or another way. But it is the characteristic of this type of *asing'anga* that they buy both medicines and information about diseases from somewhere, and that they try to compensate for their lack of credibility by emphasizing that they are experts (*akatswiri*) in those medicines.

(c) Asing'anga who communicate with spirits (group 5 and 6, but also many in group 4)

Perhaps by far largest and most spectacular category of *asing'anga* is those who communicate with spirits, some of them practising divination, and all of them claiming that their knowledge comes from parents or grandparents who have died some time ago. This kind of *using'anga* (medical practice) is age-old and has been handed down from parents and grandparents. It is knowledge that is thought to come through dreams (*umabwera chifukwa cha maloto*).

From time to time it happens in the village that a certain person experiences persistent dreams. Perhaps at that time this person has fallen ill with a disease that does not respond to any sort of conventional treatment. Then it can happen that the spirits of relatives who have died long ago appear to him in a dream and say: "You! The disease you are suffering from can be treated with such and such plants. Go, find them and thereafter do such and such to make those medicines work." During such dreams the sick person acts as if he had been seized by spirits (*ngati wagwidwa azimu*). In some cases he or she speaks as if in a delirium (*amabwebweta*); in the middle of the delirious speech the person talks various things about the medicines he or she was shown by the spirits in the dream (*walotetsedwa*). This confirms his or her relatives' conviction that the disease was also originally caused by the *azimu* and that it all has some meaning. If everything goes well, and the person is able to get a cure from the medicines revealed in the dreams, he or she might begin to learn about many other different kinds of medicines. Eventually he begins to help others who are ill, particularly if the spirits who began to send him dreams in the first place, appear again and reveal to him more knowledge about medicines and also whether more troubles will come in the future. This is the type of *asing'anga* who are knowledgeable about medicines, but they do not practice things like divination (*koma osachita za maula*).

Within this group of *asing'anga* characterized by dream revelation there are some who are regularly possessed by spirits (*omwe amagwidwa ndi mizimu*) and in such states they carry out medical practice. Such individuals are referred to as *asing'anga amambo. Amambo* are animal spirits (see also Malamusi 1992:87-88). The term *asing'anga amambo* is used to indicate (*kusonyeza*), that those medical practitioners, when they want to find out the cause of an ailment of a patient, would retreat to their rooms, start to sing songs until all of a sudden they would utter sounds like wild animals from the bush (*amachita kukhuluma ndi mau achinyama chakuthengo*, such as a lion or leopard. In the middle of the spirit possession they then change their mode of expression and begin to reveal in human language what sort of trouble the patient has.

I first witnessed a person being seized by the *amambo* as a child in my home village, Singano near Chileka, Blantyre. My father and my mother had an argument, and it happened that my father beat her. My mother then took us and left our house to spend the night with a remote relative, the mother of Anyerere who is the wife of the leader of the secret *nyau* (masked) society in our village. When we arrived there, she did not tell our host the reason why we had come. She only asked for a place to sleep. The mother of Anyerere gave us a place to sleep. But in the middle of the night I woke up and heard her produce strange animal noises, what we call *kukhuluma*. Animal spirits had seized her, because she wanted to find out the real reason why we had come to stay with her. I heard her husband come and speak to her words such as "*igone pansi mizimu*!" (let the spirits get a rest!) trying to appease them. The next day, when it was all over, the mother of

Anyerere asked my mother: "why didn't you tell us the truth about the reasons for your arrival here. The animal spirits had to come and tell me! (*Amambo anabwera anandiuza*)". That woman was a small *sing'anga* in our village, and she was keeping a shrine, a little house for the *amambo (kanyumba kakang'ono kaamambo)* behind their residence.

The *asing'anga amambo* are not found with all ethnic groups of Malawi, but especially in Chisena, Chimang'anja and Chinyungwe speaking areas of the Lower Shire river. People are very afraid of this type of *mizimu* in the areas concerned. For this reason they feel compelled to do something for them any time of the year. For example, they can do an offering (*nsembe*). In order to prepare it, they would produce some cooked food (*amaphika zophikaphika*). There may be a small shrine about which the owner says that it belongs to the *mizimu*. Frequently he would kneel down there and speak to the spirits, explaining some of his troubles. If the person gets possessed, he can transform into some other kind of being, such as a lion or leopard (*amatha kusanduka kanthu kena monga nkango kapena kambuku*).

Since these small sheds, sometimes not higher than 70-80 cm are explicitly referred to as *kanyumba kaamambo* (little house of the *amambo* spirits), the question is raised what the *amambo* really are. Local perception is that these are animal spirits and <u>yet</u> they are the spirits of people (*mizimu ya dzirombo koma imakhala yawaanthu*); they only <u>resemble</u> animals according to the manner in which the person who gets possessed by them produces animal sounds (*dzirombo nkungofanizira malingana ndi munthu wogwa azimuwo akukhulumira*). The person can speak with the voice (*akukhuluma*) of a lion (*nkango*), leopard (*kambuku*) or baboon (*nyani*) and the like.

My impression is that the *amambo* are perhaps spirits of people who had a lot of witchcraft power during their life-time. It is known that *amfiti* can transform into an animal. But this is my tentative interpretation. I do not know whether it is correct, or whether there might be something else behind, historically. It is difficult to reconstruct the matter, because those ideas come from our ancestors in the remote past. A clue to further thoughts might also be that the *amambo* spirits constitute a phenomenon that is concentrated in the lower Shire river area, into the Zambezi valley in Mozambique whose histories are connected (cf. Chafulumira 1948; Mandala 1978; Phiri 1979; Malamusi 1992). The *amambo* can also bewitch a person (*angathe kulodza*) and people in those ethnic groups are afraid that they would do harm to them (*amaona kuti ingawachitire zoipa*).

Using'anga wa mizimu, ie. medical practice with the help of spirit possession exists in many different types, and *using'anga wa amambo*, i.e. that of *amambo* spirits is only one of them. For example, *mazooka* is another type of spirits a person can get possessed with. It is found especially among the Akhokola and Alomwe in southern Malawi; among the Asena the corresponding term is *mabzoka*. In 1987 my sister, the late Lidiya Malamusi, Gerhard Kubik and Donald Kachamba made a film of *mazooka* among Chimarenje-speaking refugees from Mozambique at Muloza Refugee Camp in Mulanje District, Malawi. In the course of the performance which was audio-recorded, several persons got possessed by the dissatisfied *mazooka* spirits. The ceremony with drum, had the purpose of appeasing them. The ceremony with drums had the purpose of appeasing them. (Cf. Research film no. 69, *Mazooka ndi Using'anga*, by Lidiya Malamusi /G. Kubik, July 3-4, 1987, copied to BETACAM-SP, stored at the Museum für Völkerkunde, Berlin).

An important difference between *mazooka* and *amambo* spirit possession is that the *mazooka* can seize any ordinary person (*munthu wamba*), while it seems to me that the *amambo* usually seize a person with some instruction in *using'anga*. These are not necessarily experts, but "small" *asing'anga* like the mother of Mrs. Anyerere in our village. It seems that such persons get possessed especially when unpleasant things happen in the village. The person with access to that type of animal spirits, i.e. the *munthu wa amambo*, gets possessed by his spirits, and temporarily transforms into an animal, because of his or her concern and annoyance (*kupsya ntima*) with those unpleasant events.

There are still other types of *mizimu* which are found among the Asena. People call them *mizimu ya mfukula*. The etymology of the word *mfukula* in not clear, perhaps it is a word in the Chisena language. They are similar to the *mazooka*. During research in the area of Nsanje in 1995 I witnessed the occurrence of possession with my own eyes. On October 14,1995 we had arrived at a certain village called Tsatsirina, within the traditional authority (T.A.) Chimombo, in Nsanje District. We visited a certain man, Chanazi Jailosi, about 60, who was a *sing'anga wamizimu ya mfukula* (medical practitioner of the *mfukula* spirits). He used to invoke the spirits with the help of a drum, also called *mfukula*, which he played, whenever a sick person arrived asking for his help. We asked him whether he might be willing to play for us that drum which he used to play when he wanted to cure a person (*kuchiza munthu*) of his or her ailments. At first he was reluctant, but then he agreed and took up that drum which he held in front of his breast. But what ensued from this was starling. After he had played three songs which we recorded (original tape no. 95/8, collection Moya A. Malamusi; archived at the Institut für Ethnologie und Afrika-Studien, University of Mainz), he began to shiver all over his body (*kunjenjemela*) and to speak strange things which we were unable to understand, even a bit. We stopped recording and he also stopped his performance with the drum. When we asked him thereafter what had happened he said that the spirits were beating him (*mizimu inali kuwamenya*), because he had been playing this drum without the presence of any patient!

This should suffice as a preliminary overview of the great variety of *mizimu* (spirits) whose power can be activated by *asing'anga*. However, there is one more subtype of medical practitioners who communicate with the spirits: these are called *asing'anga amizimu ya mbendela* (the medical practitioners of the spirits of the flag). They are found particularly in the areas of Ntcheu and Dedza in south-central Malawi. They are *asing'anga* who acquire everything they know about spirits from learning. In the section about *mizimu*, later in this introduction I will explain more about them, and the meaning of the flag (*mbendera)*. Here it will suffice to say that nobody is able to be sure about the authenticity of their *mizimu.* What they do is to belch out *(kugeya)* and then speak things that are not understood by their audiences; so they usually employ an interpreter who "translates" to the patients what the spirit says. But people sometimes label those *asing'anga* "toughs", because if the patients fail to reply quickly with "yes" or "no" to what he tells them, then he beats him or her with a stick! This takes place during screening or divining sessions (*kuombeza). Kuombeza* is a method of discovering what is behind the ailment or complaint of the person who consults the *asing'anga.* Apparently possessed by his spirits, the latter speaks out anything that occurs to him in connection with the complaints of the patient. If he decides to accuse the client of having practised witchcraft, and the person denies it, he beats him or her in order to extract a confession. In fear of that, some clients agree to everything the *sing'anga* says. This is an example of the sort of transformation the practice of *using'anga* has undergone in some areas. The last mentioned subtype of those healers referred to as *asing'anga amizimu* has absorbed Christian influences and their songs are based on those of Christian congregations in Malawi. (See also the section on *mizimu* in this book, and the large chapter with my field research results on the *sing'anga* Paulo Luka of Ntcheu).

(d) Famous *asing'anga* (group 4)

Asing'anga ochuka (famous *asing'anga*) is a category that from the point of view of European-style logic would seem to cut across some of the other categories. However, it cannot be my objective here to "correct" popular conceptions. In fact, we may fare quite well following the "fuzzy logic " (Kosko and Isaka 1993) of popular thought, in order to get a picture that reflects the culture closely.

It often happens that in a certain place a famous *sing'anga* has taken up residence. Many people will then flock to him or her with their various problems. In Malawi, the tasks performed by local medical practitioners are many, and the one who is able to attract many people usually praises himself that he possesses knowledge of a wide range of subjects, and that he or she can provide medicines of many types such as;

(1) medicines to make a person become wealthy (*mankhwala opezetsa chuma munthu)*;

(2) medicines to induce pregnancies, if the person (woman) has no child (*mankhwala obeleketsa munthu ngati alibe mwana*);

(3) medicines for the protection of the body, so that a wizard/witch would not be able to bewitch the person (*mankhwala wotsitikila thupi kuti mfiti zisamulodze*);

(4) medicines to allow a person to know who is a wizard/witch in a group of people, or perhaps in the village community (*kudziwa yemwe ali mfiti pakati pa gulu kapena pamudzi*) etc.

Asing'anga who claim to have these abilities usually attract many people seeking help according to their problems. Most of the famous *asing'anga* also use a lot of herbal medicines (*mankhwala amitengo kapena mankhwala adzitsamba*). Many of them tend to stay in one place, sometimes their home village, or they settle in a place where they can expect to be consulted by many people.

Here I would like to give the names of a few *asing'anga* in southern Malawi who have been famous in recent history, because of their treatments, and who are or were resident either in their own village or in places that are densely populated (*anthu anali kuwapeza mwa unyinji wawo*). This is based on observation I made from the 1970s into the 1990s.

One man to whom many people came to obtain medicines for becoming rich (!) was Bwanali who stayed at Lisungwi in the administrative area of Mwanza. His residence was far from any roads, and yet many people arrived there on foot every day. Another such famous man, Asapesa, resided at Khungulu near Chileka. And then there was the *sing'anga* Simbazako at Ntchisi in the Central Region (see also the discussion in the Moni magazine, Blantyre, Anon. 1997, Simbazako 1997). Many people visited his place.

Equally, another *sing'anga,* Paulo Luka whose personality and work I studied in detail (see Chapter II) used to attract many people to his clinic near Ntcheu. I met crowds of people and some of them even slept there, while they were under treatment. In the area of Mulanje (see map), there was a female *sing'anga* who was known by the name Tetete. The list could be continued indefinitely.

Those *asing'anga* who have become very famous, sometimes have their own sort of fouls. It can happen that some famous ones begin to think of themselves as indispensable. People then say that a particular *sing'anga* was already born with a bad character inherited from his or her parents (*sing'angayo anabadwa kale ndi makhalidwe woipa kuchokera kwa makolo ake*). And he begins to cause hardship to others who come in search of help. Here I can give two examples of criticism expressed by many people about the *sing'anga* Paulo Luka of Ntcheu. It concerns his habit to beat people in his clinic. When he identifies a client as a wizard, and the client rejects the idea, it can happen that he beats him, thereby forcefully extracting a "confession". Badly hurt, the person then admits everything he has been accused of, while in fact he may be innocent. It is one of the many things that have upset the public about certain *asing'anga*, such as that particular one.

The second example concerns the following behaviour found among some other (male) *asing'anga.* When he gets a female client who has come to ask for help and stays at his place for treatment he may begin to make advances, if he finds her beautiful. The tactics can be vicious. He may begin to tell her frightening stories about her illness, dramatizing her state of health and thereby make her feel afraid and totally dependent on the "doctor". Eventually she sees him as the only one able to help her. This opens the gate to blackmail. In response to her increasing dependence, the *sing'anga* then asks her for sexual favours. Reports of this kind are heard from many places. An example from my own research concerns an incident that happened at *sing'anga* Simon Banda's place who had come from Ntchisi and settled in the area of traditional authority Kunthembwe in Blantyre District (see section on Simon Banda in Chapter II of this book). He died because of adultery (*chigololo*) with the wife of a client,. A couple had come to him seeking help for their child, but when the man left his wife at the *sing'anga*'s place, he persuaded her to sleep with him in exchange for his continuing support. The story ended with Simon Banda breaking his spine after sleeping with the woman (see the full story, later in this book).

Other famous *asing'anga* such as the one who called himself Eliya (after the apostle) and who also came from the area of Kunthembwe was known for beating clients in his "hospital" (*chipatala chawo*) with a special walking stick (*ndodo)* about which he claimed that it responded to messages from the spirits (*amati ndi ya zauzimu).* He beat a client especially after finding him guilty of one of two offenses: (1) that the person had come to his place with the intention of being insolent to the *sing'anga* Eliya by trying his witchcraft on him (*munthuyo wabwela kuti awachite chipongwe);* (2) that the person was a *mfiti* in pursuit of his former victim who was seeking help from the *sing'anga;* and he wanted to finish him off, i.e. kill him right at the *sing'anga*'s place before he would be saved and the wizard/witch discovered.

Eliya (no. 13 in the list) told me, he would then take one of his walking sticks which he used to keep in the little room where he did the "screening" of his patients (*mukachipinda komwe amaunikila*) and the stick would automatically beat any person identified as someone who was "trying" the *sing'anga*, to prove that he was more powerful. But some other people who feel innocent declare that this is extremely unfair.

There are yet other things committed by the famous *asing'anga* which have met with public disapproval. Someone may arrive seriously ill, only to find the *sing'anga* saying that the disease came from witchcraft. He then prescribes more medicines than needed, mercilessly asking a high price for each in the hope of increasing his income. Often the patient is unable to raise so much money. Then the *sing'anga* demands from him or her a deposit of something valuable such as a watch or a pocket radio etc., forcing the person to go "hunting for that money" (*kukasaka ndalamazo)* from his relatives or acquaintances, in order to get the valuables back. It may also happen that the patient does not recover at all, while the *sing'anga* insists upon receiving his remuneration. Those *asing'anga* who start this sort of behavior, however, often lose many customers and end up closing their practice. Conversely, there are also *asing'anga* who claim that they treat their patients free of charge. They depend on "gifts" which are sometimes extracted through psychological pressure. The most frequent and therefore common practice is that a patient pays a small sum upon arrival, before receiving treatment; he is expected to pay the full amount if the treatment works. However, if it does indeed work and he or she fails to pay, there are reprisals (see the section on the female *sing'anga* Akina Thomas, Chapter II).

The practice of divination (*kuombeza*)

Divination (*kuombeza)*, also: "to try the *ula* (lot, divining-sticks)", is an essential part of a *sing'anga's* practice. Various objects may be used for that purpose. When a client arrives at a *sing'anga's* place, perhaps he or she is ill, or complains about some misfortune, what will be done first will be that the *sing'anga* begins to divine or try the lot *(amayamba kuchita ndikuombeza ula wawo).* The term *kuombeza* is associated with those *asing'anga* who activate phials (*nsupa)* or other objects with medicines in order to find out the reasons why a certain person has come to be consulted (*asing'anga omwe amagwiritsa nchito nsupa kuti apeze dzifukwa zomwe munthuyo wabwelela*).

However, nowadays the practice of divination is often carried out under surrogates. Many clients avoid those *asing'anga* who openly declare what they are doing is divination; they fear the phials, they fear divination, because many times the "oracle" *(maula)* "does not catch a tree, but a person (*pakuti nthawi zambiri maula samagwila ntengo ai, koma munthu)*!" The "oracle" likes to say: "Such and such a person is a wizard/witch who has bewitched you! (*wakuti ndi wakuti ndi mfiti yomwe akukulodza iwe!)"* When this happens, the sick person or perhaps his or her relative with whom they have arrived at the *sing'anga's* place, will begin to demand from the *sing'anga* to tell them exactly who the *mfiti* was who haunted them in their home village. Some of the *asing'anga* who work with divination may actually identify the person or persons in that village. Many times, however, they will not give a name, but only a description of the person, such as saying that it is a man or a woman, that he or she is tall or short, and that their house's entrance faces the east or the west (*nyumba yake yayang'ana kumadzulo kapena ku mmawa*).

Hearing those words from the *sing'anga* the patient and his or her relatives will draw their own conclusions about who it might be who bewitched them and in the process they end up losing their temper (*amakhala woopsya ntima)* thinking of revenge (see the section on Akina Thomas and how my friend Kambazithe reacted to the news about who bewitched him, Chapter II).

The problem here is verification, "what about if all this is not true?" It can happen that the suspect gets into trouble within the community, because the people who have returned from consulting a *sing'anga* arrive with considerable anger and sometimes they beat up the suspect without any explanation, an act that raises anxiety (*kudetsa nkhawa)* in other members of the community, concern and sadness (*komvetsa chisoni).* These may be some of the social consequences of divination and people having trust in what the diviner says *(zomwe wamaula wanena*).

Occasionally, such incidences reach the point that a witchcraft suspect who was beaten up and seriously hurt by his relatives reports the matter to the local police, and then it remains the police's task to find out for what reason the person was hurt. Such reports are frequently found and discussed in the *Police Magazine* of Malawi which contains a wealth of written information on witchcraft cases. (See also chapter III of this book where I am dealing with written, including archival, sources). In such cases it can happen that the police call the *sing'anga* to provide evidence, if he is implicated because of telling his client that such and such person was a *mfiti.*

As a consequence, many people who consult a *sing'anga* doing divination simply declare from the start, "but myself, what has instigated me to come is that you help me through the benefits of good medicines, but not through the oracle *(ai, ine chomwe ndabwelela nkuti mundithandize mwayi wa mankhwala koma za maula ai!)".* Sometimes it also happens that a *sing'anga* finds himself with a legal case, because of incitement to violence, that people beat each other because of *kuombeza maula*, or that a person was caught and beaten up. It can happen that the police then warn the *asing'anga* not to give any names or descriptions of the witchcraft suspects during their divination practice.

This has led to some changes in the practice and also changes in terminology. Many *asing'anga* no longer use the expression *kuombeza maula.* Instead of using *nsupa* (phials), some of them hold a walking stick in their hand with which they strike the ground. And they call their procedure no longer divination but *kuunika,* a verb whose basic meaning is to throw light on some object or person, such as by holding up a lamp to someone's face, or use a torch, for the purpose of recognizing something or somebody in the darkness. The word is related to the noun *muni* which was the torch of long ago, a grass bundle lit with fire, and held up to find one's way in the darkness. In a figurative sense , *kuunika* means "to illuminate", to make something to be seen clearly such as the hidden witchcraft practice, and if for that purpose the "holding up of a lamp at someone's face" is repeated with many clients, one can also translate the word with" screening".

Clearly, in practice and terminology, *kuunika* and the use of a stick is only a form of displacement of the original idea (cf. Moore/Fine 1990:48 on the term) generated through social pressure. If the *sing'anga* strikes his walking stick on the ground during the "screening" sessions, it is of course also a form of *kuombeza* (divination). But with a new name and a different divining object, this practice allows many people in Malawi who belong to Christian congregations also to consult a *sing'anga* without running the risk of having to say about themselves: "Ndikupita kwa Satana!" (I am going to see Satan!)

Nsupa (phials) and *nyanga* (horns)

Nsupa, usually translated into English as "phial" (of. Scott/ Hetherwick 1929:408)[2] is an object used by people who are knowledgeable about medicines. Sometimes wizards and witches also use their own phials with dangerous medicines that kill people. *Nsupa* can have a variety of shapes. Since the remote past the experts of medicines have used the gourds of the *mphonda* fruit[3] but also the horns of antelopes and other animals of the bush, to serve as containers for these substances. When a person possessed phials in his house, people were thinking of him or her as someone with great strength from those medicines, even from magic *(matsenga).*

A phial which comes from a gourd is a vessel which people like to use for keeping medicines that are often rubbed into the skin of a sick person after scarification (*kuchekela anthu ngati akudwala),* but there are also some phials from gourds which the wizards and witches (*amfiti)* use putting in their medicines and other things such as pieces of glass. Those pieces of glass allow the wizard to see far and target the person he wants to harm or kill. The *amfiti*, when they aim at a person to be killed, they first spot him or her in one of the glasses inside a phial.

But those individuals whom the general public considers to be the most dangerous, are the ones who keep a phial from an animal horn (*nsupa ya nyanga za nyama*), because the usage of this type of phial is predominantly to kill people. Sometimes it happens, that a *mfiti* (wizard/witch) wants to kill someone, but fails to do so, because his victim has powerful protection, usually with medicines that were rubbed into scarifications of his skin. In such a case the *mfiti* can approach a friend in the witchcraft profession and hire from him a more powerful horn (*nyanga ya mphamvu)* in order to penetrate the victim's protective shield.

Under these circumstances phials (*nsupa)* are like weapons (*zida)*; their possession gives people a feeling of security in their lives, because they think that if anyone ever tried to show insolence to them, their phials would work and finish off that person. According to each owner's needs a phial is used in many different ways.

What I have explained so far is only one aspect in many, of what is generally known by the public, in contrast to specialized knowledge by the wizards and witches, and that by medical practitioners *(asing'anga),*namely that phials are used in connection with medicines. Where does this general knowledge come from? – It comes from various sources. For example, there are some people who have come to the conclusion that they possess extraordinary strength (*anakhwima kwambiri)* and they get tired of their "horns" (*nyan-*

[2] In English "phial" is described as "a small bottle, esp. for liquid medicines", Longman 1990: 770

[3] *mphonda* (botanical name: Lagenaria siceraria, Cucurbit.) is a type of fruit similar to pumkins (*dzungu,* pl. *maungu*). The gourd-cup (*dende*) is obtained after the seeds are scraped out and the gourds left to dry (*amaziumitsa*). (Inf. Monika Malamusi, April 21, 1999). Jessie Williamson 1975:142 has described this plant as follows: "An annual usually allowed to straggle over the ground, flowers white, fruits of varying shapes, some edible and some used only for gourds, some have a prolonged base to the fruit which forms a natural handle to the gourd. Common at Lake levels and to a lesser extent at higher elevations all over the country. – The fruits of some kinds are cooked to eat as an extra food. The leaves are cooked as *ndiwo* among some tribes ... The ripe fruits are boiled, then the seeds are scraped out and the gourds allowed to dry out to use as a receptacle for beer, milk or for ladling-out purposes."

ga) , i.e. of practicing witchcraft. A former wizard or witch might begin to boast about his or her previous deeds (a) in a state of drunkenness, or (b) during a dispute with someone else (*kukangana munthu ndi munthu).*

It then happens sometimes that the person begins to talk openly (*amayamba kulankhula poyela)* about things related to witchcraft (*nkhani zina ndi zina zanyanga).* From such reports people patch together basic knowledge about the usage of phials (*nsupa*) or horns *(nyanga).* I remember that some time during 1970's, Wilingtoni Chagwanumbi who is the leader of a *nyau(*masked*)* secret society in our home village, Singano near Chileka, Blantyre District, and another man, Daliyon Fred Binya told stories about how they had acted as wizards in the past. They told us that wizards eat the human flesh (of a corpse) with a tool similar to a long toothpick, a sharp-pointed stick which we call *chisonga,* to pick up pieces of meat, in the manner one eats cucumber (*nkhaka). "Amfiti amadya nyama ya munthu ndi chisonga ngati nkhaka*"! The stick (*chisonga)* can be cut from the hard material of bamboo (*nsungwi*).

Some other public knowledge about these things comes from the medical practitioners (*asing'anga)* who identify and capture wizards and witches, when they "take out" (*kuul-ula)* the power from their "horns", i.e. deactivate their magic. That is the moment when one can obtain information about *nsupa* and *nyanga,* as I did on many different occa-sions.

Some of my other sources, besides the systematic fieldwork I carried out with medical practitioners and their clients, are casual. Here I have to relate a story which I heard some time in 1994 at the funeral of a certain child from another family in our village. When such a sad event takes place, it is the custom in the village that people sit down on the veranda of the relatives of the deceased person, to exchange views. I also went to the house of that family. Many elders had assembled, and as we were sitting and talking, our discussions turned to the subject of persons who appear to be invincible (*nkhani ya an-thu wokhwima),*i.e. individuals who somehow have the power to resist and defend them-selves against any attempt to bewitch them. Such people normally include the *amfiti* (wizard/witches) themselves and the *asing'anga* (medical practitioners). One of the per-sons who were present, whose name was Thomas Mtekesa, and who is a remote relative of mine, began to tell us the following story:

"At Khombwe (a place about 6 km from Chileka) there was a certain man who was well-versed about herbal medicines (*mankhwala azitsamba);* he was a well-known medical practitioner (*sing'anga*), but at the same time an amazing wizard (*mfiti yolapitsa).* As a wizard he had already eaten many of his nephews, nieces and grand-children (*anadya kwambiri zidzukulu zake*). Some other people in that village had tried to consult various *asing'anga* in the area, but they had all failed to finish him and provoke his death by magic (*pa matsenga).* That man boasted a lot about his witchcraft (*iye anadzitama kwambiri)* and that he was an expert (*katswiri)* of "horns*"(nyanga)* and that he was in-vincible (*kukhwima).* For this reason many men who had married into a family of that place[4] ran away because of fear that if their wives got pregnant, that invincible wizard would destroy and 'eat' their children."

[4] The social order in southern Malawi is mostly matrilineal, with uxorilocal marital residence, i.e. men live in the villages of their wives; when they do so they are referred to as *akamwini.* Often their children become victims of a brother of the wife, who "eats" them (i.e. kills them off to eat) by witchcraft. The

"However there was one young man who had the courage (*anapezeka olimba ntima)* to marry into that place, after he had encountered a very beautiful girl in that village. He married her and soon she became pregnant. However, her pregnancy did not get far, and the girl died. Her husband was unable to accept that fact, and his head stopped working properly. He was convinced that she had died through witchcraft exerted by that wizard. And he developed an intense desire to take revenge and kill that man. That was very difficult though, due to his protection. What the young man did in the end, was that he began to follow that man everywhere he went, monitoring all his movements and looking for a chance to finish him off."

"It was in the month of February, four months after the girl had died. It appeared that the wizard had long forgotten that he had killed her who was his niece or grand-child. One day it happened that people came to his house asking for medicines, because he was also a *sing'anga* and as such knowledgeable about various herbs that are effective for many kinds of disease. Then the man set out to the bush for digging up medical plants. After he had left his house, the young man followed him at a distance, as usually. His heart was in such pain due to the loss of his wife, that he had become obsessed following the suspected killer everywhere."

"Since it was the rainy season with the riping of maize (*nthawi ya dzinja ya chimanga*) he could hide anywhere without being noticed, while the invincible wizard had no suspicion at all that someone was watching him or anything bad might happen to him. After he had entered the bush and begun to dig in the ground for tubers and other parts of plants to be used as medicines, he apparently felt something burning in his abdomen (*ananva mmimba kuotcha*)[5] so that he wanted to relieve himself. He put his axe down and went hehind the trees in order to defecate. The young man observed everything from his hiding place, and he devised a plan to outwit the invincible wizard and eventually take revenge."

"When the old man had finished, and begun to resume his work, his pursuer at first did not do anything but continue to watch. After some time the wizard took his axe, the medicines he had dug up and went back to his village. At that juncture the young man said to himself: 'This is my chance! That wizard is extremely powerful, everyone has failed to hurt him, but I will show him my superiority, I will show him something amazing!'"

"As soon as the old wizard had left the place to go home, in order to help his clients with his medicines, the young man came out of his hiding; he broke off a big pumpkin leave (*nkhwani*) from some field, and went to the spot where the wizard had left his excrements. He collected them from the ground, wrapped it all up in that leaf and went with it to his home in the village. He kept the wizard's excrements at home up to late in the evening. When the village was quiet and everyone at rest, he sneaked out, to the house of the wizard, noticed that everybody inside was sleeping, and put those excrements down at the backdoor of the house of that man. Then he went back home and fell asleep, greatly relieved."

---

maternal uncle is called *malume* (see also Gwengwe 1965; Kubik/Malamusi 1987; Makumbi 1955; Mwale1952; Ntara 1969; Nurse 1978; Phiri 1983)

[5] This is a polite way of expressing to audiences the fact that he was in need of seeing a lavatory.

"It happened that in the middle of the night the invincible wizard had to go out of this house to urinate, and – by bad luck – he stepped on the excrements! With a curse about his mishap, he wondered who the person might have been who had the insolence to defecate in front of his entrance, so that he would step on it ! He became extremely annoyed and as he entered his house, he thought that such a person deserved capital punishment, indeed. So he took his phials and some lethal medicines quickly, and began to mix them with the excrements at his door, while pronouncing a curse that the person, whoever he was, should die: ' I want that without delay he gets ill with diarrhea (*mutseguka mmimba)* and dies within a short time!'"

"Since he did not know that these were his own excrements which he had left in the bush there, he was surprised that early next morning he began to feel trouble in this abdomen. His abdomen began to swell terribly, but he did not know, of course, that this was the effect of his own witchcraft medicines. Instead he now tried to treat himself with various other herbs, even those which can remove magic (*matsenga*), but all failed. His condition quickly deteriorated, and he ran out of all medicines that he knew. Eventually, when his abdomen blew up to enormous proportions, he just died."

When I heard this report from Mr. Thomas Mtekesa, I could not help being amused and rejoice about the outcome. This was an example of the fact that some medical practitioners (*asing'anga*), according to many people's opinion, may also practise witchcraft, and instead of healing people, they would also destroy innocent persons.

Nsupa and *nyanga* can therefore be both tools and weapons. A phial can be in possession of a *sing'anga* or a *mfiti.* And a *sing'anga* is naturally suspicious of anyone having such vessels in his or her home. This reminds me of a story my wife told me about someone who kept a bottle with medicines in his house for the treatment of his back, and a *sing'anga* came and accused him of witchcraft. This is the story my wife, Ananjeza, told me in 1997:

"I was sitting at the enclosure (*kumpanda)* of our house, and saw people passing along the way that leads from the shops to the village, close to our house. As the two men were passing I saw that one of them was the headman Maneya (from a neighbouring village). The views they were exchanging while walking was about the *asing'anga* these days. Headman Maneya said: 'Nowadays those medical practitioners cause us a lot of discomfort, because sometimes it happens that we elders keep medicines in our houses, so that, if for example we get afflicted with rheumatism (*nyamakazi)* we cut them ourselves into our skins (*tidzidzitemela),* but in case one of our relatives goes to a *sing'anga* for divination (*kukaombeza)* you might end up being identified as someone who keeps medicine bottles in your home, and that it is you who finishes the people in your village. Perhaps the *sing'anga* comes with his client to your house, after he spotted you by divination, and finds your medicines, not knowing that these are medicines which you use to help yourself. Otherwise, your relative has heard from the *sing'anga* there that <u>you</u> are the *mfiti*, thereafter he comes and searches your house, finds the bottles and makes a lot of noise (*phokoso)* . In both cases you get accused that it is you who bewitches your grand-children. And since those bottles are found in your house, it is difficult for you to deny any vicious practice; if you did, they would consider you a liar, in view of the apparent evidence. Your grand-child might even start to beat you (*kukunyetsa*) for being a *mfiti*, while you are innocent!,"

Matsenga (magic) and *ufiti* (witchcraft, sorcery)

The Chichewa terms *matsenga* and *ufiti* can only be translated customarily into English terms such as "magic", "witchcraft" and "sorcery". Because their finer meanings get inevitably blurred in the translations.

Matsenga is a plural form. The singular *tsenga*, often translated "trick", cf. Scott / Hetherwick 1929 {1970:553} is not much used. The term *matsenga* is applied to plots and devices by people, often of ill intent, against somebody to be tricked out, or to make him or her ill or cause him or her to encounter bad luck, misfortune and disaster (including accidental death), – events that are summarized under the term *matsoka.*

To give an example: a certain boy left his home in the morning to go to school. But before he arrived at school, while he was on the way, he suddenly thought of returning home. Eventually, he did not return home at all, but instead he entered the area of mountains far from human settlements, and there it happened that he was bitten by a killer bee and he died on the spot. The question that remains is: what was it that made him change his mind that he would think of returning home on the path from school, but then instead of actually going home go to the mountains, and there again get bitten by a killer bee?

People say that behind such a chain of events there is *matsenga,* and there must be a person behind it who staged it all by putting his medicines on the path to the school, and while doing so, pronouncing the words: "if such and such a child passes here he should feel compelled to do such and such ..." according to what the man has arranged for him to happen. We can say that *matsenga* is one type of action with medicines by which some people inflict harm upon someone, cause him to encounter hazards, or die where he goes.

I can give another example: if a person has a problem with his leg which is swollen and he tries to apply all sorts of medicines, such as rubbing in medical cream, without his condition changing, and the swelling even gets worse, then people say that the disease is caused by human beings (*matenda amenewa ndi amunthu)* perhaps through *matsenga.* It implies that on a certain day, the sick person was walking on a certain path, but there was another person who was thinking negative about him *(akumuganizila zoipa)* wishing that he would fall ill. That person took his medicines whose application he alone knows, and put them on the path where he knew that his enemy would cross. On the medicines he would bind a thin thread (*kaulusi).* When the victim passes the place the thin thread begins to do its work and enters the body of the person to do harm. This happens because of the words the one who sets the trap pronounces against the victim, while placing the evil medicines on his path. One could say that *matsenga* is one avenue of practising witchcraft in the sense that the person with evil intent uses a device which he activates secretly, but with ingenious trickery to avoid that the victim would know about it; then he ambushes his victim, for example by putting the tiny device on the path where he habitually walks so that he would step on it, or jump over it, without knowing that it is medicines (*mankhwala).*

But not all *matsenga* are designed to cause harm to another person. A characteristic of *matsenga* is the trickery. The intent to deceive, surprise somebody. For example, children can practice *matsenga* in the following way: one of them takes a string (*luzi*) and makes a series of knots (*timfundo),* perhaps four. Then he puts the string into his mouth, secretly biting off one knot and hiding it in the mouth's corner. Then he tells his companions: "Look! I am going to pierce my tongue with this string !" He closes his mouth again, pushes the knot he bit off back to the top of his tongue , holds the end of the string with the three remaining knots under his tongue so that it looks as if the isolated knot on top were still part of the string, and says: "Look , I have pierced my tongue with the string! " This kind of pastime of children *(zomwe ana amasewera)* is also called *matsenga.* In fact any sort of trickery that surprises audiences, a technical device of playfully cheating others, can be referred to as *matsenga.* This includes the "magic" shown to the public by trick artists.

By contrast the following action would not fall under the category *matsenga:* there is a certain insect which is called *mwayi* (luck); it is about 1.3 cm large, oval in shape, black and has white patterns on its back (*malembo oyela pansana).* When you encounter this insect on your path through the forest, or in fact, on any path, you draw with your finger a circle around it in the sand clockwise,to make sure that the luck will be yours; your act, however, would not fall into the category of practising *matsenga.* It seems that *matsenga* always implies interaction between people, deceptive interaction.

What is the difference between *matsenga* and *ufiti*?

I will try to work out a descriptive definition both in Chichewa and in English translation. But the fact is that these terms overlap in their meanings. There is no sharp distinction between them (*ufiti ndi matsenga sunasiyane kwenikweni*), because if somebody applies *matsenga,* people tend to believe that he is a *mfiti* (wizard/witch).

Matsenga ndi ngati gulu limodzi lamankhwala lomwe anthu ena angathe kugwilitsa ntchito kufuna kupweteka munthu wina. Matsenga alipo amitundu-mitundu. Makamaka matsenga cholinga chache ndi chopweteka munthu, komanso zinthu zina zomwe ana amasewera nkumanena kuti ndi matsenga. Matsenga angathe kupangidwa masana osati usiku, iyayi. Matsenga amapangidwa ndi munthu mmodzi kuti apweteke wina.	*Matsenga* is like one category of action with medicines whose power certain people can activate, if they want to hurt another person. There are different types of *matsenga*. Although the purpose of *matsenga* is to harm another person, there are also other devices which children employ playfully that are called *matsenga*. *Matsenga* can (only) be prepared during daytime, not in the night. *Matsenga* are prepared by a single person so that he or she should hurt someone else.
Pomwe ufiti ndi gulu limodzi lamatsenga, atha kulodza munthu ndi kufa, koma nthawi zambiri amagwira ntchito za usiku. Ndipo ufiti ungathe kupangidwa ndi munthu mmodzi, kapena gulu la amfiti. Amfiti akapha munthu amene akufunayo, amanena kuti amadya nyama yache, pomwe munthu wa matsenga akapha munthu amene akumufunayo, nyama yake samadya.	Conversely, *ufiti* is a subcategory of *matsenga*, namely the one which is used to bewitch a person until he/she dies; but many times it is a nocturnal practice. Also: *ufiti* can be carried out either by one person alone or by a group of *amfiti*. When the *amfiti* kill a person whom they want, they say it is for eating his or her flesh, whereas a person of *matsenga* after having killed the one he wants, will not eat the corpse.

Mfiti amachita matsenga ndi ufiti. Chitsanzo: mfiti itha kulowa munyumba ya munthu. Chimenecho ndi chiyani? – Matsenga. Kumulodza kuti ayambe kudwala ndi chiyani? – Ufiti. Pamene munthu wamatsenga chabe pa njila sangathe kubwera nkulowa munyumba ya munthu ngati mfiti.	A *mfiti* carries out both, *matsenga* and *ufiti*. An example: A *mfiti* is able to enter the house of a person (through the walls or roof). What is this? – *Matsenga*. To bewitch him/her so that he/she would begin to fall ill, what is that? – *Ufiti*. Conversely, someone with ordinary *matsenga* on the path, cannot come and enter the house of a person in the way a *mfiti* can do.
Munthu yemwe amadziwa matsenga nthawi zina sangakhale kuti ndi mfiti, koma amangodziwa okhawo.	A person who is knowledgeable about *matsenga* need not be a *mfiti*, but only knows *matsenga,* nothing else.
Mfiti zonse zomwe imapanga pakufuna kupha munthu ndi matsenga. Chifukwa pali kusiyana ndi munthu wa matsenga chabe.	Everything a *mfiti* does in his/her intent to kill a person, is *matsenga*, but there is a difference between him/her and someone who practises ordinary *matsenga* (i.e. *matsenga* that is not *ufiti*).

Ufiti: the wizards' and witches' designs

I can think of no better way of transmitting something about the world of witchcraft and the wizards' and witches' designs upon their victims than quote directly from conversations I had in 1995 with two renowned *asing'anga,* B.S. Nyalugwe (see no. 11 in the list) and Yesu Samson (no. 10). Here I will give extracts from our talks recorded on tape, in English translation.

B.S. Nyalugwe was 65 years old, when I first met him. His home was in Mulanje (see map). But he had come to Chinkango village near Chileka in 1980. This is where I recorded him in 1995 (orig. tape no. 95/3). He had been a medical practitioner since 1970 and was ranking among the very famous ones (*asing'anga otchuka).* He had a particularly good reputation in treating infertility among women, but he was also good at removing threatening magic, such as "… when people in a house can't find sleep because of a scraping sound, *gwegwele gwegwele* harassing them, as if magic *(matsenga)*were being tried out. If those people call me in my capacity to help them, then I sprinkle medicines on those spots and the wizards or witches, whoever they may be, will not be able to come again. When this is accomplished, the inhabitants of that house will acknowledge that they were being helped. Their friend will then ask them: 'From where did you get help? I also have problems that hurt me.' – 'Ah! At Nyalugwe's place.' And so there are ever increasing numbers of people coming to see me."

… "Indeed *mfiti* and *sing'anga* are different entities, because between the two, a *mfiti* can never excel a *sing'anga* in power. If he did, it would mean that the *sing'anga*'s work was insufficient. *A mfiti* is afraid of the *sing'anga,* because as soon as the cause of sickness is identified, and medicines applied, the *mfiti* has no chance of coming again, and the person gets cured. For this reason we say that between *mfiti* and *sing'anga*, the *sing'anga* is superior…."

..."There are two or three kinds of medical practice (*using'anga*). One kind is carried out by those who customarily go from village to village, perhaps practising divination (*maula kuombeza)* in order to find out what happened... Those *asing'anga* have their own form of training. There is also another kind of *asing'anga* who do not engage in divination, but administer herbal medicines to those who need help, as is the case with me. And then there are those *asing'anga* who identify wizards and witches and chase them away. This is yet another type, because their training is different."

... "As concerns the wizards and witches , the one aspect I know in great detail is that when they enter somebody's house and find the person sleeping, they blow at him or her substances which anesthetize, so that he should fall into a very deep sleep. Then they carry the person away. If it is a child they dance with it (*kumabvina naye)*! That is what their witchcraft is like, their tricks. After the person has been treated in that manner, he or she will get ill. In the case of the child, if it manages to escape you will find that the child has its spine broken. When people bring the child to us and demand consultation, we say 'Oh the wizards and witches were dancing with it!' Then we take medicines for bathing the child, and then, should those wizards and witches try again to kidnap it, they are unable to do so. They are afraid of the protective medicines. They say: 'If we touch that child, we only hurt ourselves!' *Eya* ! this is what I know concerning these matters."
...
... "It is also true that *amfiti* (wizards and witches) can bewitch a person who is far away, over a distance, such as I have explained before that there are many types of magic (*matsenga).* The wizards call out the name of the person who is far away, and indeed that person comes to them as a shadow image (*chithunzithunzi).* Then they play around with that image, and by doing so they manipulate harmfully the real person who is far away. If there were no herbal medicines to counteract them and convince them that they are defeated, they would be very powerful. But luckily , the wizards and witches are quickly subjected to obeisance, because they are afraid of the plant medicines; if they played around with them they would die away fast..."

Thrilled by the idea that a person could be lured by calling his name, and that his shadow would respond and fall into the hands of the wizards, I asked Mr. Nyalugwe what the outcome was, after they played around with the shadow image. He said:

...."Now that person is beginning to get ill. The wizards can see this through his shadow image and say : Aa! That person. I have hurt him/her, I have finished with him. Or else, the wizard will get confirmation from others that his victim over there has fallen ill. If the person afflicted does not find help quickly, he or she may die there.".....

My final question to Mr. Nyalugwe concerned the rumours circulated in the villages that *amfiti* can even fly and arrive at some other place. I asked him to comment on that issue.

... "Yes, a wizard or witch is able to fly. However, I cannot explain that aspect of witchcraft very well, because it would be necessary to experience personally what they do. As far as I am concerned I know about these things because of what my grandmother told me. She used to tell us children that a *mfiti* can fly, and once she gave me medicines, saying ' you wash your face with them, and you will actually see the wizards and witches!' Then I really saw the *amfiti* how they fly in the night!....And I was extremely frightened. Afterwards I told my grandmother that by no means would I want to experience these things again... What people say is that wizards and witches board an aeroplane.

But their aeroplane is a flat basket (*lichelo)* as used for winnowing grain, and they can stand inside, and in this way even arrive at the top of Mulanje mountain, have their conversations there and return; because all that is magic (*matsenga*). These things are like the plots of dreams…"

…." There are certain people who have no witchcraft (*ufiti*), but only know magic (*matsenga*), and they can make a person sick by magic. There are also some others who have nothing at all, but because of hating each other, they go to the experts who know magic, complaining that such and such individual was troubling them. If the expert is paid money he might tell his client: 'All right! Take these needles and cut out that person's footprint from the soil. Then you pierce it.' And indeed if he pierces it again and again, you will find that the victim begins to feel shot into the foot; alternatively he feels pain in the legs, even the whole body. In the extreme case, if nothing is done the counteract it, he can die. That is magic (*matsenga*)."

The other person with whom I have talked much about the workings of witchcraft was Mr. Yesu Samson. About 54 years old he had originally come from Lilongwe and settled at Nkungwi village, T. A. Nankumba, in Mangochi District. He claimed to be a *sing'anga* with a wide range of knowledge, who could treat all sorts of problems and cure a person who was already bewitched. The complete recorded interview in Chichewa is on my original tape no. 95/2 and dates from July 19, 1995. Below I am only giving extracts in English translation showing some highlights.

…" The nature of wizards and witches is of the most diverse kind. Therefore they also have many different methods for killing a person. When they intend to kill somebody, they first sit down with the members of their group at their regular meetings and discuss the matter. If there is just one among them who refuses to do the kill, then they are all blocked by that person. It is then necessary for the others to persuade him or her that the targeted person should indeed be eliminated. When they have come to an agreement to kill, they carry out their plan by penetrating the house of the victim through their magic, invisibly."…

…" Now, wizards and witches enter a house at the edge where a wall and the roof meet (*mmalenga molekezela*). That's how they are able to enter … Then they seize that person, harass him and do with him whatever they desire. The person then begins to feel sick. His body can't get well again. And thereby, he has delivered himself to the will of those wizards supplying them with an opportunity to 'process' him….When that stage has been reached, they become the owners of his body. Then they can relax and wait until the person falls ill. From now on the wizards or witches can enter his house even just by knocking at the door, and the person will himself open, or rise up from his bed to open while, in fact, he is in deep sleep. When the time has come for the wizards to leave, they can tell their victim to close the door behind them."

…"The wizards and the witches act after they have dressed up in their witchcraft costume. On the path a wizard or witch will perform a dance with strange contortions (*ikutamba)*. Many of them like to wear small pieces of white cloth, and also, after they have annointed themselves with ash, their eyes will appear very much enlarged, and their lips become very long. Judging from their appearance one could think they were something else, not real persons. They seem to have transcended their human bodies.That is what the *amfiti* are! … For example, if they are in the middle of the village doing their contortions (*motamba),* their manner of walking would appear to conform with ours, except that it is miraculous, because you cannot see a *mfiti's* footprint as he or she is walking, due to their magic."

"In the work I have carried out, I am getting acquainted with everything in connection with the wizards and the witches. They are quite bizarre (*amfiti ndi wopusa*). If a relative has left their home to stay far away, and the *mfiti* wants to kill him, first he will call out his name by means of his witchcraft. This causes the man over there to experience a strange acceleration of his heartbeat and he feels that he wants to go home to his village. This is the *mfiti*'s method of "processing' him (*akamukonzele*). Eventually, when that person has set out to return home, the wizard or witch will implant a spider in the man's big toe and make it come out at the heel. That spider functions as a pilot positioning signal so that the *mfiti* should always know the whereabouts of that person. Those wizards or witches can then fly there with their aeroplane which is a woman's basket (*lichelo*) or even a plastic plate. They can board any of these objects in order to follow the pilot signal which is that spider guiding them to the exact location of that person. In this way they can harm a person even if he should be in Lilongwe while the wizards are elsewhere. When he dies far from home, people will say "oh yes, he died in Lilongwe" while, in fact, his killers were all the time staying here."

I decided to ask the *sing'anga* Yesu Samson the following question: ".. if a *mfiti* is on such a journey, and someone comes and knocks at the entrance of his house, would he find him in the house or would he perhaps find that he has gone out?"

He processed my question this way:

"Wizards are quite bizarre (*ndizopusa).* When you knock at their house, you will meet something else, the phantom of a person (*chitsanzo chabe cha munthu)* which stays at the very same place while the owner of the house is, in fact, on a journey … He is not at all in the house. That is the odd behavior of a *mfiti.* I am thinking of the time in Ulongwe[6] where I was invited by a certain Mr. Kalembo from Mangochi to construct a clinic. Now, at Ulongwe there was a certain *sing'anga* who had identified wizards who were staying up there in the mountains –- on high ground. The police asked me to help them to arrest those wizards. When I went there, I saw for myself that they were *amfiti*; they were one woman and three children, four people in all.The aeroplane they used was a plate, and their hammers for killing people were nails from a railway track[7]…

When the police arrived there they put them in chains (*atawanjata unyolo).* But is it not so that those arrested are still on witchcraft? And when you put them in chains, they are still on what? Witchcraft. So then there is really no reason that they should sleep in a police cell, because they still have the power of witchcraft. Sleeping there, they simply return to their home by witchcraft, and they can be found there! So I warned the police …. And I set off to my house, dipped plant medicines in water, and arrived again at the police station of Ulongwe. I sprinkled those medicines on the *mfiti.* Suddenly the big witch became frightened and began to insult me with obscene words."

---

[6] Place in Machinga District, south of Mangochi.

[7] Perhaps from the railway passing at Liwonde in direction Mozambique

"… When *amfiti* begin to learn their craft they go to an expert of those things who is their elder or leader…. The *amfiti* have their own meeting points: they meet regularly at one place. That is their assembly, in the manner as we people arrange our meetings, for the purpose of planning what they should do. … In their midst there can also be a person who does not know how to bewitch, he just attends the meeting to eat with them."

At this point I asked Yesu Samson, whether there was any form of exchange or payment between the *amfiti* who were members of a group. He replied that that was the case, and that it could not be otherwise, because they were selling knowledge, skills to each other. Then I asked him whether they paid each other in real money or merely in images of money. He replied:

"We cannot say about those people that they pay each other in images of money, because how could one expect a man who has bewitched his brother in order to kill him and eat his flesh to eat it alone? He will share it with the other *amfiti* in the group, and thereby pay back a debt to those who once fed him with their meat. If some of the meat remains, they put it up for sale ! They sell it for money !"

"When we *asing'anga* want to be insolent to the *amfiti* we try to detect them at the very place where they divide their prey between themselves. That is why sometimes wizards and witches are caught red-handed while they are still in possession of that human flesh. .... If I want to be insolent to the *amfiti* I begin my actions at the moment someone has died. I fence off that funeral with medicines. When I have finished protecting that funeral, I proceed to protecting the house of the deceased person (*nyumba ya malilo*) which means that I am preventing the *amfiti* to come and carry out their designs. Thereby I guarantee that the person who has died is left in peace to go to the grave. When the body has been taken away from the house and buried by his relatives, I also go to he grave to protect the grave. Now I have prevented the wizards and witches from doing anything in both places: village and graveyard. If one of them still arrives at the contest, he will be discovered by the power of my medicines with his things of witchcraft exposed in his hands. Because it is not so that a *mfiti* really eats the corpse of a person, but he eats its magical representations (*zibinje zawo zomwe)*[8], perhaps we could say by his magical tricks (*matsenga awo omwe*). He just creates an image expressing that he eats the flesh, while in fact he eats the product of this own magical tricks.

Mizimu (Spirits)

Many *asing'anga* (medical practitioners) these days employ the term *mizimu,* declaring: "I am a *sing'anga* of the spirits (*ndine sing'anga wa mizimu).*" But the real meaning behind the fact that he or she should describe themselves in that manner, is not well-known.

As concerns *mizimu,* we can say that many people think that it is something which cannot be seen by human beings (*chinthu chomwe sichionedwa ndi anthu)*, but that it helps

[8] I am not familiar with the word *binje* (singular), *zibinje* (plural), but think it is close in meaning to *chifano* (pl. dzi-) : an image, phanton, likeness. The type of Chichewa spoken by Yesu Samson was Chichewa proper as spoken in the area of Lilongwe where he originally came from; it is a bit different from the way people speak in the south.

a person in varouss ways so that he or she should find something good. However, it can also cause someone to encounter mishaps, under the circumstances in which that person is found. There are many *mizimu* about which people think that they are good. When a person obtains something beneficial, he or she thinks that all this is due to the spirits of their relatives who died long ago. Conversely, if a person encounters mishaps in his or her life, he or she will assume that it is caused by ill-meaning spirits, perhaps because he does not look well after his relatives (*samasamala abale ake*), and the spirits in the graveyard are annoyed; and so it comes that he or she is only having bad luck (*matsoka okhaokha*).

Pressed by feelings of guilt, some of these people will then go to see a *sing'anga* in order to find out what is behind. Perhaps the *sing'anga* will say that it is dissatisfied spirits and that the client should make a sacrifice (*sadaka*) so that the spirits would leave him alone and find a rest (*igone pansi,* literally: that they should sleep down there). If thereafter, the person gets better, or at least does not encounter any more bad luck, he or she might say : "Indeed, it was the spirits of my parents who were not happy"— (if the parents are already dead).

One type of *mizimu*, already mentioned earlier in this book, is especially found in the belief system of Chimang'anja -, Chisena- and Chinyungwe-speaking people. They are called *amambo*. In my research on the *ngororombe* panpipe dance of Chinyungwe-speaking groups from Tete Province, Mozambique, 1990 and 1992, I came across the fact that *amambo* spirits when they seize a person, can also ask for the panpipe dance to be performed for them. Elsewhere I have given a detailed description of the socio-cultural setting of this dance (Malamusi 1992, 1997) and I would like to reproduce here the following observations from my earlier work:

> While some persons in the group explained the character of *ngororombe* as just an entertainment dance (*chamba chamasewela chabe*), there are also certain events which may be associated with it. For instance it can be that there is a funeral somewhere, and then it is possible that the *ngororombe* group is invited to dance there. Perhaps one reason why the group often plays at funerals is because they play *ngororombe* as if crying. At other times, the same *ngororombe* is capable of being played for ancestral spirits (*mizimu*). If someone gets possessed by a spirit (*agwa azimu),* it can happen that through the possessed person the spirit says that he wants a *ngororombe* group to perform; the *ngororombe* people are then called there, in order to make the spirit desist from that person.
>
> To explain further about ancestral spirits, it may happen that a funeral takes place, perhaps of a grown-up person. Then after some time has passed, that dead person wants such and such action taken, so that he/she and his/her ancestral spirits (*mizimu yake*)* should rejoice. Then the spirit of the dead person may arrive at the village to make a certain person sick who appears to be a relative.When the sickness develops, that person suddenly speaks any sort of strange things, but in what he /she says there are certain themes which come from the spirit of the dead person, i.e. it is explained what the ancestral spirit wants the living to do for him/her. Other people in the village try to understand and interpret what the sick person is saying, that the spirit of so and so wants such and

* In the plural, because it is believed that a person who has died has "many *mizimu* within him/her" where he or she stays after death. Everyone who dies incorporates several *mizimu* which have different characters and can move about independently. What is it that makes a person good at times and bad at other times? It is believed that it is the different spirits in the same person. After death these spirits, some good, some bad demand different things from the surviving relatives (Note, Nov 14,1990).

> such things. After some time the people in the village begin to provide what the spirits wants; if it is beer – always millet beer (*mowa wa masese)* – the people begin to brew it so they may drink because, they say, without doing that, the sick person would never recover, and die. But if they hurry to do the spirit's bidding, the sick person quickly gets better.
>
> When a person dies, he or she can have medicines (*mankhwala pakuziteteza muzinthu zina,* medicines to ward of certain things) remaining in the body, which had previously been given to that person by a *sing'anga* (traditional doctor) for protection against witchcraft. Sometimes, however, other substances are mixed by chance or mistake into these protective medicines, and may begin to work after death to transform the person into a wild animal which then stays in the forest. After some time has passed the people begin to realize that "Our relative who died has risen up to be such and such an animal", because the person afflicted by illness behave, in a way reminiscent of the animal into which the deceased has been transformed. If this is perhaps a lion the sick person acts out things which that lion acts out, or if he had turned into a leopard, he acts accordingly.
>
> The beings into which the deceased can transform include lion, leopard, python and many other creatures that are dangerous. This animal, they say, comes regularly near the house to see how things are going on. When something of this kind happens, many people in the village live in fear because of those spirit-animals, believing that if they do not carry out the spirit's demands they will experience a lot of difficulties. If this happens in the village – somebody afflicted with the illness by spirits – then elders perform a rite, so that the bad spirit should desist from making this person sick. This is when they invite the *ngororombe* players, so that while they drink free millet beer, there should be a performance of the *ngororombe* dance.
>
> As they perform they receive money from the people who have called them to dance, to give their spirits pleasure. The beer and money come from the person who was afflicted with disease.
>
> (Malamusi 1992: 87-88)

Then there are those *mizimu* whom many *asing'anga* in the region declare to be their ultimate source of inspiration. Among all the *mizimu* it is this type that raises questions about their provenance and their objectives (*cholinga chache chenicheni).* Where do those spirits come from? – This question is raised because those *mizimu* seem to come into existence only after a client has arrived at the *sing'anga*'s place with his complaints and after he/she has explained that they are suffering from such and such problems. The *sing'anga* then begins his task by calling his *mizimu* through the method of belching out (*munjila yogeya kwambiri).* Thereafter he intones spiritual songs (*nyimbo zauzimu),* then he prays, continuing the songs after finishing the prayers, until all of a sudden he begins to speak out messages to his client. The issue to be raised here is whether everything he says during that state really comes from the *mizimu*, or perhaps from his own ideas about the illness of his client. Someone like me cannot help but wonder about those kinds of claims. Perhaps what really is behind it is deception; that the *sing'anga* became accustomed to say that it is the spirits which tell him what has happened to his clients and where their illnesses came from.

Nowadays many *asing'anga* act like that in their performances. They anticipate that many people, if they heard that he was a *sing'anga wa mizimu* (medical practitioner by virtue of the spirits), would arrive seeking help from him. This is so because they also find a way to underline their claims; they adopt for themselves names from the bible, such as Paulo Luka, Petro, Eliya, even Yesu (see my list). By doing so, they wish to demonstrate that everything they do conforms with the doctrine of the bible. Some of them always keep a bible at hand when they perform, and often they quote directly from the bible. This creates confusion by giving the impression to the public that what they do perpetuates the work of the apostles (*aneneri)* whose names they frequently invoke, while downplaying the fact that it is their own ideas which they propagate. Perhaps it is even their intent to make people think that the work of the *asing'anga,* i.e their medical practice, was inspired by the spirit of an apostle. One of those with whom I worked in Kunthembwe and who had adopted the name of Eliya, claimed all the time, that his medicines were coming from the apostle Eliya, and that the latter had revealed to him one medical tree whose ingredients he used to prescribe to all his clients. He did not activate any *nsupa* (phials) during his work, but instead he always took recourse to the bible.

For me it is difficult to obtain a comprehensive picture of what is behind such practices, because those *asing'anga* would simply insist upon everything as coming from the *mizimu*. Some of them also say their strength comes from the white flag (*mbendela yoyela*) which they plant at the place of their practice. It is only the *asing'anga amizimu* who do that. On the flag a cross is often written in the middle, perhaps in red, in other cases blue.The *sing'anga* then says, when the wind moves the flag, the wisdom (*nzeru*) of the spirits (*mizimu*) enters his head. They say that much of what the spirits transmit, passes through the symbols of that flag to get to him (*zimadzela pa mbendela imeneyo*) .This is what the *sing'anga* Eliya from Kunthembwe has told me from time to time.

Some other *asing'anga* such as for example, Paulo Luka (see the section about him, Chapter II) have also adopted the name of a famous apostle in the bible, and certain things he accomplishes are comparable to what those do who carry out "medical practice of the spirits" (*using'anga wa azimu*). A flag is also there at his place and the clothes he wears when doing his work are white, with a cross written upon them. When he wants to start his work he begins to say prayers to the Lord (*Ambuye)*, and he also sings spiritual songs (*nyimbo za uzimu),* the same which are sung in various churches in the area. But he insists upon what he is doing is not *using'anga wa uzimu,* and if anyone called him *sing'anga wa mizimu* he would be his enemy because of that epithet. He carries out a lot of work concerning witchcraft, and he identifies and denounces individuals whom he thinks are *amfiti* (wizards/witches). By contrast, other *asing'anga* of the spirits, such as Eliya, would never say that such and such person is a *mfiti.*

What has given me a lot of thought during my research, is that I have been wondering why certain *asing'anga* do things like the people in the Christian churches do, and why among other things there are so many motifs that come from the bible. This is a question which those who are better informed may answer. For example, Gerhard Kubik who worked on witchcraft in southwestern Tanganyika 1960 to 1962, with the *sing'anga* Chikanga Chunda in Nyasaland in 1962 and 1967, and about religious syncretism in Gabon 1964, 1966 and 1969 (see field-note copies Phonogrammarchiv Vienna) has proposed the following historical and psychological explanation:

"When in 1876, the first missionaries came to what would be called the Nyasaland Protectorate by the British administration, many other Christian missions soon followed, such as CCAP (Church of Central Africa Presbyterian) which was established on the Shire Highlands in a place called Blantyre (after David Livingstone's place of birth), the

Dutch Reformed Church, Roman Catholics etc.: they all felt that their work was threatened by indigenous religious beliefs. So they tried to suppress the local religion with its focus on ancestral spirits. Especially the *asing'anga* were targeted as an obstacle to Christianization, and the community of Christian converts was instructed that witchcraft was something that did not exist, that it was all just superstition. However, while they were successfully implanting the major figures of their own spiritual world into the minds of their converts, they failed to convince even the members of their own congregations that local spirits, witchcraft and magic did not exist (only the foreign ones did). If somebody lost a child, or a relative, or suffered from a mysterious illness which hospital doctors were unable to treat, that person would continue to seek the cause in witchcraft activities by a close relative, in spite of Christian teachings. The church was unable to disperse his suspicions and destroy his belief in the world of *mizimu, ufiti* and *matsenga* as a psychological reality to be accounted for."

"Public beliefs always create a market. Where hospital doctors fail, and where the church is unable to provide comfort, that is where the *sing'anga* comes in, because he or she is able to address their clients' psychological problems directly, and help them to find relief. However, in view of the repression and discrimination their profession had suffered, particularly by the early Christian missionaries, they had to adapt in order to make their profession survive. Many of them adopted Christian symbols and ideas to give themselves legitimacy in a world that had changed. Familiar with the Christian teachings, some of them decided to derive their legitimacy directly from the Christian reference book, the bible. That many of them adopted the names of the apostles, as their personal names, as if they were reincarnations of them, testifies to an intensive process of identification with those famous Christian ancestors who – in conformity with traditional beliefs—are simply considered to be remote ancestral spirits. Christian beliefs and local African religious concepts began to converge and overlap in many areas, most of all in the common belief that there are spirits, that words (e.g. in prayers) can help, and that symbolic action can be effective. Central to these beliefs is also that one can get help from those who have died, including archetypal personalities such as Jesus or the apostles. However, since the belief in local spiritual beings had been discriminated against, and many people had internalized the missionaries' teachings, some *asing'anga* in contact with Christianity, instead of turning to local spirits, turn to Christian ancestral figures for inspiration, hoping thereby also to attract clients who belong to one of the Christian congregations operating in the country."

(Interview with Gerhard Kubik in Vienna, September 7, 1999)

Nsembe

The words referring to *nsembe* are words of long ago, indeed. If someone talks about *nsembe,* it always means that there are things concerning *mizimu* (spirits). *Nsembe* is a word which expresses the idea of petition, of asking, begging for something (*kupempha*), because whenever a person says he or she will "pour out" *nsembe* (*akuthila nsembe*), it means that he or she will beg things from the spirits whom he thinks that they are capable of helping him in his needs. There are many ways of *akuthila nsembe*, i.e. "pour out" something for the spirits, make an offering in the hope of a reward, but the basic meaning is always the same that the person doing so, begs something from the spirits. And it always includes an offering. This is what distinguishishes *nsembe* from other forms of communication. When Gerhard Kubik asked me whether it could be called *nsembe* when in November 1997 he deposited his written wishes in a Shinto shrine in Kyoto, Japan, my answer was "No". (Conversation, September 8, 1999). *Nsembe* always involves an offering to the spirit by the person who expresses his or her wish. He didn't offer anything.

There are many different occasions for *nsembe*, such as *nsembe* "poured out" by a *sing'anga* who uses maize flour (*ufa*). I observed such *nsembe ya ufa*, the offering of maize flour, with the *sing'anga* Lichapa in Mulanje, eastern Malawi (see list of the medical practioners I have worked with; no. 9). *Nsembe* is part of medical practice. Someone who is ill and requests quick relief may seek advice from a *sing'anga*. In many cases the latter will diagnose that perhaps the person was afflicted with illness because of ancestral spirits (*mizimu ya anthu akufa omwe anamwalila kale kale);* and that those ancestors were not happy in the place where they had gone, and that from their place they would send any kind of disease to haunt the person about whom they were thinking that he or she was doing bad things in the village. In such a case many people are convinced that thinking about an offering (*maganizo ansembe*) can bring relief. Psychologists will agree,[9] but if you tell this news to people in our region who pray in certain churches such as the congregation of the Seventh-Day-Adventists, they will deny passionately that it could be true. In this environment, *nsembe* has no meaning at all for some people.

There was another type of *nsembe* which people performed a long time ago. People in the village believed that if rain did not come in a certain area, an offering (*zithila nsembe)* would help. Indeed, many ethnic groups were practising this. People would go to the mountain to make the offerings there, such as killing a domestic animal (*kukaphelako chiweto*), perhaps various domestic animals; on some occasions songs were sung, and perhaps maize flour was sprinkled towards the sky (*mwina ndikumawaza ufa kumwamba*). Thereafter, rain would perhaps fall on their villages. Such offerings for rain were common before the Christian creed arrived in Malawi. This is well-known because some authors have reported about it (cf. Gwengwe 1965 [1970: 19-31]) and there is also the oral tradition. Whenever there was drought there were offerings for rain (*kuthila nsembe ya mvula*) until it arrived.

The different ethnic groups in Malawi make a variety of offerings to the spirits. Some of the offerings I am describing below concern the needs of small social units, such as extended families, people who have consanguine relationships (*omwe ali pachibale pawo*). When a person is constantly pursued by nightmare dreams, and always feels ill, he or she may one day become delirious and say strange things. Such a person is considered to suffer from an infliction called *matenda wobwebweta*. The verb *kubwebweta* means: to speak out anything phantastic, and it is thought that the words uttered come from *mizimu* and concern their wishes, what they want people to do for them (*kulankhula zili zonse zomwe zikuchokera kwa azimuwo zimene akufuna kuti anthu awachitire*). The relatives begin to listen to the sick person and the delirious speech. They then perform *nsembe,* perhaps offering millet beer (*mowa wa masese*), perhaps they prepare food of one or another kind, handing it out to people free of charge.

Some other time it can happen that the person in trouble is a member of the *nyau* masked secret society (see also Kubik/ Malamusi 1987) or has a close relative who is a

---

[9] See the work by ethno-psychoanalysts summarized in Reichmayr 1995 [2003]; also Multhaupt 1990 on Africa.

member. In the name of the spirit he or she can call upon the society and its members to dance the "big dance" (*gule wankulu*) for him or her. It is then possible that the sick person finds relief without any need for herbal medicines. Here I can report one case. In 1994, a certain girl in our area was repeatedly seized by a spirit and began to speak in delirium(*nkumabwebweta*). In such states which people interpret as spirit possession, she always called out the names of masks and that they should perform for her (*ankatchula gule kuti aimbe*). On February 6, 1994 I and my recording assistant, Mr. Donald Kachamba, went to the place at Golowa village, T.A. Kuntaja, near a popular spot called "10 miles" on the Chileka/Blantyre road, to see the performance taking place for the girl. (Cf. recordings and documentation, orig. tape no. 94/28, archived at the Institut für Ethnologie und Afrika-Studien, University of Mainz, Collection Moya A. Malamusi). This is a so-called *gule wa Achipeta* (masked dance of the Achipeta) style, and the owner of the dance (*anu ake agule*) was called Changalala, a man of about 60 years. People had alredy assembled and they were drinking millet beer. One of the masked dancers took the girl by her hand and went with her to a place where a tree was. I was unable to observe in detail what was going on there, but I noticed that the owner of *gule* had an animal's tail (*nchila*), a small axe (*kankhwangwa*) and a plate of maize flour (*ufa*) in his hands. It is sure that an offering took place at that tree.

There are other types of *nsembe* which people carry out in the name of a prominent village ancestor, a founder or first occupant. In many communities there is usually an elder who is greatly revered, beyond his or her death. Even thereafter, the place continues to be known under the name of that person, and remembered by his name. Often he is associated with the tree he planted when the place was settled. Our small area at Singano village, Chileka, for example, is referred to as "at Kazunguza's " (*pamene timakhala ife amati paKazunguza).* Kazunguza was the brother (*mulongo wawo*) of Achiri, my grandmother in the matrilineage who died in 1987. Kazunguza thereafter, was the maternal uncle (*malume*) of Anasoko, my mother. There is a mango tree in our village which was planted by him, and in the past offerings were made there.

Such a prominent ancestor continues to exist in the mind of the offspring as their ancestral spirit (*ngati mzimu wawo*) whom they fear a lot. Consequently, anything they undertake, they may undertake in the name of that ancestor. Even if they brew beer for sale (*mowa wa malonda*), the producer of that beer would not hesitate to fill a large vessel plaited with bamboo (*nsungwi*), called *chipanda*, with millet beer and put it there under the mango tree planted by the ancestor, or any other tree that is close to the place. Leaving the beer there he would call out the name of the ancestor so that he should help the community and that he should drink this beer together with those alive who have produced it.

Many times in our village I observed that when they brew millet beer they would put a vessel down at that tree which is close to our compound. But it is now many years that have passed since I saw this. Even the vessel called *chipanda* which is plaited from bamboo, is no longer found, and so far, I have not even obtained a specimen for my "Museum of Ethnographic Objects" next to my office. It might be possible to find someone at Madzi a Bango, in Chikwawa District, who could make one for our museum. But in the past, when people had offered millet beer to the ancestral spirit, a certain man used to come who was the gravedigger of our village. He had been responsible for many funerals. His name was Sawasawa. On many occasions I saw him come and drink the millet beer that had been placed at that mango tree. The gravedigger (*sabwila*) has a special social status. He can arrive at the village and do anything disagreeable, even insult people, but there is never any legal case (*mulandu*). The term *sabwila* is also a taboo word. It would be extremely impolite to address a professional gravedigger, who gets money from every funeral, with that term. It can be used as an insult in conversation with an ordinary person, but it always triggers a vehement response, even a violent reaction.

II. Field research data in detail

Talking to *asing'ana* in Malawi is not a recreational activity. At first I encountered many obstacles detracting my interlocutors from understanding the purpose of my research and why I had come to see them. Initially, many among the *asing'anga* I have worked with did not want to give me any kind of information about their work. Sometimes several days had to pass until I was able to converse with them productively. Only after a long time did some of them eventually explain to me a few things, usually what they considered to be of no particular secrecy.

But in the process of talking, some topics came up which encouraged me to ask deeper questions. Since I have always carried a tape recorder with me, I recorded our conversations. Unexpectedly, this proved to be an asset. I was able to play back to them the recorded conversations and I found that they greatly enjoyed hearing their words on the tape. No doubt, it contributed to the fact that relationships between the various *asing'anga* and me were soon straightened out. Sometimes a friendship developed. And if there were things they did not like to tell me in the beginning, they now began to talk freely, and they also had no objections to being recorded.

Of course, I also wanted to learn something from the patients' viewpoints, those who were receiving help from the *asing'anga*. This turned out to be even more difficult, because the patients were afraid initially, not only of me and my unusual work, but even more so of the *sing'anga* who treated them. On many occasions I found that the sick persons were not at all happy to say even a word about why they had come for consultations and what kind of trouble had instigated them to arrive there. It has happened repeatedly that in the places to which I went, it was the patients who would show the greater resistance to share information with me.

Here I discovered a recipe that would help. As soon as I was formally accepted by the owner of the place, the *sing'anga,* I simply begged him to encourage his patients to respond to my various questions. With some luck, I then received reasonable information, though probably never completely uncensored, from one or another person among the sick. Much more background information became available, however, in those cases when it happened that the sick person was my acquaintance, such as Kambazithe Makolekole, the xylophone player (see section on Akina Thomas).

In this chapter which is the central part of this book. I will reproduce in the original, translate, annotate and discuss some of my conversations with four *asing'anga* out of the thirteen in my list. These are:

(1) Akina Thomas (Mrs.) (no. 4 in the list)

(2) Simon Banda (Mr.) (no. 1)

(3) Jonas Masangwi (Mr.) (no. 2)

(4) Paulo Luka (Mr.) (no . 3)

I have chosen those from my earliest fieldwork in four different districts, Blantyre, Thyolo, Ntcheu and Chikwawa; but I also decided upon those four people because each was a personality quite different from the other, including one female *sing'anga*: Akina Thomas. Their work presents a cross-section of what *asing'anga* in Malawi usually do.

Due to limitations as to the book's size, it was not possible to spread out in extenso the material I possess about all the thirteen individuals. But the database is always my original, preserved field notes.

In my transcriptions of the Chichewa-language interviews. I have followed meticulously the individual pronunciation of my interlocutors. For reasons of historical accuracy and faithfulness to my field sources I have not edited the texts to conform to the so-called standard Chichewa. The Chichewa-speaking reader of this work will be aware of the fact that there are various dialects of the language. My spellings are intended to reflect as closely as possible local and individual pronunciation. Therefore, you will find, for example that Paulo Luka whose home was in Mozambique would say at one point: "chafukwa kumeneko nkodula, ndiye lero pita ku chipatala chaboma, asati cha private..."and in another place he would address one of his clients as "*m'bele wanga*".

These are not typing mistakes. Paulo used these pronunciations instead of those in standard Chichewa, such us "chifukwa", or "osati" and "mbale wanga", especially in conversations with clients who shared his original dialect.

There are also sections of text in my transcriptions in which Chichewa is mixed by the speaker with another language, such as for example, Chisena. This is the case of *sing'anga* Akina Thomas in Chikwawa District. Here, as elsewhere, I have strictly observed the rule of accuracy in relation to the sources which I hope any serious fieldworker respects.

The English translations appear next to the Chichewa originals.They appear to be longer which is due to the nature of the English language. Bantu language structure often allows us to convey an idea much more quickly than in a European language. In part this is due to the existence of noun classes and concordial prefixes (see also : Salaun 1969). There is no gender distinction in personal pronouns. *Ali bwino* can refer to a male or female person or many persons; in translation it can mean " he is well ' , "she is well" or "they are well" while in English we are required to make a choice between gender in the singular, or otherwise use the plural.

In the translations, therefore, it was important for me to render the original meanings as closely as possible in the other language. Since the Chichewa terms, like those in any other language, rarely have translations that would match a word exactly, the method I have used to tackle this problem, was to explain many of the terms and their meanings in extensive annotations (which are numbered as footnotes). This will enable the English-speaking reader to get as close as possible to the meanings in the original text.

Akina Thomas (Mrs.)

Among the many different personalities of *asing'anga* in southern Malawi, there is also a good number of women professionals. One of then is Mrs. Akina Thomas Wakhuta Moyo. This is her complete name, including the descriptive epithet "*Wakhuta moyo*" (= the one who has had enough of his/her life). This phrase described her claim of extraordinary powers. Any wizard or witch *(mfiti)* trying to play their medicines on Mrs. Thomas is doomed. Those who want to do evil to her, die fast. *Mfiti wakhuta moyo, safunanso moyo* (the wizard/witch has had enough of his/her life, he/she does not want live again).

Akina Thomas is a medical practitioner who helps people in the areas of Chikwawa and Nchalo in Chikwawa District. Her type of *using'anga* can be characterized in her own language, Chisena, as *kwa amambo* (= for the *amambo* spirits). In Chichewa the term is *azimu*, but of course not the *azimu* (spirits), as conceptualized by Christian churches, but spirits which can inflict bad dreams or disease. *Amambo* is a term in the Chisena language, but these spirits can also be described in Chichewa as *mizimu ya amambo* (spirits of the *amambo*-type). The *amambo* are thought to be animal spirits, *mizimu yofanizira ndi chirombo* i.e spirits which resemble wild animals such as a hyena, monkey etc. This is evident in possession. The medical practitioner or even the ordinary person who gets possessed begins to act like any of these animals (see also Malamusi 1992:87-88).

Many times we hear people say about some medical practitioners that these are *asing'anga amambo* (= medical practitioners of the animal spirits). Usually this means that such a person, before he or she became a *sing'anga*, first fell ill and was perhaps sick for along time. In their desire to recover, such people begin to express many different things which they were "shown" by animal spirits appearing to them during their state of illness. And it is precisely what he or she experienced during those states as "shown" by the spirits, will then constitute the practice of this *sing'anga* to help other people. The kind of experience will determine whether the person will take up the work of a so-called *sing'anga wamankhwala*, i.e a medical practitioner who hands out beneficial medicines, or otherwise the work of someone who is not even a *sing'anga* in the true sense, but a diviner (*mulosi*)[10] who can foresay things that will happen in the future. All this arises from the experience of disease, perhaps from dreams, or otherwise from inspiration by the animal spirits (*mizimu ya amambo)*. Mother Akina Thomas got possessed by animal spirits when she was still very young, but only when she had grown up did she begin her work of medical practice (*ntchito ya using'anga)*. She explained to me that first she tried hard to refuse the demands of the spirits, but she failed. Eventually, she had to give in to the spirits' insistent calls and become a medical practitioner. Summarizing, we can call Mrs. Akina Thomas a *sing'anga wa mizimu ya amambo* to characterize the way she had been introduced to her profession.

This is how I first made her acquaintance: For some time, Kambazithe Makolokole who is an eminent band-leader and composer of *valimba* (xylophone) music and lives at Lauji village near Chikwawa in the Lower Shire River area (cf. Malamusi 1993, 1995, Tracey 1991) had suffered from a personal problem: he no longer managed to have proper sexual intercourse with his wife. While he had always slept successfully with his wife in the past, not haunted by any problem, all of a sudden he discovered that he was unable to have an erection.[11] so he decided to see and obtain advice from various *asing'anga* in the

[10] *kulosa* = to predict, foresay, prophesize; *kulosela* is the applied form of this word.

[11] In Chichewa/Chinyanja this can be expressed by saying: "*mpeto yawo siyinadzuke nkomwe*" (cf. Scott/Hetherwick 1970:324). Correctly to be written *mpheto* refers in a polite way to something "be-

area, hoping that they would be able to uncover what had happened to him. He remembered having once visited – with the very same concern – a female *sing'anga* whose name was Akina Thomas, when he was still living at Kakoma, a place close to the residence of the parental Makolekole family. Akina Thomas had given him some medicines to be administered orally, but she had also instructed him to come back to her after finishing the medicine she had prescribed. Kambazithe however, as soon as he began to experience some relief and thought that he was cured of the trouble, did not feel like going back to that female doctor, allegedly because he had heard that she had moved to a remote place – in fact to the place where we would eventually find her.

At least this was his version of the story. Since he had been fine for a while, with everything normal between him and his wife, he began to think that perhaps his former sexual problem was positively resolved, and that it would not recur. But all of a sudden he experienced that the trouble resurged, just as it had haunted him before.

It was precisely at that juncture that I arrived in his village. When he complained to me about his problem, I offered him transport to take him back to the same *sing'anga*. When we arrived I realized that the place was indeed remote from the village of Kambazithe Makolekole. However, I soon discovered that contrary to what he had claimed, there was yet another reason for why he had never come back to her: because during his first visit he had not paid the consultation fee, but had negotiated an arrangement with the *sing'anga* that he would pay the bill as soon as he found relief. Unfortunately, he never honored his promise. As soon as he experienced that he was getting better, he decided not to reveal the fact to her, knowing that he would then have to pay the sum they had agreed upon.

Not surprisingly then, at the reception in her place, Tizola village, on February 2, 1995 she asked him (in my presence): "So you have come again now after a full year has passed? What have you been doing all the time?"

In the conversation that developed between the two and which I have recorded, the female *sing'anga* talked in Chisena language [12], but she talked as if she was speaking like the animal spirits called *amambo* (*kulankhula ngati mizimu ya amambo*). Neither myself, nor Kambazithe Makolekole understood everything the *sing'anga* was saying, but her husband provided a translation explaining the meaning of her words in Chichewa.

This conversation between the *sing'anga,* her translator and her client is followed by an interview which I conducted the same day and whose transcriptions also follows below.

---

tween the legs", "also the secret parts". *Siyinadzuke*, literally: it did not wake up, it did not rise. *Kudzuka* (v.) = to get up, to rise up.

[12] Chisena (the language of the Asena = people of Sena, named after a town in Mozambique) is classified by Malcolm Guthrie (1948:59) as N.44, a language of ZONE N, Group 40 of the Bantu languages. On the history and culture of the Asena see also Kubik/Malamusi 1989:28-32, Pampalk 1982, Phiri 1979, Rita-Ferreira 1975).

Recorded consultation at the village of medical practitioner Mrs. Akina Thomas, aged 52, at Tizola village, T.A Lundu, Chikwawa Disrict, February 2, 1995. 0rig. Tape no. 95/1

A. = the female *sing'anga,* Mrs. Akina Thomas

K. = Kambazithe, the patient

W. = the Chichewa translator

M. = Moya (myself)

A. Kwaiwo kwaiwo shamwali!13)	A. *Kwaiwo kwaiwo shamwali*![13] [speaking to Kambazithe]
W. Akuti moni!	W. She is giving you greetings!
K. Zikomo, zikomo, mphandule! 14)	K. Thank you, thank you, *Mphandule*![14])
A. Uli dzyadidi?	A. *Uli dzyadidi*? (Are you well?)
K. Aaa,tili bwino pang'ono	K. Not quite, We are just a bit well.
A. Kwaiwo shamwali!	A. *Kwaiwo, shamwali*! [speaking to me]
W. Ati moni –	W. She is giving you greetings!
M. Zikomo	M. Thank you!
W. Ati muli bwanji?	W. She is saying, how are you?
M. Tili bwino kaya iwo?	M. We are well, what about her?
A. Nanga siwawona wekha, pomwe umati ngati wachenjela, hehe ndaseka ine Kaburunga.15)16)	A. [Speaking to *Kambazithe* with the voice of the Spirit *Kaburunga*]: [15]) After all, don't you see yourself how you have acted like a treacherous person? [16]) [But] *hehe*! Myself I am justl laughing, me! *Kaburunga*!
K. Ndabviona eee.	K. I have seen these things, yes!
A. Sha, shilingi ibodzi yokha yomwe akundipatsayo, ngati chanukho?[17] Ameneyo ndi wochenjela safuna kupeleka ndalama.	A. [continuing to speak, as if the spirit spoke through her]: *Sha*! If he just gave me one shilling only as something that I could sniff! [17] This person is treacherous, he doesn't like to reimburse me.
W. Anayikhila.18)	W. [turning to the *sing'anga*]: He has just paid something. [18]

---

[13] shamwali (Chisena language) = *munthu ndi nzake*, a person's friend; a companion, comrade

[14] Mphandule is a honorific title in Chisena, a way to address a person of higher rank; perhaps something like "Your Excellency!" "Your Highness!"

[15] Kaburunga = *nzimu wina wa ukazi* (name of a female spirit).

[16] Kambazithe did not pay the fee for the previous treatment. The spirit accuses the client of thinking of himself as particularly clever (*ochenjera*), believing that his problem was over (*ankaganize kuti bvuto lawo latha*), but "you were not clever at all, but stupid, and so you have come to see me again" (*koma siunachenjere, koma wapusa chifukwa wabwelanso kwa ine*).

[17] This is a metaphor, referring to the way a dog, e.g. a police dog sniffs to check whether it is the object wanted. In a similar way the *sing'anga* takes the coin which the patient gives her as a down payment and sniffs at it *(kuti anunkhizile)*. A client pays some money before treatment starts. This is called *ndalama yoombezera* (the money for divining) or *ndalama yamaula* (the money for the lot)

[18] Kambazithe had paid a symbolic amount, such as 20 tambala. (Malawi's currency is the Kwacha. One Kwacha has 100 tambala).

A. Shamwali ukupeza deletu tayu?19)	A. [asking Kambazithe] Shamwali! How have things turned out? [19]
K. Aaa! NKhabe.20)	K. Aaa! Not quite well. [20])
A. Waaa iwe ndiwe psyiru, akuti pamudzi panupo bvuto yanuyo iripobe?	A. [Speaking with the voice of the spirit]: *Waaa* you are an idiot! [telling Kambazithe what the spirit said]: She says, is your trouble still there in your village?
K. Yakaleyo? Aaa imeneyi ikukhala ngati yayambanso, yandiyamba nthundu winangombo.21)	K. The one of long ago? No, it seems that it has started anew, it is a different type that has afflicted me. [21])
W. Akuti ntenda yanuyo ndi yakale sikuti akukuzungulilani iyayi, kuteleku akungokumbutsa yakale yomweyo.22)	W. She says that your disease is the very one of long ago, the witches don't circumnavigate you. It is just the old disease that comes back as a reminder! [22]
A. Shamwali samachela nsampha umodzi, koma amachela iwiri, itatu, inayi.23)	A. Shamwali someone will not just set one trap, but he will install two, three, four. [23])
W. Akuti kodi sanakuuzani kuti muli ndi matenda asanu mthupi limodzi, ndiye matenda enawo adachepa, ndiye akukumbutsira matenda enawo.	W. The *sing'anga* says, did she not tell you that you have five different types of disease in one body? And while some diseases have decreased, she is reminding you of the continuing presence of others.
K. Monga matenda anji amenewo, poti ena ndiwo bisalabisala sindingathe kuwadziwa iyayi.	K. Such as which diseases? Since some others are just in permanent hiding, I cannot know them.
W. Akuti matenda akutsailani kwambiri, ndi mmimbamu mumakupotani 24) kwambiri nthawi zina. Ndipo nsanau umu mu nthitimu, mumakupwetekaninsoni nthawi zina.	W. She says that among the diseases that are still very much with you, there are those inside your abdomen which wrap you up [24] from time to time; and there are those of the spine and the ribs where you also often feel pain.
K. Eyaa.	K. Oh yes.
W. Ndinso nthawi zina mukamalowa mnyumba	W. And also at other times, when you enter the

[19] This phrase is in Chisena: it translates into Chichewa approximately as "*Anzanga, ukupeza bwanji tsopano?*"

[20] *nkhabe* (Chisena) corresponds to *palibe* in Chichewa.

[21] Kambazithe tries to avoid the embarrassment of his debt default by claiming that he had come to Akina Thomas with a different disease.

[22] The spirit detects the lie quickly and discredits the idea that the witch or wizard would have given him another disease. Kambazithe should not deceive himself. The problem was that he did not keep his promise to pay the *sing'anga*. She then alludes to the fact that she herself might have been the one who brought the disease back to him as a reminder.

[23] *Samatchela nsampha umodzi* (one will not install just one trap) is a phrase like a proverb (*mwambi*). She wants to instruct her patient, that one treatment (trap) is not sufficient to catch the "animal" (the disease), but repeating and different treatments are necessary. The term *nsampha* covers several types of traps, such as for mice, rats and bigger animals.

[24] *kupota* = to twist (like a thread); to wrap around. For example, if a dog eats grass, the grass wraps up the worms in his abdomen and they go off. Here the phrase only refers to abdominal pains.

nthawi zambiri mumafuna kufooka ndiye mumachitabe mophanitsa 25) kuti aa ndine mamuna.	house, you often feel very weak and tired, and yet you continue to act upon that pit, 25)), boasting: Ah! I am a man!
A. Wandinva shamwali, ndanama?	A. Have you understood, comrade? Have I told lies?
W. Akuti ngati akunama mudzitsutsa, ndiye akuti kodi munthu uta wako umodzi 26) ungaphe nyama?Inu munatenga mankhwala kamodzi basi nkupita nkupitilatu basi osabwelelanso, ndiye sadakutayeni ai.	W. She says, if she has told you a lie, you must contradict her. And also she is asking you: Do you think that just one bow 26)) and arrow in your possession can kill a wild animal? You took medicine only once, that was all, and then you continued your habitual ways, without coming back. But she had not abandoned you!
W. Akuti panyumba panupo iwo akhala two weeks akukudikililani,27) akazanunso osabwela nawonso namudzakhala ngati mwachenjeletsana,28) monga munachenjelela inu mujaa. Ndiye amfiti akumabwela nkumazonda akazi anuwo.	W. She says she was actually waiting for you at your house 27)) for two weeks and also that you failed to come here together with your wife so that I could have strengthened her (against witchcraft) as I had strengthened you at that time. 28)) And so the wizards/witches continue to come and spy upon your wife.
A. Wapinva shamwali?	A. Have you understood that, comrade?
K. Ndapinva eee.	K. I have understood, yes.
W. Ndiye akuti muli ndi mafunso?	W. So she says, do you have any other questions?
K. Eeee, ine ndikufuna kuti ndidziwe amene akuchita izo, ndipo weniweni amachita izo, kuti ine pano ndidzilephela kugona ndi nkazi wanga mnyumbamo, kundipatsa utenda ngati umenewo sikundipha kumeneko. 29)	K. Yes, Myself, I would like to know the one who is doing these things, the very one who practices the witchcraft which causes me to fail to sleep with my wife in the house. Inflicting a disease like this one upon me, is it not equal to killing me off in my existence? 29))

[25] *mmalo mophanitsa* = in a place like a pit that is narrow at the bottom and wider at the mouth like *mbuna* (a game-pit). This is a symbolic description of the vagina.

[26] This is a restatement of the same *mwambi* about *nsampha* (trap) with other words, in a new metaphor, bow and arrow instead of a trap. *Uta wako umodzi* (your only bow). *Uta* stands for the patient's weapon, the medicine (*mankhwala*). The doctor is asking the patient whether he thinks that the medicine she gave him long ago would be sufficient" to kill the animal", i.e. to finish the disease.

[27] *asing'anga anapita pa matsenga kunyumba kwa Kambazithe* (the medical practitioner travelled by magic to the house of her patient, Kambazithe).

[28] *kuchenjeletsa* is the causative form of *kuchenjera* (to be cunning, to be able to outwit others, to be-treacherous etc.) *kuchenjeletsa* = to make someone superior, to strengthen someone, make him/ her more clever in relation to others. The *sing'anga* blamed Kambazithe that he had neglected the fact that the body of his wife (and not only his own body) should also be strengthened against the evil designs by the one who bewitched them. *Thupi lankaziyo likhale lochenjera kwa mfiti* (the body of the woman should become superior in strength to the *mfiti*'s designs).

W. Akuti inuyo ndinu osabvuta,bvuto lanuli alitha ndi mankhwala omwe mutenge pano, ndipo mankhwalawo mukamwa katatu, kapena kuti mukabviika katatu, choyamba mukakabviika nkukamwa mpaka kutha, ndiyenso kachiwiri nkubviikanso kumwa nkutha mpaka katatu. Kungotha mankhwala amenewo mukakhala nga nga 30) osafooka mkomwe mukamakagona ndi nkazi.	W. She says, yourself you are not seriously troubled; your problem will finish with the medicine which you will receive now. You should take these medicines home and drink them on three successive occasions. Perhaps first you divide them into three portions and soak them into water. You soak the first portion and drink the solution until you have finished; next time you soak again a portion and drink the solution; in all you do that three times until those medicines are finished, and you will be very strong [30]) when you sleep with your wife, not getting weak again.
A. Wanva shamwali, taphatizana apo?	A. Have you understood, comrade? Have we come to an agreement now?
K. Eee ndanva, koma tsopano ine ndikufuna kumudziwa weni weniyo akumaseweletsa nchuno mwangamoyo, nanga monga munthu ameneyo kundimalizila kwake sikundipha basi, ndiye ndimudziwe ndi ndani?	K. Yes, I have understood. But still I want to know that very person who continues to play around with my waist, because if this person intends to finish me, is it not just the same as killing me off? So I should like to know who he/she is?
A. Monga kalelo iwe sudali mamuna kwambiri, moti nkazi wamba osakuseweletsa?31)	A. Is it not so that long ago you were a real man? And no woman would have been able just to play around with you? [31])
K. Iyayi ndidali mamunadi, koma pano zachisoni kwambiri, kuti ndikulephela. Ndafa ine ndithu.	K. Certainly, I was a real man before; it is only now that these sad things have happened, that I should fail. I have really died.
A. Tayu tayu, inalamuka imeneyo wanva tayu.	A. Take it easy! It will rise again, you understand? Relax!
K. Koma amene akundiphataphatayu 32) ndinkafuna ndimuganizile pinango.	K. But the one who continues to touch me ,[32] would really like to curse him/her.
A. Akuti mukufunsa nkhwangwa, nkhwangwa iri nchiuno?33)	A. You are asking for the axe? Now the axe is in your own waist! [33])
K. Eee ndinkafuna ndidziwe, chifukwa afika paupandu,34) inenso ndachinjambo	K. Yes. I just wanted to know , because this person[34]) is reaching out for the evil;

[29] The word *kumeneko* does not refer, in this case, to a particular place or spot, but to the very existence as a human being (*ya umunthu*).

[30] *nga nga* is an ideophone ; it really should be *nga nga nga* meaning: very strong, firm; in this case it means that his penis will rise up with strength (*mbolo idzuka kwambiri*).

[31] She wants to say that long ago Kambazithe with his sexual strength would have "finished" any woman.

[32] Chisena: *Kuphata* = to touch. This refers to the action of the wizard/witch who continues to play around with his body.

[33] This is a symbolic, proverbial reply. *Nkhwangwa* (axe) stands for the wizard. The doctor tells the patient that the "axe" i.e. the wizard/ witch is part of the patient's own waist. In symbolic language the doctor wants to say that the one who has bewitched Kambazithe is to be found among his relatives; in fact it is the wife of his elder brother.

[34] *munthu wachifwamba* (someone who "steals" a person) or *munthu wa upandu* (A person who boasts with bravery). The phrase *afika paupandu* in Kambazithe's words therefore implies that his sister-in-

maganizo anga.	so myself I will also change my thoughts.
A. Pali nkazi modzi, yemwe amati ndikamwa umuna wa mulamu wanga ndiye pali mulandu pamenepo? Iwo ndiyemwe akukubvutitsa iwe, kwinako udziwa wekha.	A. There is one woman who says "I will drink up the virility of my brother-in-law." So will there be a lawsuit? She is the one who is troubling you, everything else you should know yourself.
K. Ai, ndimulamwanga eti? Ine mwina ndinkaganiza mwina ndi nkazanga wothoyo. Ee kunyadoyo ndili naye ndi poison kwambiri.	K. Oh! It is really my sister-in-law? Myself I had thought that otherwise it might be my own wife. But no, if it is indeed my sister-in-law, I possess a lot of poison.
A. (kulankhula zina ndi zina)	A. (passages of no concern to the subject of the interview)
K. Inembo ndimafuna ndimubwezele chipongwe.	K. Myself, I want to return to her this impertinence.
A. Ziri ndiwe shamwali, ngati ukufuna kubwezela.	A. That is up to you , comrade, if you want retribution.

The result of the consultation was that *sing'anga* Akina Thomas eventually identified the person who had bewitched Kambazithe, when he instisted upon knowing. However, contrary to his suspicion that it was his wife, she pointed to his sister-in-law, the wife of his elder brother (cf. fig.2).

Witchcraft within Kambazithe's family relationship:

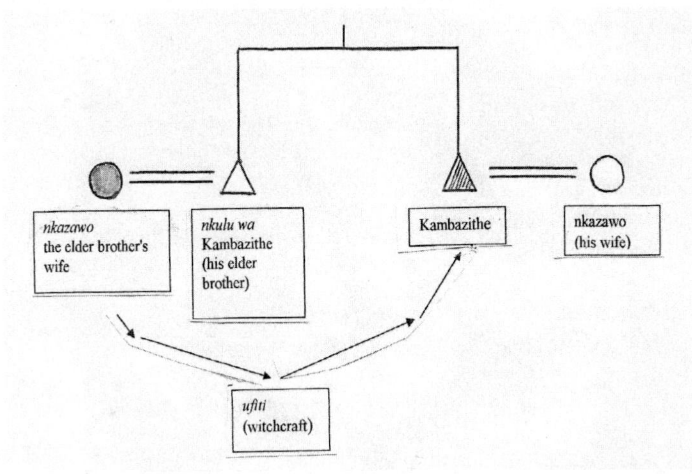

The situation within his kinship was such that Kambazithe and his wife had several children. But the other couple, his elder brother – who was about ten years older– and his elder wife had none. Thus, jealousy of the barren woman stands out as a plausible motif for practising witchcraft to make her brother-in-law impotent. Kambazithe was furious when he heard the news from the *sing'anga* and swore to take revenge. But she told her patient that it was really up to him, whether he intended retribution or not.

law had reached a stage in which she wanted to be a hero, boasting with bravery, trying to steal away a person. He is determined, however, to cut her down to size, even by using poison.

Interview with Mrs. Akina Thomas at the same place, on the same occasion, on February 2, 1995. Orig. Tape 95/2

A. = the *sing'anga*, Mrs. Akina Thomas

M. = Moya (myself)

M. Ineyo choyamba ndimafuna kuti ndidziwe mudzi wanu munabadwila, nanga ndi ntchitoyi munayamba chotani?	M. Myself, first I would like to know whether Your village (here) is the one where you were born? And how you started your work.
A. Oho, ntchitoyi ndidaiyamba ndiona chaka chino pano cha 9 ndikugwila ntchito imeneyi. Mudzi wathu unaberekedwa ine pano ndi kwa Masache, boma la Chikwawa lomwelino.	A. Oho! I think I began this work nine years ago and I have continued ever since. Our village where I was born is at (chief) Masache 's place, here in Chikwawa District.
M. Ndiyeno kuti muiyambe ntchito imeneyi munayamba motani?	M. And what was it precisely that made you start your profession?
A. Uhuu, ntchito iyi kuti ndiyambe, chosadziwa chilichonse iyayi, malingana mizimu kundigwila, idandigwila ndili wang'ono, ndiye malingana kuikana mpaka ndalimbikilabe, mpaka kupita ku chalichi osatheka basi mizimuyo kumangobwela basi. Ndiye mizimuyo nkumangobwela kunena kuti iwe tikufuna kukhala sing'anga, ndipo using'anga wako ukhale wa azimu, ndipo ife sitikufuna zonse zomwe asing'anga ena akuchita ai, 35) koma ife timangofuna nsalu yoyela ndi mpango woyela 36) kuti udzigwilila ntchito yakoyo.	A. Uhuu, I did not have any anticipations at all that I would one day start this kind of work, and that perhaps spirits would take possession of me. They actually caught me when I was still a small girl. But although at that time I rejected very firmly to do this kind of work, and even went to church [for my protection] it was all in vain. The spirits kept coming all the time. And those spirits were coming to say to me: you! We want you to become a *sing'anga*, but your medical science (*using'anga)* should be of the type based on communication with the *azimu* (spirits). Also we don't want you to rely on all the things some other *asing'anga* employ, [35] but we just want that you procure yourself a white cloth (*nsalu yoyela*) and a white hood (*mpango woyela*) [36] for taking up your work.
M.Uhu!	M. Uhu!
A. Ndiye kuyambila pomwepo zinalimbadi,37)	A. Starting from there, things eventually gained momentum. [37] First there came a

[35] There are other a*sing'anga* who for example try to find out something about human problems by using a *nsupa*, i.e. vessel from an animal horn, gourd etc. containing a black, burned medical substance. The *mizimu* (spirits) told Akina Thomas that they would not want her to use any of these devices.

[36] The kind of hood identified here as *mpango* can also be called *nduwira* translated by Scott Heatherwick 1970:376 as"head-dress of calico". The spirits told Akina Thomas that if she wore that cotton garment with the hood while receiving her patients, the spirits would quickly enter her head, helping her to identify her patients' problems.

ndiye panabwela munthu wina yemwe anatha zaka 22 osabeleka, mpaka ndidamusumika,38) pambuyo pake adabeleka. Mamunanso kutha akazi ambiri kwabasi,39) kusemwa 40) nkazi kuchoka kusemwa uyo kuchoka.Ndiye atafika pano ndidamusimika mpaka kubeleka ndi nkazi wake yemweyo anamukwatila. Chifukwa kuteroko timakhala ngati tamuchulula 41) basi, ndiye nthawi ina iriyonse amakhala wobeleka mpaka kale.	certain woman who had stayed for twenty-two years without giving birth to a child, and I treated her successfully. [38]) Thereafter she became pregnant. A man also came who had slid from one divorce into another, who had got divorced from many women, getting married -- leaving his wife, [39]) getting married with another one – leaving her, and so on. When he came here for consultation, we were able to put him alright, until he even produced a child[40] with the woman he had recently married. Through my treatment he apparently got turned on again, [41]) and ever since they have had children.
M. Ndiye paja dzina lanu lija ndi ndani?	M. And at that time what was your proper name?
A. Natembo.42)	A. Natembo. [42])
M. Ndiye dzina limene mumachuka nalo limenelo?	M. Is this the name with which you became famous?
A. Uhu, Natembo Thomas.	A. Uhu! Natembo Thomas.
M. Kaya mukudziwa muli ndi dzaka dzingati dzakubadwa?	M. Do you know how old you are?
A. Iii, sitingathe kudziwa iyayi.	A. Iii! I cannot know that.
M. Tsopano kunoko matenda amene mumachilitsa inuyo ndi matenda amitundu ingati?	M. Now here, the diseases which you normally cure, how many types there are?
A. Matenda akuti ndichilise, monga tsempo 43) nimbachilisa, nchofu 44) nimbachilisa, chibayo nimbachilisa, monga nthenda zambiri monga padziko lapansi pano, zina zake ndimbatani? Ndimbachilisa, koma chinalephela ine ndi	A. The diseases which I am said to be able to cure include for example, *tsempo*[43]) (swollen face), I can cure that, *nchofu* [44] (vomiting yellow liquids) I can cure that, *chibayo* (pleurisy, pneumonia)and many other diseases

[37] *zinalimbadi* (= things gained force, momentum). As a young girl, after the spirits had appeared to her, Akina Thomas did not want to take up the profession of *sing'anga*. but then she found the energy, the inner force, to do so.

[38] *kusumika* (also *kusimika* in Chisena language).

[39] The reason why the man got divorced from all those women was that they did not get children, and he did not contemplate that perhaps the fault was with him, but he accused his marriage partners of being infertile, until one of his ex-wives gave birth to a child from another man. That was the point he went to consult the *sing'anga* Akina Thomas.

[40] *kusemwa* (Chisena language) = *kukwatila* (in Chichewa) = to marry, to get married.

[41] *kuchulula* (Chisena) = *kuyambitsa* (Chichewa) = to get someone started, to turn someone on.

[42] This is a clan name (*mfunda*).

[43] The correct pronunciation is *tsempho*. The term describes a disease in which the face gets swollen around the eyes (*kutupa ku maso*), swellings can also appear on the hands, the llegs etc. and the patient might cough (*kutsokomola*) very hard. People believe that this disease is caused when a woman commits adultery, and thereafter, from the salt she puts into the food, the husband may get ill, develop *tsempho*; even the children can develop the same ailment. Western-trained medical doctors, however, believe that *tsempho* is due to malnutrition, lack of vitamins, even kwashiorkor.

[44] This could be caused by problems of the gall-bladder or liver.

edzi sindinganame kuti ndingaikwanitse mankhwala ake palibe.	that can be found on earth, how do I cope with them? I can cure them. But with AIDS I have failed, I would not want to tell lies and claim that I have sufficient means against it; there is no medicine at all.
M. Oho,	M. Oho!
A. Mhhu	A. Mhuu.
M. Chabwino iyayi zikomo kwambiri.	M. All right, thank you very much!
M. Ndiye ndinaona nthawi ijayi kuti mumagwiritsa kenakake ntchito monga ngati mumaimba kenakake, ndi nthawi zinanso mumaimba nyimbo, chimene mumaimba chija chinali chichani?	M. At that time [referring to the recorded consultation, cf. tape 95/1] I saw that you include in your work other activities such as singing songs. When you were singing what was that instrument which you were playing?
A. Chimene timbaimba chija, timbati muleji 45) wathu, ehe kuti mizimu ija ibwele, Imabwela naimene ija.	A. That thing we were playing, we say it is our *muleji* [45]) so that those spirits should come, they come with that song.
M. Imabwela ndi imene ija?	M. They come with that song?
A. Ehe tingaimba nyimbo yawo ija. Basi mijimu iyenela kubwela.46)	A. Yes, if we sing their song, then the spirits are induced to come. [46])
M. Muleji kodi ndi maseche?	M. *Muleji* is it a rattle?
A. Ehee maseche.	A. Yes, it is a rattle.
M. Ndiye kupanda chimene chija mulejiwo?	M. And without that rattle?
A. Iyayi.	A. Oh no!
M. Osabwela mizimu?	M. The spirits don't come?
A. Koma ibwelabe, malingana nyimbo zawozo zinaimba iwowozo angagundidwa, eee afika.	A. But they still come, from the moment their songs are sung, they are feeling excited, and in turn, yes, they arrive.
M. Tsopano nyimbo zimene zija zimakhala muchinenelo chanji?	M. Now those songs are in which language?
A. Oho nyimbo zimene zija zimakhala ngati bzyoka 47) la Chisena.	A. Oho! Those songs are like the talking of Chisena spirits (*bzyoka*). [47])
M. Nyimbo zimene zija mumachita kuphunzilanso?	M. Did you learn those songs regularly?
A. Ambaimba naniyachewo, mzimuwo umbayimba okha.48)	

[45] The translation of *muleji* (in the Chisena language) is uncertain, although later in the interview, Akina Thomas states that the term refers to her rattle which in Chichewa would be called *maseche*. Scott/Hetherwick 1970:310 list a similar word, *mlezi*, and translate it as "nurse", even as "God" as "the one who nourishes all things and whose is the bow *utawaleza*, the rainbow". If Mrs. Akina Thomas perhaps misunderstood my question, *muleji wathu* might well refer to some supernatural power, perhaps in association with playing the rattle, so that the spirits would come.

[46] She explains that it is the spirit who sings through her voice.

[47] *bzyoka* (plural: *mabzyoka)* refers to a type of spirit. In 1987, the research team Gerhard Kubik, Donald Kachamba and Lidiya Malamusi filmed a *mabzyoka* spirit possession ceremony in a camp of Chimarenje-speaking refugees from Mozambique at Muloza, Mulanje District. (Cinematographic document no. 69/ Kubik, July 2, 1987, private collection Prof. Kubik, Vienna).

48 She wants to say that it is not herself who sings those songs, but the spirits use her vocal cords.

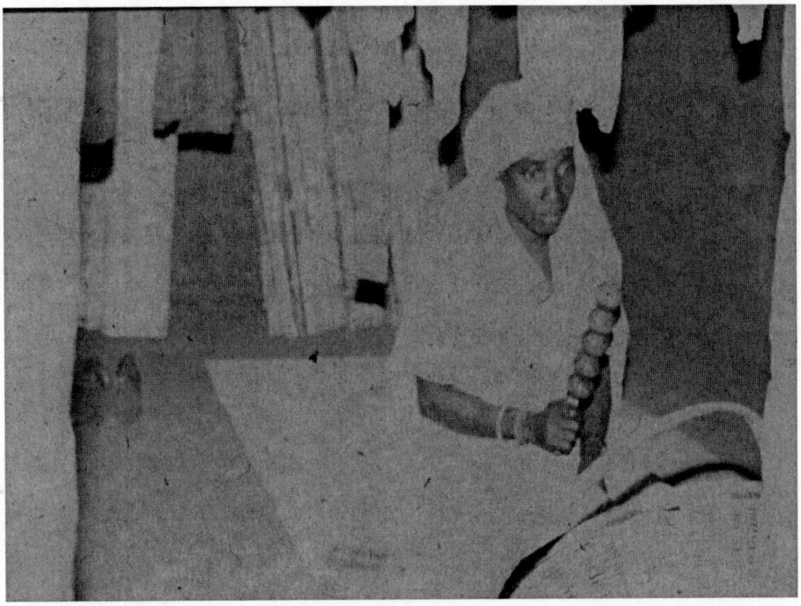

The "doctor of spirits "(*asing'anga amizimu*) Akina Thomas sitting in her room where she regularly holds spirit sessions. In order to diagnose the kind of trouble of a patient who seeks her advice, she sings songs. In her hand she is holding a rattle to accompany her singing, calling the spirits so that they should tell her exactly what kind of problem her patient has.

At Tizola village, T.A. Rundu, Chikwawa District, February 2, 1995 (Photo no. 95/2/7, author).

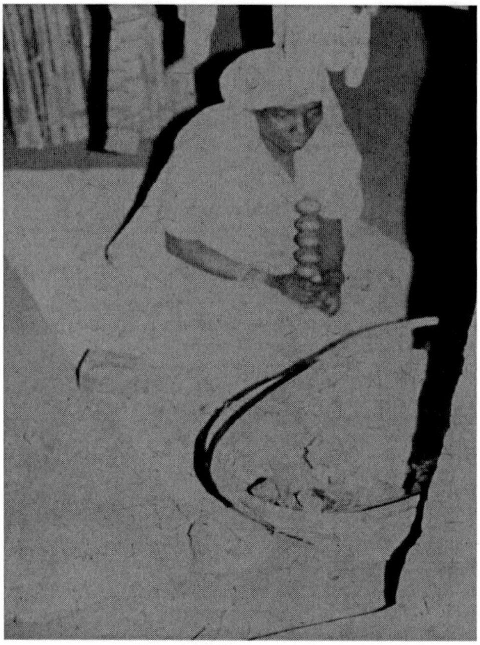

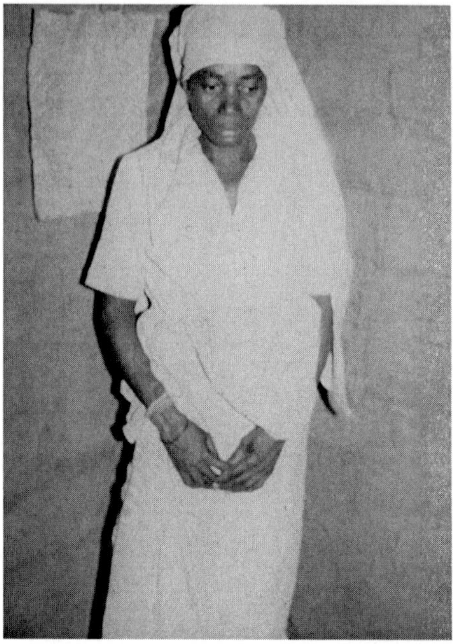

Mother Akina sings her songs while whistling and shaking a rattle. On the occasion of a spirit session she would only wear her white cotton garment and hood, no other type of clothes. She insisted that if she used other clothes while performing the songs, the spirits would not come to her head.

At Tizola village, T.A. Rundu, Chikwawa District, February 2, 1995.
(Photo no. 95/2/8 and 9, author)

Simon Banda
(Mr.)

Simon Banda was very famous as a medical practitioner (*sing'anga*) in the Chileka/ Blantyre area. He had come from Kasungu in the Central Region of Malawi to settle within the traditional boundary of Chief Kunthembwe. It was here that he opened a surgery. By the time I met him, he had not actually lived here for a very long time, but approximately for two years, as he informed us when we found him. The exact place where he resided was Khumbirina Village within the jurisdiction of Chief Kunthembwe, in Blantyre District. Only a short time after he had established his surgery, however, many reports about his expertise began to circulate, and many clients flocked to him, some of them getting admitted to his surgery as if into a hospital, sleeping there. Not only did he know many kinds of herbal medicines, but he also helped people by other ways of treatment.

The only disagreeable thing that was reported about him was the fact that he was addicted to alcohol, and that he liked to court, even seduce women among his patients. Upon arrival in the village he had brought along only one wife from his home area in the Central Region, but very soon he was seen with three wives, picked up locally, while his original wife was virtually abandoned.

Some people became worried about this state of affairs. But the worst thing that happened regularly was that female persons who arrived alone, seeking medical assistance, or fell ill while staying at the *sing'anga*'s place were regularly pressed into having a sexual relationship with him. Sometimes the kind of prescriptions he gave were dependent on their compliance. This went on for a long time and eventually it ended in disaster (see below).

The following account is translated from my Chichewa fieldnotes dated December 17, 1993 when I was compiling information about the *sing'anga* Simon Banda whom I visited that very day at Khumbirina village, T. A. Kunthembwe in Blantyre District. Originally, these notes were written to accompany the recorded interview on original tape no. 93/13 of my field recordings. (Copies of the recordings were made for the Archive of Sound recordings established by Wolfgang Bender at the Institut für Ethnologie und Afrika-Studien, University of Mainz).

It is common wisdom in Malawi that whenever the news spreads that in a certain place there is a medical practitioner who helps people, then many people set out on a pilgrimage there with all sorts of personal problems. So it happened in the area of Kunthembwe in 1993, that reports were heard, beginning in September, that a *sing'anga* called Simon Banda had arrived in order to start a medical practice. After having checked reports about that person I felt like going there to see for myself what exactly he was doing. On December 17,1993 I set out together with my companion, the composer Donald Kachamba, so that we should get a first-hand field experience of that man's skills and how they were applied. After we had arrived at a place called Chikuli, in the same area, we contacted a certain young man who had already helped us on a previous occasion to find people who would be able to tell and sing stories *(nthano)*. From him we inquired about what sort of things that *sing'anga* was doing. He told us that that person was performing very well, to the effect that many people had already found relief at his place. So we decided to visit him there, discovering that the place was not even very far from Chikuli.

When we arrived we found Mr. Simon Banda together with some women, about whom he told us that they were his "secretaries". Speaking to us in Chichewa he actually used the English term with a Chichewa plural prefix *ma-*. He said: *masekilitale*. Surprisingly, already after a short while we found ourselves chatting with him, and in a recorded interview (see below) he explained to us many details of his work and how he had become a *sing'anga*.

What follows now is my own observations, i.e. what I noticed with this *sing'anga* stirring considerable interest in me. This *sing'anga* used many different methods, and many astounding things took place there in his practice. He used to help people with medical substances (*mankhwala*), but also with magic (*matsenga*).[49]) Among the various things which he showed us was one that surprised us a lot: he used a certain paper, a special sheet of paper in his possession, for a magic action to give retribution to people for possible acts of insolence towards him. But he would also use this method if for example one of his clients who was identified by him as the victim of somebody's witchcraft, demanded retribution. In any case, Simon Banda, after having identified the wizard or the witch would ask his client: "Do you want retribution for the acts of that person?" In all these cases, in order to produce such evil magic for punishing a person and make it work, he himself would use that sheet of paper together with the iron blade of an axe *(nkhwangwa)* in his possession. He would take these two objects and cause them to interact by putting the paper on the ground and the axe blade on top while speaking certain words (a curse). But now, when he showed it to us, we observed to our astonishment that fire came suddenly out of those juxtaposed objects, with an explosive sound. The fire first lit up, just by itself, and smoke spread, and then the fire suddenly lit up very much in an explosion. The purpose of all this was that the targeted person, far away, would then perhaps be hit by lightening or his or her home would burn down by the effect of this magic. As the fire diminished and faded out, we then saw that the axe had disappeared from the place where it was. He told us, however that he knew where it had gone. But he emphasized that, in this case, since he was just showing to us what he was able to do, it would not fly like a missile to kill somebody, but would come back by itself to the place where he used to keep it. This was something with which this man really puzzled us.

Thereafter he also showed us the phials (*nsupa*) which he customarily used for his work when he wanted to administer curative medicines to the people; he had several types, also some for being insolent to certain persons. He had many different types of phials. Among them there was one about which he said that he had brought it from the Indian Ocean, and indeed it looked like a conch (*chigabado cha nkhono*), the large, twisted shell of a snail-like tropical sea animal (*mnyanja ya madzi anchere*). The information he gave us was that the things he kept inside the shell were extremely dangerous, because they included medical substances which people who were called *ambvala-mimba* had brought to him from the graveyard. The term refers to fabulous creatures who wear no clothes and have very big abdomens, as if they were "wearing" their abdomens. I have no idea where such people are supposed to be found and, although the term is widely known in southern Malawi, I was unable to get more information out of him or from anybody else.[50] It seems to be a "tribe" or kind of people (*ntundu wa wanthu*), and they

---

[49] Chichewa terms such as *tsenga (*plural: *matsenga*) cannot be translated in a linear manner into European languages, by equating them with English terms. See my delineation of the semantic field of this word elsewhere in this book (pages 38-41).

[50] In Malawi there are several stories about "short people" in relationship with the remote history of the country. They are called by various names: *akafula* (cf. Nurse 1967), *mwandionera-kuti, ambvala-mimba,* etc. People's idea about these beings is that *akafula* are short, but it is not known whether they

seem to be connected with graveyards. He said that these were short people, or small people, and that they would appear and come only in the night. He continued saying that under certain circumstances, if he himself wanted to kill a person with his phials (*nsupa*),but failed to do so because of the internal strength and resistance *(wokhwima kwambili)* of that person, then he would send those little people to do that job of killing. This was like hiring them, he said, and he would pay the *ambvala-mimba.*

After he had finished showing us the various objects and demonstrating the actions he used in his work, he began to tell us about how he had started the work of *sing'anga* in the first place. He told us that he himself had once been a very dangerous wizard *(mfiti yoopsa*). Before starting to do the work of healing (*using'anga)* he had actually studied the skills of sorcery (*ufiti*) to a great extent, and only thereafter had he become knowledgeable in the practice of *using'anga.* And it was because of that knowledge that eventually he began to be feared by the wizards (a*mfiti*); because they knew that he had once been a wizard himself, but had abandoned sorcery and started to cure people. He stressed that his past as a wizard was an advantage, because anyone who had been a wizard before, would have no problems identifying another wizard, or finding out that such and such a person had been bewitched (*walodzedwa*), because of his previous experience in witchcraft. Even about medicines of all kinds he was well informed, he said, and could remove any type of magic; for example, if a person had been trapped *(wacheledwa)*[51]) by a wizard or witch, or also, if a person had been trapped literally with a string hidden somewhere in the fields so that he would fall and hurt himself (a kind of body trap set by a malicious person who was his enemy and jealous of his real estate). Such problems, as described by his clients, did not constitute any particular revelation for him, he said, but he would handle them quickly.

In the interview transcribed below, he elaborated on much of this information. But my portrait of the man is also based on what I was told in conversation by sick persons whom I met at Mr. Simon Banda's place while they were waiting to obtain treatment.

Three weeks after we had visited the *sing'anga* Simon Banda and talked to him, we decided to see him again, this time for consultation, in the hope of receiving some medicines, because I had begun to suffer myself from an infection that did not want to disappear. Actually it was something like intertrigo [52]) a type of dermatitis: the skin between my legs appeared infected with bacteria and fungi. First I had tried to procure treatment in a local hospital, but it was all to no avail. Instead, the affected area increased, because to whatever hospital I went they washed it with some kind of desinfectant, not very appropriate for use in the genital area. The wound increased as if it had been burned by fire. I even went to the renowned Malamulo Hospital at Makwasa, 80 km away from my home in Chileka, but there also they gave it the same sort of treatment. In my despair I

are dressed or naked, *mwandionera-kuti* are short people with big heads, while *ambvala-mimba* are conceptualized as short people with a big abdomen.

[51] *wacheledwa* is the passive form of *–chera*, v. = to set a trap, e.g. *kuchera nsampha*. A wizard can set a magical trap so that his victim will be caught.

[52] "Dermatitis occurring between folds or juxtaposed surfaces of the skin and caused by moisture, warmth, and the overgrowth of resident microorganisms" (Compact American Medical Dictionary, 1998: 235)

began to think of the *sing'anga* Simon Banda and what I had heard from many people about his medical resources. So I went there again, explaining to him everything about my infection between the thighs, and that it would not heal. He replied: "These are trivial matters, I am giving you some medicines and in two days that infection will have disappeared". I did not feel like believing him. After we had talked he went into his private room to look for those medicines and he brought a very small quantity of a kind of powder of brown colour, probably obtained by pounding bark *(khungwa)* of a tree. I could not ask him at that stage, while I was seeking help, what kind of tree that was, it would have been inappropriate to ask. This medicine was so small that I had doubts about how it would work. He said "This medicine looks small, but its power is enormous. When you go home to your house, first you bathe well, and when you have finished, you should take this medical powder and sprinkle it on the place of the wound, then leave it like that for two days."

When I arrived in the village, I applied his prescription meticulously. After bathing I sprinkled the medicine on the infected area, but to my surprise I noticed that as soon as I had administered the powder, it seemed to enter the wound very fast, and it stayed there as if glued on. There was no way of removing it again. It was like an adhesive. I left it there for two days and indeed I saw that eventually the wound dried up and the pain disappeared completely as a sign that the infection was finished. I was wondering about how this could have happened and the *sing'anga* had such powerful antibiotics like the one he had given me and which he had obtained from a certain tree. I desired to go there again to report about the success of his treatment within just a few days. But then, what happened was that in the middle of my return journey to the place, I met with a young man, Mr. Trango Makanjila with whom I had worked before on another research trip. When I told him that I was on my way to see again Mr. Banda, he gave me the shocking news that "this *sing'anga* has died. They buried him the day before yesterday."

I did not trust my ears, because just a week earlier I had been talking to him. I asked the young man to tell me what had happened. He said the news that could be heard was that a certain man together with his wife and his child had arrived at the private clinic of the *sing'anga.* The child was very ill. The three people were Mozambicans who were staying in the refugee camp at Chifunga (on the way to Mwanza) and who had come all the way from there. They stayed with the *sing'anga* Banda for several days, and gradually the sickness of their child which they had brought with them began to disappear, because of the medicines administered by Banda. The two parents were very happy that their child was getting better. However, as the child continued to be treated, after more than two weeks they ran out of food. To obtain better food for the child, the man thought of going back to Chifunga in order to procure it.

Leaving his wife and the child behind, he then left for Chifunga. While he was still on his journey, the *sing'anga* Banda became aware of the fact that the wife was very beautiful. Knowing that they had come to ask for his help to cure the child, he calculated that if he demanded anything from her, she would not refuse. Gradually, Banda began to court the married woman. She tried hard to reject his advances, explaining that she only had come there because their child was ill, but not for the purpose of adultery. Banda did not listen to her arguments, but pressed her hard to have sexual intercourse with him. The woman explained that she was sure that her husband had put medicines into her, so that if she ever slept with another man, that other man – whoever he might be – would die. The woman tried to convince Mr. Banda about these facts, but his answer was: "Don't you know that I am a powerful man? Those medicines are ineffective with me; I can sleep with you without problems at all."

The bad luck which had descended upon him, was increased by the fact that the woman's husband delayed his return with the food he was trying to obtain. A full week passed and he did not come back, because he had actually continued his journey to his home village in Mozambique for some unrelated reason. And so Mr. Banda found a chance to continue pressing the woman with his demands for sexual intercourse, because she was left without any resources and the food they had carried was used up, while her husband had not come back. And then one day, Mr. Banda began to give her money so that she could help herself with food, and when he asked her again to have intercourse with him, she eventually agreed.

But that was the end of Mr. Banda, because – according to my informant – the moment he finished the act, he was unable to rise. Until he began to cry at that place, and people hearing his distress came only to find that his back was spoiled and he was unable to stand upright again.

Thereafter people tried to carry him to the hospital of Kunthembwe, but when they arrived there he was no longer alive and the officer at the hospital just told the people that this person had already died, and that there was nothing one could do to help him. So the people just carried the *sing'anga* Banda to his funeral; they transferred him to his local residence and tried to contact his relatives. The other day his relatives came from Ntchisi, in the area of Lilongwe, where his original home was, and they took the body there.

This was the death of the *sing'anga* Banda who had coerced the wife of somebody from Mozambique to have sexual intercourse with him; and his destiny was that he would die during the act.

After hearing this story I really had no comment, but I still wanted to reach that place; eventually I decided to return home, because I knew that the people there would not tell me many things that would surpass what the young man had already told me. I also anticipated that the people would be reluctant to say anything, because the death of Mr. Banda looked like he was killed, and they might think that I was a policeman who wanted to investigate the matter. So I was quite sure that even if I went there, I would find no useful replies to my questions. So I just returned, although there were many questions I would have liked to ask, but it all failed, since there was no one else who could have addressed my personal questions which I wanted to ask the *sing'anga* Banda.

Recorded interview with Mr. Simon Petro Banda, aged ca.50 at Khumbirina village, T. A. (Traditional Authority) Kunthembwe, Blantyre District, December 17, 1993. Original tape no . 93/13

Simon Banda's original home was in Ntchisi, in the area of Lilongwe, Central Region, but he stayed in Blantyre District up to his death. However, the aim of his moving here, the thoughts behind it, are uncertain. Perhaps he had professional reasons, thinking that here he would find many people who needed help.

The conditions of my interview with him were not particularly favourable, because he had just consumed alcohol, and therefore his discourse was not really satisfactory, he seemed to hurry up. And yet, lots of things about his work he explained to me well. I have slightly shortened the interview, however, not transcribing a few passages that are irrelevant to the subject. The omitted parts are marked.

B. = Banda

M. = Moya

U. = a patient, male, about 18years old (the letter is arbitrary, it does not stand for his initial)

B. Ntchito yanga ndinayamba 1963 pa 10 October, ndipo inali nthawi ya 9 o'clock mmawa, ndipo ndinakhala ku boma la Ntchisi, ndipo ndinakhala kuboma la ku Mzalanyama 53) uko ku Lilongwe.	B. I began my work [as a medical practitioner] on the 10th October 1963. The time was 9 o'clock in the morning, and I was at the administration of Ntchisi, actually I stayed at the post of Mzalanyama [53]) there in the Lilongwe area.
M. Tsopana mwangoyamba kunena chomwechi, koma dzina lanu simunatiuze?	M. Oh, you are just starting to say those things, but don't you want to tell me your complete name?
B. Simon Petro Banda	B. Simon Petro Banda.
M. Tsopana dzina limene mumadziwika nalo pa ntchito yanuyi?	M. Is this the name under which you are known at your work?
B. Ndimadziwika ndi Dr. Banda. 54)	B. I am known as Dr. Banda. [54])
M. Ndiyeno mukupezeka kuti muli m'mudzi momuno mwa Khumbirina kwa T.A. Kunthembwe eti? Ndiye mungatiuze chiyambi cheni cheni kuti muyambe kugwira ntchito imeneyi?	M. You are now found in this village of Khumbirina, at the Traditional Authority of Kunthembwe, aren't you? Would you tell us about the beginning of it all that you should start to do the work of a medical practitioner?
B. Chiyambi cheni cheni cha udokotala	B. About the beginning of my doctoral

[53] This is a place near the game reserve.

[54] "Doctor Banda". By coincidence this is also the way former Life President of Malawi, Dr. Hastings Kamuzu Banda, who was a medical doctor, would have been addressed by patients. However, I do not think that Simon Banda identifird with the ex-president, Banda is a frequent and important *mfunda* (clan name) in Chichewa-speaking areas of te Central Region of Malawi.

wanga, ndinayamba ufiti, ndinayamba kuuluka.55) Ndinayamba ufitiwo 1958, ndipo ufitiwo ndinausiya mu chaka cha 1963,ndi chifukwa chake kuti ndidzikhala sing'anga.	practice, at first I had started witchcraft, I had started to fly, [55]) I began to practice witchcraft in 1958; eventually in 1963 I renounced witchcraft, and it is because of that, that I was to become a *sing'anga.*
M. Tsopano chiyambi chake cheni cheni alipo amene anakuphunzitsani?	M. Now at the beginning was there anyone who instructed you?
B. Bambo wanga 56) amene anandibeleka Ine ndamene anandiphunzitsa ndipo kudziwa za ufiti wa iwowo.	B. My biological father[56] was the one who taught me, from him I obtained the knowledge about *ufiti* (witchcraft).
M. Kodi bambo anuwo anali sing'anganso?	M. Was your father also a *sing'anga*?
B. Anali sing'anga amaphatikiza using'anga ndi ufiti omwe.	B. He was a *sing'anga*; and he used to combine *using'anga* (healing practice) with *ufiti* (witchcraft).
M. Ndiye inuyo munangophunzilapo ufiti wokhawo?	M. And what you learned there, was it only *ufiti*?
B. Ndinaphunzira ufiti ndi using'angawo zonse ziwiri, koma pa nthawi imene ndimazasiya ufiti, ndinawapempha iwowo muchotse ufiti umene mwandipatsa mundisiyile using'anga, ndi chifukwa chake ndili sing'anga kuchokera nthawi imeneyo kudzafika munthawi ino.57)	B. I learned both, witchcraft and medical practice together, but at the time when I decided to abandon witchcraft, I begged from him [my father] that he should remove the power of witchcraft he had conferred upon me and leave me only with the power of medical practice. It is because of that I have been a *sing'anga* from that time on until now. [57]
M. Ndiye kuti tinganene kuti ntchito yanu yomwe mwakhala mukugwila ndi yomweyi ya using'anga?	M. Can we say then that the work you have been doing is exclusively that of *using'anga* (medical practice)?
B. Ya using'anga sindinakhale pakampani iriyonse, kapena pena paliponse iyayi.	B. Yes, medical practice. I have never worked for any company or in any other profession.
M. Kodi nthawi imeneyi nkuti inu muli ndi zaka zingati?	M. How old where you at that time?
B. Ndinabadwa 1951, 58) koma ndinene kuti kukula kwanga konse ndakulila mukukhwima.	B. I was born in 1951, [58]) but I should say that during the whole period of adolescence

[55] *kuuluka* = to fly; here a symbolic expression for "being a wizard".

[56] *bambo wanga amene anandibeleka*; this seems to suggest that his mother had married different men during her life, from whom she had children. So he refers here to his real (biological) father. (Information by Monika Malamusi, April 15, 1999).

[57] This also implies that he still had the strength to remain unaffected by witchcraft. *Munthu wokhwima* is a phrase that can refer to someone invincible by the sorcery of others. (Information by Monika Malamusi, April 16, 1999).

[58] The dates given by Mr. Banda, 1951, the year of his birth, 1958 for the start of practising witchcraft, and 1963 for the start of becoming a *sing'anga* would suggest that he had become a wizard at age seven and a medical practitioner at age twelve. This is quite possible. It is even normal that wizards and witches, according to my documentation (see also the newspaper article about Sowa Kabango from Chileka; Kachinziri 1997) begin to practice their witchcraft during childhood. On the other hand, it is possible that Mr. Banda did not remember exactly the year of his birth. Most people in Malawi have no birth certificates. When I visited him in 1993, I estimated his age as about 50.

	I grew up assimilating the internal power [of my parent].
M. Tsopano mutadziwa za using'anga zija, kudela la kwanulo chimene chinachitika pambuyo pake ndi chiyani?	M. After you had obtained knowledge about *using'anga* in your home area, what happened thereafter?
B. Kudela la kwathuko kuti kokha anthu akangondiopa, malingana ndi ndime 59) imene ndinatenga.	B. It was in my home area that people would just be afraid of me with reference to the stage of expertise[59]) I had attained.
M. Monga ndime yaufitiyi kapena ya using'angayi?	M. Such as the expertise in witchcraft or perhaps medical practice?
B. Ya ufitiyi, chifukwa ankaopa ndithu.	B. Of witchcraft, because that is what they feared, indeed.
M. Kuti munali wodziwa kwambiri?	M. And you were an expert in this?
B. Wodziwa kwenikweni kwambiri.	B. Yes, I was a real expert.
M. Tsopano inu chimene chinakuchititsani Kuti munene kuti mukusiya ufiti?	M. Now what actually happened to you that you would renounce witchcraft?
B. Ndinayamba kupemphera, ndiye ndinapempha bambo wanga asanamwa lire kuti mundichotse ufiti ndikhale ndi kukhwima, using'anga ndiyo ndi imene ndinayitenga ine. Ndiye ndinakasanza ku phiri la Ntchisi.	B. I began to pray [to God], and so I begged my father before he would die to remove the power of witchcraft from me, so that I should have strength in healing practice (*using'anga*), the specialization which I had taken up, And there on the mountain of Ntchisi I vomited!
M. Kuphiri la Ntchisi?	M. On the mountain of Ntchisi?
B. Ndikumene ndinakachotsa ufiti wanga.	B. Precisely there that is where I exorcised my witchcraft.
M. Munansanza zinthu za mtundu wanji?	M. What sort of things did you vomit?
B. Njoka 60) ndi zinthu zina zambiri.	B. Snake[60] and many different things.
M. Zosiyanasiyana.	M. Different things.
B. Ahaaa.	B. Exactly.
M. Zinthu ngati zimenezi zinaikidwa ndi ndani mu thupi lanu?	M. Who planted things like that into your body?
B. Bambo wanga aineyo wondibeleka	B. It was my biological father.
M. Bambo wanu eti?	M. Really, your father?
B. Mhu.	B. Mhm.
M. Ndiye mutasanza pamene paja ndiye chinachitika china chachiwiri ndi chiyani?	M. Now, after you had vomited there, what happened next?
B. Chinazachitika ndinazafa kwa Masiku awiri	B. What happened was that I died; for two days I was unconscious.

[59] *ndime* can be translated in more than one way. In this case it refers to a higher level of expertise in *using'anga*. It is important to know that in their apprenticeship *asing'anga* (medical practitioners) move successively through different levels, stages of skill and expertise. Obviously he stressed that he had reached a high level of specialization. In Scott/ Heatherwick 1929:373, the word *ndime* is translated as"boundary", "limit of work", also with reference to gardening; here the most accurate translation might be "level of expertise".

[60] *njoka* in Chinyanja / Chichewa is singular or plural. People believe that a wizard habors terrible things in his abdomen, including snakes. It cannot be reconstructed in this case, whether Mr. Banda was talking about one snake or several snakes he vomited.

ndili chikomokele.	
M. Muli chikomokele?	M. You were unconscious?
B. Ahaa, ndiye anthu ena nkumaganiza kuti iyayi, mpaka kukhoma bokosi kuti munthu uja wapitadi ndithu, ndiye apo ndinazazizimuka ndili wa moyo.	B. Yes, and some people were thinking that I had indeed passed away, to the point that they began to nail a coffin. And then all of a sudden I woke up, I was alive.
M. Aaaa pamene munakomokapo ndi pamalo omwe munasanzilawo kapena mutachoka kupita kumudzi?	M. Did you faint at the place where you had vomited or was it after you had left for going to the village?
B. Nditafikano kumudzi, anthu atandisa-kasaka ndikundipeza nkupita nane kumudzi, kumeneko ndikomwe ndinakakomoka kwa masiku awiri.	B. After I had arrived at the village; after people had hunted me down, spotted me and escorted me to the village. It was there that I lost consciousness for two days.
M. Koma tsopano ndifunsebe ngakhale zili za nkati mwathupi, kuti panthawi imene munali chikomokeleyo pali mwa zina zimene mukuzikumbukila kapena?	M. But now let me still ask you, even if those things are deep inside the body, whether at the time you were unconscious you had any experience you would remember perhaps?
B. Zina nditha kuzikumbukila, koma zina nditha kuziyiwala, chifukwa chakuti ilo linali dzana.	B. I can remember certain experiences, but some others one can also forget them, because that day is so remote.
M. Tatiuzani mwazina zimene mukuzi-kumbukila zingakhale zotani?	M. Tell us then the nature of those experiences you remember?
B. Ndimaona angelo, 61) mizimu ina ndi ina ndipo yopanda maina, ndiye mizimu imeneyo inali kumandimenya kwambiri, ndiye pakati pa mizimu imeneyoyo ine poithawa,62) ndi chifukwa chake kuti ntchito yanga sindinaitaye.[apo akungonena zilizonse zomwe zilibe tanthauzo nkomwe].	B. I saw angels *(angelo)* [61] and various spirits (*mizimu*) without any names, and those spirits were beating me very much, but eventually I escaped from them.[62] It is because of that, that I have not abandoned my work…… (UNRELATED PARTS NOT TRANSCRIBED)
M. Ndiye tafika pamenepo, ndiye zitatha pamenepo ndiye munatani?	M. When everything was over at that point, what did you do?
B. Nditachoka apo ndinadzayambano kudziwa mitengo kwambiri, monga m'mene bambo aja anali kundiuzila.	B. When I had passed that stage, I began to know about many (medical) trees such as those which my father had identified for me.
M. Monga tinganene kuti ilipo mitengo ina yomwe munaidziwa chifukwa cha kufa kwanuko?	M. Could we say that there are perhaps some more (medical) trees which you knew because of your dying?
B. Panthawi imeneyoyo nkuti ndikudziwa Kale mitengo yambiri ya ntchito zikuluzikulu, ndiye kuchokela nthawi iyo kufika lero ine sindimalephera matenda aliwonse. Aliyense amachila…………..	B. At that time I already knew many trees for the immense work, I was going to undertake, and from that time until now, I have never failed before the challenge of any disease. Everybody

[61] *angelo* is the Chichewa rendering of English word "angel (s)" (sing and plural), in early missionaries' translations of the bible and virtually all Christian religious books on sale in the country.

[62] The scene is like a dream sequence and depicts primary anxiety as in nightmares; when the dream becomes unbearable one wakes up. *Anathawa mizimuyu ndiye nkudzidzimuka* (he ran away from the spirits and all of a sudden he woke up).

[kudzidumpha zopanda phindu]	gets cured. [UNRELATED PART NOT TRANSCRIBED]
M. Kodi inuyo kuyambayamba kwa ntchito yanuyi, ndimatenda ati omwe anafika kwa inuyo ndikupezeka kuti inu ndikuwachiza?	M. As you were beginning your practice, which ones of the diseases that came to your attention did you find that you could cure?
B. Pakali panopa chimene ndingakuuzeni, ndikuuzeni chowona chokha chokha, palibe matenda amene akulepheleka kwa ine ai, ndiye matenda amene ndinayamba ine kuwachiza ndi matenda poyambilila peni peni misala itabwera kwa ine inatha, masiku atatu nkuchila. Yachiwiri khunyu, yachitatu ndiye panabwera zosiyanasiyana mudziwe kuti nthupi mwa munthu simumakhala utenda umodzi ai. Koma zonse ndakhala ndikuthana nazo.	B. Anything that I have told you so far, I am telling you only the truth; there is no disease which my clients bring to me that I would fail to cure. The types of disease I began to cure were those that affected me personally, such as *misala* (mental disorders). When mental disorder came to me, it was finished within three days and health was restored. Next came epilepsy *(khunyu)* and thereafter came various diseases. You know of course that it is not merely one disease that resides in the human body. But whatever disease there may be, I finish it off.
M. Mukuthana nazo. Aha, ndiyeno mutatha apo ndiyeno munachitapo chiyani?	M. You finish it off, o.k., and when you had reached that stage, what did you do next?
B. Chimene ndinachita ine nchakuti utenda uja ndaudziwa uliwonse koma chimene ndingachite ine koma ndisegule chipatala,63) choti ndizithandizanso anzanga amene ali wosowa, amene akulephela kuti akanathandizidwa ndi masing'anga 64) wena ndiye ineyo onse waja ndinawatenga pamodzi, ndi chifukwa ndinali wodzidalila 65) kuti nditha kuchilitsa utenda omwe ungafike.	B. What I was doing in view of the fact that I was familiar with any disease was that I intended to open a medical practice *(chipatala)*[63] for consultation, so that I would also help my fellow beings in need, those who had failed to obtain help from other doctors. [64] Myself I took all those together into my surgery, because I was convinced[65] that I was able to heal any disease that would arrive.
M. Kodi chipatalacho chinali kumudzi kwanu komweko?	M. Was your surgery there in your home village?
B. Kwa a Dikison 66) uko ku Mdzalanyama.	B. It was at Mr. Dikison's[66] place there in Mdzalanyama.
M. Ku Mdzalanyama?	M. At Mdzalanyama?
B. Mhu, kumalile ndi Mozambique, Zambia mpaka Nchinji.	B. Mhm, at the border with Mozambique and Zambia up to Mchinji.
M. Tsopana chipatala chimenecho mwakha-la	M. How long did you have your surgery?

[63] In Cinyanja / Chichewa *chipatala* means (a) a hospital, and (b) the medical practice (surgery) of a private physician.

[64] Here he chose the term *masing'anga* (instead of *asing'anga)* to express the idea that those patients had previously visited many different healers without finding help.

[65] *kudzidalila* = *kudzikhulupirira*= to be convinced, to have self-confidence.

[66] Mr. Dikison (engl. Dickson) might refer to a famous person in his home area, a chief or the like.

nacho nthawi yaitali bwanji?	
B. Aaa! koma ndinene zoona zokhazokha, chipatala kunjako pakadali pano chikadalipo, ngakhale ndabwela kunoko mayi wanga akuyendesa chiyani? Chipatala chimenechocho, chifukwa mankhwala ambiri omwe ndikugwiritsa ntchito pano akuchokera kumeneko ndipo ena akuchokera ku Tanzania.	B. Aaa! To tell the truth, that surgery is still there up to now, even if I have come here. My mother what does she maintain? Precisely that surgery, because many herbal medicines which I am applying here in my work, actually come from there, and others come from Tanzania.
M. Mwanena kuti mankhwala ena amachokela ku Tanzania, amabweletsa kuno ndi ndani?	M. You are saying that some other medicines come from Tanzania. Who is bringing them here?
B. Amashazi, 67) abvala mimba, aja anthu samabvala chovala iyayi, iwo zomwe amachita nkuti amakhumula mimba ukuku,68) iwo amabwela nthawi ndi nthawi, mwezi ndi mwezi.	B. The *amashazi,* [67] the *ambvala-mimba,* those people who don't wear any clothes. What they do is pulling their abdomen to make it long (*amakhumula mimba ukuku*). They come here from time to time, from month[68] to month.
M. Kodi mumachita kuwatuma kuti ndikufuna mankhwala akuti akuti?	M. Do you place orders that you want such and such medicines?
B. Malingana ndikukhwima m'mene kunalili ndi m'mene nyanga 69) ndimaziziwila, ndiye iwowo ali ngati antchito anga omatumikila.	B. Due to my internal power, and since I have nowledge of the horns *(nyanga)* [69] those people are subordinate to me ; they are like my workers to be sent around.
M. Kumatumikila kumakatenga mankhwala nkubweletsa kuno?	M. Sent around that they should obtain medicines and bring them here?
B. Ali ngati ndondocha,70) abathwa tiyanthu tifupitifupi tija. Nditimene timakhala bize 71) yomakagwila ntchito iti? Ntchito imene ijayo.	B. They are like *ndondocha*[70] those very short people like pygmies (*abathwa).* It is those who are very busy[71] carrying out those works consigned to them.
M. Kodi kunoko mumadziwa bwanji kuti matenda omwe abwelawa akuchokera pati?	M. How do you know the cause of the diseases brought to your attention?
B. Ndimadziwa ine ndili ndi galasi,72) galasi limenelo ine ndimatha kuunikila ndipo	B. I know because I have a glass.[72] By means of this glass I am able to look at things in

[67] I have been unable, so far, to identify the linguistic origin of that term.

[68] Monika Malamusi has described the act as something like pulling the skin of his abdomen forward, or as if pulling chewing-gum out of one's mouth. (Conversation, April 18, 1999).

[69] *nyanga* (horns) are the tools used by a *mfiti* (wizard, witch) to send evil magic to its destination (see also my introduction, pages 23-26).

[70] Monika Malamusi has given this definition of *ndondocha* (April 18, 1999); *kachinthu kakang'ono kakafupi kamachokera ku manda* (A small and short being that comes out of the cemetery). Mr. Banda compares *ndondocha* with pygmies. The closest geographical point where pygmoid people are found in the area is at Lake Bangweulu in Zambia. *Abathwa* is an interregional term for pygmies, known in many language from Zambia to Rwanda.

[71] *bize*= from engl. busy.

[72] *galasi* = from engl. glass. It refers here to a glass with magical powers in possession of a *sing'anga* which can be pointed to any place at any distance to enable him to see. It penetrates houses and rooms.

ndikuwona kuti iyeyu wachoka kumudzi wakuti ndipo dzina lako ndiwe wakuti wakuti, malingana nanga sigalasilo m'mene lilili limayang'ana nyumba ya munthu? Ngakhale m'mene mwabwelamu nditha kuona kunyumba kwanu onse ndi banja lomwe kumaliwona pa galasi paja malingana ndi sayansi 73) imene ndili nayo.	the distance and so I can see for example that such and such a person comes from this or that village, and that your name is such and such; is it not this special glass that penetrates the house of a person? Even you, as you have come here, I can look from here as far as into your house, and see everybody; and your family appears in that glass, accordingly this is the science[73] I possess.
M. Mhu, imene muli nayo, ndiye mwachitsanzo osalephela nthawi zina kuti ngakhale kuchipatala kumene matenda ena amalepheleka?	M. No doubt, you have your science. But couldn't it be for example, that sometimes you fail to find a cure for diseases, if even in the hospital they fail with certain illnesses?
B. Chimene ndimachita ineyo ndichonena kuti – pepani ndafulumiza kuyankhula mwansanga,74) – ngati matenda aja ndikuwalephela ine ndimawatumiza kuchipatala cha boma, chifukwa ntchito imene ndikugwila ndi yabomanso limodzi. Ndiye ngati ndidziwa kuti matendawa sindingawathe ndiye ndimamupatsa chikalata kuti apite kuchipatalacho, ndikawona kuti mwina kufunika kuchitidwa opareshoni, kapena kuonjezela magazi amunthu chifukwa ine sindingathe kuonjezela magazi pomwe iye watha magazi 75) ai. Chomwe ndikupempha ineyo nkuti boma landitaya, chifukwa sakundipatsa mankhwala wowonjezela magazi pachipatala chimene ndili nacho pano.	B. What I am doing can be explained—I am sorry that I have been talking in a hurry. [74]– If I fail to cure a certain illness, then I send the patient to the government hospital, because actually my work and that by the government are identical. So if I realize that I am unable to give treatment, I give the client a letter of referral of the matter to the hospital; for instance, if I see that he or she should have an operation, or perhaps a blood transfusion. Myself, I am unable to increase somebody's blood, if he or she is anemic. [75] What I am asking for, the government never grants to me, because they don't provide me with medicines for the treatment of anemia in the surgery which I maintain here.
M. Ndiye kuti inuyo simungathe kupeza mankhwala ati munthu angamuonjezele magazi muthupi mwake?	M. Does that mean that you are unable to find medicines that would increase somebody's blood in his body?
B. Mankhwala alipo, koma kuti ineyo ndil-ibe zoyezela kuti ndidziwe kuti uyu alibe magazi, zoyezela zomwe ndili nazo ine ndi galasi basi.	B. There are such medicines, but I possess no testing devices to know whether somebody lacks blood, the testing devices I have that is my glass, and that's all.
M. Ndiye monga pali ena ameneno mukuwaphunzitsa ntchitoyi?	M. Is there anyone whom you are teaching your work?
B. Pamakhala pobvuta, chifukwa using'anga	B. This is difficult, because *using'anga* is

[73] *sayansi* = from engl. science.

[74] referring to the fact that earlier in the interview he said that he could cure every disease.

[75] What he actually suggests in this discourse, is not necessarily a contradiction to his earier claim of being able to cure any disease (*matenda*). His concept seems to be that if somebody needs surgery, or a blood transfusion, even if he/she suffers from anemia, that this is not *matenda,* or at least it is an illness beyond his reach, because of a lack of technical equipment and not lack of personal skills.

ndi chinthu chapadela, chifukwa munthu amene akuyembekezela kuphunzila using'anga aziwepo kaufiti pang'ono. Tsopano munthu sangangomuphunzitsa chisawawa 76) osadziwa ufiti.	a special thing, because a person who is a candidate for the apprenticeship of *using'anga* should also know a bit of witchcraft (*kaufiti pang'ono*). One cannot involve anyone indiscriminately [76] and hand out this knowledge to a person who does not know *ufiti.*
M. Ndiye simunapeze ameneyoyo?	M. And you did not find any suitable person?
B. Ameneyo sanapezeke [onse akuseka, ndipo nkazi wawo woyamba naye akuthilila umboni kuti " akunena zoonadi"] kokha masekilitale angawa pang'ono [kunena azikazi wawo awiri] pang'ono paja inu ndinu mai ndani? [nkaziyo akuyankha kuti "Eliza"]	B. Such persons cannot be found--- [At this point everybody was laughing and his first wife confirmed it by saying: "he is telling the truth"]—a bit of an exception is my secretary [pointing to his second wife] you there you are Mrs. who? [she answered: "Eliza"]
M. Amenewa ndiye asekilitale anu eti? Ndiye mwina nawonso ali ndi zina zofuna kukambapo, asendezeko pafupi ndi maikolofoniwa.77)	M. So this person is your secretary? Perhaps she also has something to tell, let her move closer to the microphone! [77])
B. Munthu wosadziwa ufiti sangadziwe using'anga, chifukwa using'anga ndi ufiti.	B. A person who does not know *ufiti* could not know *using'anga* because *using'anga* is identical to *ufiti.*
M. Pamenepotu, inu mukunena chilungamo.	M. That is it. You are really telling the truth.
B. Pali nsupa yoyenda yokha pano, yomwe ngakhale akazi wangawa sanaigwile m'manja mwawo, imeneyo imathandiza miyoyo ya anthu sanakhale nayo m'manja mwawo iyayi, ndimakaniza kwambiri kuti agwile.	B. There is a phial (*nsupa*) here which operates alone; even my wife [pointing to the secretary, his second wife] does not touch it with her hands. It helps the life of many people, but they don't keep it in their hands, I refuse very much that anyone touches it.
M. Chifukwa chake ndi chiyani?	M. For what reason is it prohibited?
B. Chifukwa chake chimene ndikuchidziwa ine, ayeni ake ansupayo ndi awa, akazi wanga akuluwa.	B. It is only me who knows the reason. The owner of this phial actually is this person [pointing to his first wife], my senior wife.
M. Aha! tsopano pamapezeka kuti pali anthu ena nawonso wozama kwambiri. 78)[andidula mawu]	M. Aha! Now couldn't it be that some Individuals exist who also have internal strength...[78] [Mr. Banda cuts into my words]

[76] *chisawawa* is a word often used in connection with public strife which can begin with two people quarelling until everyone is involved. It refers to chaotic, arbitrary ways of selection, or indiscriminate hand-outs of anything, papers, knowledge etc.

[77] My suggestion did not lead to any result. She preferred to remain silent and let her husband talk.

[78] *Kuzama* = to be powerful, to resist, to persevere; a term similar to the verb *kukhwima*. Here I wanted to continue saying: *kufuna kuononga nsupa yanuyi* (…. and want to spoil your phial). Knowing that there are many wizards or witches who have tricks even against the medicines of a *sing'anga,* and that the result is a constant power struggle between the two which is never resolved, I wanted to confront Mr. Banda with this possibility.

B. Ndichifukwa chake kunoko ndege 79) za wanthu za ufiti zasiya kuyenda. Chifukwa cha ife kuti tili kuno, ngakhale mafumu amene akuti akumadandaula kuti ndege zawo zasiya kuyenda kuopa zida zathu. Ndiye apo ine ndikuwakanila kuti ai, ife ngati ndege zathu zili ndi mphamvu ndi mabvuto awo amenewo osati athu aife ai.	B. It is because of the power of my phials that the aeroplanes (*ndege*) [79] of the people of witchcraft have been grounded at this place. It is because we are here. And even if several chiefs [and many of them are wizards] have been complaining that their aeroplanes have stopped operating in fear of our weapons, I myself reject their accusations saying that if our aeroplanes are more powerful, then it is their problem, not ours.
M. Ndiyeno nthawi zina pamapezeka munthu wina wamakani 80) weni weni kutino apa ndikayesa kutamba!81)	M. It sometimes happens that there is a very determined person[80] who says to himself: " Here I am going to do my witch dance!" [81]
B. Ameneyo atha kugwa chifukwa cha zintchito zake zimene wabwela nazozo.	B. Such person will finish up falling down, because of the witchcraft intentions with which he came.
M. Zimene wabwela nazo, koma inuyo mumakhala mukuzindikila kuti wakuti wakuti anabwela pano?	M. The witchcraft intentions with which he came, but can you recognize that such and such wizard or witch has penetrated your place [in the night while you are sleeping]?
B. Timazindikila kuti wakuti wakuti anafika malo ano, malingana ndi ntchito yathu imene tilinayo.	B. We recognize that such and such person has arrived here, since this is precisely our task, the task we are committed to.
M. Ndiye mumabwezela chipongwe chomwe amafuna kukuchitanicho?	M. Are you then returning the insolence which that person wants to throw upon you?
B. Kodi inuyo munthu akumenyeni nkhonya, ndiye kuti inuyo mukafuna kubwezela ndiye kuti mubwezela bwanji?	B. What about you, if someone gives you a blow with his fist and you want to return it to him, how will you return it?
M. Muli monse.	M. By any means.
B. Ndi nkhonya yomweyotu, bola nyonga zanu zimene muli nazo. Ndiyeno amfiti kunoko asiya kutamba ndikuphana, koma ine ndikadzachoka kunoko muzaona anthu azayambanso kuphana. Ndine sing'anga eti Simon Banda, ndayankhula ndikatero.	B. With the same fist, it depends upon the strength you have. Right now the wizards and witches here have stopped to do their witch dance and kill each other, but once I will be gone from here, you will see that the people will start again to kill each other. I am a *sing'anga*, Simon Banda, am I not? And that is what I am saying.
M. Inu apa tinene kuti tilekeze pomwepa,	M. Let me suggest that we end the interview

[79] *amfiti* are supposed to fly invisible aeroplanes (*ndege)* in the night.

[80] *munthu wamakani* = someone who in a spirit of contradiction, is always doing the opposite of what others do, or what others prohibit him to do.

[81] *kutamba* = is to dance the wizards/ witches dance. They are supposed to have a special dance.

Koma ndicheze ndi amodzi wodwala kapena awiri.	here, but let me talk to one or two of your patients.
B. Tiyeni komweko kuchipatala sopano.	B. Let us go to my consulting room!
M. Kuchipatala kuja eti?	M. In the surgery over there? [we are moving into the house where his patients are resting, myself with the microphone in my hand].
B. Mnyamata uyu anachotsa fupa 82) la bala lakeli, pomwe ndidayamba kumupatsa mankhwala apano. Mankhwala omwe tili nawo ali ndi mphamvu zazitali kwambiri. Kuteleku anachotsa yekha fupalo, fupalo linachokera apa mukuonapa [akundilozela pa nkono wa mnyamatayo]	B. This young man extracted a bone out of his wound here, as soon as I began to give him the local medicines. [82] The medicines I possess have far-reaching power. They enabled him to discover and remove by himself that piece of bone. It came out right here [pointing to a spot on the arm of that boy].
M. Malo ache amenewa, nanga iweyo mnyamata, pepani ndidzangoti mnyamata pamene ali achikulile.	M. So that is the spot. And what about you, boy, I am sorry calling you boy while you are quite grown up---
U. Ine ndine mnyamata!	U. I am really a boy!
M. Zinachitika bwanji, kuti papezeke kuti mwatulutsa fupapo?	M. How did it happen, that you took out a bone from that spot?
U. Apapa padali bala limene lidangoyamba lokha, malingana ndi kumene ndidali. Ndiye nditabwela panopa nkumatsila mankhwala ndiye linapezeka kuti linatulukila kunja.	U. Here there was a wound which just started by itself in connection with where I had been. After I had come here and sprinkled medicine on the wound, the bone was found as it appeared outside.
M. Fupalo.	M. That bone.
U. Ndiyeno patapita masiku okwana asanu ndi awiri ndiye tsiku lachisanu ndi chitatu mpamene linadzatuluka lokha nkugwa pansi. Ndithu linagwa ndi usiku ndikugona ndiyeno mam'mawa ndinaliona lili pa mphasa ndiye ine nkulitolano nkukaonetsa adokotala-wa.	U. After seven days of treatment, it happened on the eighth day that it should appear by itself and fall down. Indeed, it fell down in the night while I was sleeping, and in the morning I saw it lying on the mat. I picked it up and showed it to the doctor.
M. Panthawi imene munkafika adokotala anakuuzani kuti chiyani?	M. When you arrived there, what did the doctor tell you?
U. Adokotala anandiuza kuti ndi matchela 83) amuwanthu.	U. The doctor told me that it was traps for people.[83]
M. Ndiye inu munakhulupilila kapena simunakhulupilile?	M. Did you believe that, or perhaps you didn't?
U. Iyayi ndinakhulupilila ndi malingana ndi m'mene anafotokozela iwo inenso ndinakhulupilila.	U. No, I believe it in view of the fact how he explained all, and myself I also had confidence in it.

[82] The bone (*fupa*) extracted from his wound which did not heal, became visible after treatment by Mr. Banda. It had been planted into the body by a *mfiti* (wizard / witch).

[83] *mchera* (singular) is a spear trap used for elephants. A trench or channel is dug round a garden to prevent the animals from entering. (Cf. Scott/Hetherwick 1929: 287)

M. Koma muli kumudziko balalo munadwala kwa nthawi yaitali bwanji?	M. But how come that while you were in the village you suffered from that wound for such a long time?
U. Iyayi ndadwalako kwa nthawi yaitali koti chaka chinocho ndi cha folo.	U. Indeed I suffered for a long time, in fact this is the fourth year (I have suffered)
M. Balalo osapola iyayi?	M. And the wound did no heal?
U. Eee, balali osapola iyayi.	U. Yes, the wound did not heal.
M. Munayensanso kupita kwa asing'anga ena ?	M. Did you also try to go to other *asing'anga*?
U. Eee! ndinali kwa asing'anga ena.	U. Yes! I went to other medical practitioners.
M. Ehe!	M. Ehe!
U. Kumenekoko ndakhala zaka zitatu.	U. At one place there I stayed for three years.
M. Zaka zitatu asing'anga ena ankakuuzani kuti chiyani?	M. For three years? What did those other *asing'anga* do for you all that time?
U. Eee zaka zitatu, cha folo nchimene ndikubwela nacho kuno, amenewonso ankandiuzanso chimodzimodzi, kuti ndi zamuwanthu.	U. Yes, for three years and in the fourth year I came here. The other doctors told me the same thing, that it comes from witchcraft by people.
M. Koma analilephela fupalo kuti alichotse?	M. But they failed to discover that bone so that they would remove it?
U. Amenewo analilephela ndi njila yakuti, anamwalila nsanga ndikanadwala.	U. The one who failed to help me finding a way, died fast, while I was still ill.
M. Oho! Chabwino, ndiyeno panopa muli ndi chitsikimizo 84) kuti a basi bala ndiyeno latani?	M. Oh! All right, but now do you have any confirmation [84] of what will happen to this wound?
U. Panopa ndili ndi chitsikimizo kuti balali lipola.	U. Right now I have the confirmation that the wound will heal.
M. Tsopano paja kumudzi ndikuti?	M. Where is your home village?
U. Kumudzi ndi kwa Kunthembwe.	U. My home village is at chief Kunthembwe's place
M. Kwa Kunthembwe eti? Paja dzina lija ndani?	M. Oh, at chief Kunthembwe's place! And what is your name?
U. Driyana.	U. Driyana.
M. Labambo?	M. And that of your father?
U. Chikwanje.	U. Chikwanje.
M. Iyayi apapa tikufunilani kuti mupeze bwino nsanga ndipo mwapeza kale bwino ndimomwe zikuonekelamu [kuyankhula ndi adokotala]: Tsopano inu adokotala, kodi monga pali mapeshenti ena amene mumati akafika ndikuwatsikimizila kuti izi ndi m'mene ndikuonelamu sizamuwanthu iyayi?	M. As far as I am concerned, I really wish that you soon find some relief! Actually it appears that is already happening! [I am now turning to Mr. Banda] And now you doctor, can it be that when certain patients come to you, that you inform them that the symptoms as you see them are <u>not</u> caused by people's sorcery?
B. Pokhapokha ndimayankhula izi kawiri Kawiri mobwelezabweleza chifukwa	B. Sometimes I am saying just that, again and again, because it is not everything

[84] *chitsikimizo* or *chitsimikizo* = confirmation; from the verb *kutsimikiza* = to make sure, to confirm (cf. Scott/Hetherwick 1929:556).

chilichonse sichitha kukhala cha ufiti ai.	that turns out to be caused by witchcraft.
M. Eya!	M. Eya!
B. Koma zambiri zimatha kukhala zongobwela ndi Mulungu mwini wake, koma zina ndi zina zimatha kukhala za mwaanthu malingana ndi m'mene mmizi tikukhalila, sopano pali anthu ambiri amene tikuwauza kuti ndi zamuwanthu,85) palinso anthu ambiri amenenso tikuwauza kuti sizamuwanthu. Tiyelekeze kuti matenda a malaria kapena amalungo, tinene kuti malungo ndi amuwanthu ngati? Pano pali ana ambiri ndikulandilapo wodwala malungo amene matenda samakhala amuwanthu.	B. Many things are just inflicted upon people by God, but other things can be caused by People due to the ways how we live in the villages. We are telling many people that these symptoms are caused by people's witchcraft, [85] and there are also many whom we tell that it is not the case. By comparison, if someone has malaria fever, how could we say that this fever comes from witchcraft? I am receiving many people here who are ill with malaria, these diseases have no human origins.
M. Amuwanthu.	M. Human origins.
B. Koma amene wobwela kuti ii uyu walozedwa, ifenso timaona, koma matenda ena akangobwela malingana ndi Mulungu mwini wake namalenga wachitila, ndiye ifenso sitingathe kuchita kanthu.	B. But when it is clear that a person was bewitched, we can see that, while some other diseases would just arrive by the creative power of God, and in that case, we can do nothing.
M. Kodi inuyo kapelekedwe kanu kamankhwala kamakhala kotani pakati pa munthu yemwe wangobwela kuti akudwala ndipo palibe kanthu kena, ndi wina yemwe wabwela kuti walodzedwa?	M. What is the difference between the kind of prescription you give a person who comes as a patient without any additional problem behind his disease, and a person who comes because he or she was bewitched?
B. Aaa thilitimenti yanga ndingofotokozapo pang'ono chabe.	B. Aaa, let me explain a bit about my treatments.
M. Mhu.	M. Mhu.
B. Thilitimenti ndimapeleka ndikaona kuti utenda uja ukubwela chifukwa cha munthu, ndiyenso ine ndipeleke mankhwala ofanana ndi masenga. Ngati ndiona kuti utenda uja sunabwele chifukwa cha munthu koma wangobwela monga mmene Mulungu anatilengela ndiye ndimapelekanso mankhwala ofanana ndi utendawo momwe ulili.	B. The treatment I give when I see that the disease in question is caused by (the witchcraft from) a person is such, that I also prescribe medicines that resemble magic (*matsenga*). Conversely, when I see that the disease in question is <u>not</u> caused by a person, but has come through God's own creative power, then I prescribe medicines which are appropriate for the specific disease that is there.
M. Koma pakati pa utenda uwu wongobwela okha ndi utenda wochokela muwanthu, umene mumabvutika nawo kwambiri kupeleka mankhwala ndi uti?	M. But between the disease that comes by Itself and the one that is caused by a person's witchcraft, which one gives you more trouble finding a cure?

[85] Witchcraft can be described without using the word *ufiti.* Mr Banda often says *Za muwanthu* (literally: things from inside people) if he means witchcraft, and *sizamuwanthu* (things not from inside people) if he means the opposite.

B. Eee chimene ndimachiona ine kwambiri ndiponso chimene chimandipasa phuma oti olo kunyumba osagona utenda wobwela ndi anthu , wolozedwa wamasenga.	B. Eee! As I see it, what gives me much trouble and makes me breathe heavily, up to the point that I don't sleep in my house, is any disease caused by people, when someone was bewitched by magic.
M. Mhu.	M. Mhu.
B. Ndiumene ndimauona kuti ine olo kunyumba kuja ine sindingathe kugona. Cholinga ine ndimafuna ndimuone munthu amene wapanga zimene zija, ndiye ndikamuona ndimatha kumufunsa pamasenga usiku 86) cholinga chopweteka munthu ameneyu unalingalila chiyani? Ndiye andiuze zifukwa zimene adalakwa ndani? Wodwalayo. Ndichimene ineyo ndimapanga.	B. These are the instances that worry me much until I can't even sleep in my own house. Then it is my aim to try and contact that person who is doing such things. If I can see him or her by the power of my own magic in the night[86] then I can ask him or her about the purpose why he wanted to hurt that particular person, what were the thoughts behind it. He or she should give me the reasons and explain the wrong-doings he or she was accusing whom? My patient.—That is what I am doing.
M. Tsopano akakuuzani inu, chimene mumapanga ndi chiyani?	M. When he gives you his reasons, what are you doing then?
B. Ndiye ndiona kodi chifukwacho ndichokwanila kapena chosakwanila.	B. I then examine whether the wizard or witch had <u>sufficient</u> reason to hurt my patient, or his reason was <u>insufficient</u>.
M. Chikakhala kuti ndichokwanila?	M. And if his reasons to bewitch him were sufficient?
B. Munthu achile.87)	B. Then the sick person should recover[87].
M. Chikakhala kuti ndichosakwanila?	M. And if the reason to bewitch is insufficient?
B. Ngati chili chosakwanila kumuzuzula asabwelezenso.	B. If the reason was insufficient, then I prevent the *mfiti* from repeating his deeds.
M. Munthu uja mumuchiza?	M. And you cure the patient?
B. Munthu uja achila ndithu, aziyenda bwinobwino, koma akabweleza munthu amene ujayo ndiye pali nkhondo pakati pa iye uja ndi ine nanga iyeyo si wamasenga 88) imakhalapo nkhondo	B. Yes, the patient will recover indeed, and he should continue well. But if the *mfiti* repeats his act, then there is a war between him/her and me. It will be a nocturnal war, because isn't a *mfiti* a

[86] *kuona pamatsenga* = to see someone (a wizard/witch) through a magical device. The idea is that the *sing'anga* contacts the wizard/witch in the night by magic; he travels there, but not physically.

[87] What actually happens, is that the *sing'anga* and the *mfiti* (wizard/witch) discuss the matter and come to an agreement. This can be desribed in Cinyanja/Chichewa as follows: *Mfiti amagonja, akuti tengani mankhwala amene ndinamulozela. Ndiye sing'anga akatenga mankhwala amenewa amakasakaniza ndi mankhwala ake asing'angayo ndi kumupatsa odwalayo, kapena kumuchekera, nde amapeza bwino.* (The wizard/witch obeys and says: allright, take the evil medicines which I used to bewitch that person. The *sing'anga* takes them and mixes them with his own proper medicines, and then gives it all to his patient, or makes incisions in his patient's skin to rub them in. Eventually the patient recovers). The *sing'anga* effectively neutralizes the evil medicines of the *mfiti* with his own. For this reason, and because the two come to an agreement, Mr. Banda insists that a *sing'anga* must also know about *ufiti*.

ya usiku.	person of magic? [88]
M. Kodi pali kusiyana kwanji pakati pa munthu wa matsenga ndi sing'anga?	M. What difference is there between a person of *matsenga* (magic) and a *sing'anga* (medical practitioner)?
B. Pali kusiyana chifukwa munthu wongopanga za masenga ndi sing'anga, wopambana 89) ndi sing'anga.	B. There is a difference because between a person who only practices magic and a *sing'anga* it is the *sing'anga* who is superior. [89]
M. Wopambana ndi sing'anga.	M. The superior person is the *sing'anga.*
B. Wopambana ndi sing'anga kwambiri, ndiye ndikuonetseni zida zomwe ine ndimagwilitsa ntchito. Mwachiziwa ichi [apo akutulutsa mu chithumba momwe chinali]. Mwachiziwa ichi, kuno ku Malawi chilipo? [akutiwonetsa chigabado 90) cha chinthu china chomwe chimakhala ku nyanja ya nchere].91)	B. Very much so, the *sing'anga* is superior. Let me show you the tools I operate in my work. Do you know this thing? [he takes it out from the bag where he has kept it] Do you know this thing? Can it be found here in Malawi? [he shows us the shell[90] of something that is found in the ocean]. [91]
M. Sitinachidziwe ndiponso sitinachionepo.	M. We didn't know this, and also we have never seen it here.
B. Mutha kuchijambula pachokhanso, iyi ndiye paphela ung'anga onse chifukwa ichichi ndi nyanga imene imakhala mu Indian Ocean ya mmadzi ndiye timakhala nayo.	B. You can photograph it by itself! This "horn" is the climax of all medical practice, because this is the "horn" *(nyanga)* that stays in the Indian Ocean under water, and I possess it.
M. Tsopano ndiye mumagwilitsa ntchito yanji?	M. Now for what kind of work do you use it?
B. Ichichi kukhwima konse kwagona pati? Pamenepa, chifukwa ndati ineyo mungoona chabe, kukubonisani.	B. This thing, where does all the strength reside? In there, because I say, if you just see it you start yearning for it .
M. Ntchito yanu yonse mumadalila pamenepa?	M. So all your work depends on it?
B. Ndimadalila pamenepa chifukwa nkatimo muli mankhwala, oti ndikamupasa munthu mankhwala amenewo three days kuchila basi.	B. It gladly depends on it, because inside the shell there are medicines to the effect that if I give somebody those medicines, it just takes three days for a cure.
M. Kuchila basi. Tsopano inuyo mumapeza munjila yotani?	M. Getting cured and that's it! Now by which means did you find this thing?
B. Ine izizi kwenikweni, zimabwela kuchokela ku Tanzania.	B. These things originally come from Tanzania.

[88] Both *sing'anga* and *mfiti* are in command of *matsenga* (magic). It ends up in *mpikisano* (competition) about whose magic is stronger.

[89] Someone who just knows magic cannot cure a person like a medical practitioner *(sangathe kuchiza munthu ngati sing'anga).* Comment by Monika Malamusi, April 21, 1999.

[90] He refers to the shell (*chigabado)* which is a noun in the CHI-/DZI class with a demonstrative pointing to the N-class, and thereby to the noun *nyanga* (a wizard's horn). Through this subtle reference the idea is expressed that this shell is a very important "horn" for him.

[91] *nyanja la nchele* (literally: lake of salt) referring to the Indian Ocean.

M. Ndiye kuti mankhwala amene amakhala mmenemu ndiwothandiza anthu?	M. Does it mean that the medicines inside the shell are designed to help people?
B. Ee ndiwothandiza anthu, kuchiza siwokupha ai, mankhwala ambiri omwe timakhala nawo siwokupha munthu ai, koma kuchilitsa moyo wa munthu. Ndicho chifukwa chake tikukhalabe ndi moyo mpakana chaka chino.	B. Yes, they are for helping people, they are meant to cure, not to kill. Many medicines I possess are not at all aimed at killing a person, but sustain human life. And it is because of that we are still alive up to this year.
M. Iyayi, chabwino, nanga pali zina zimene zoti mutifotokozelenso?	M. All right, are there other things you could explain to us?
B. Aaaa, ayi.	B. No, there aren't.
M. Zikomo kwambiri.	M. Thank you very much.

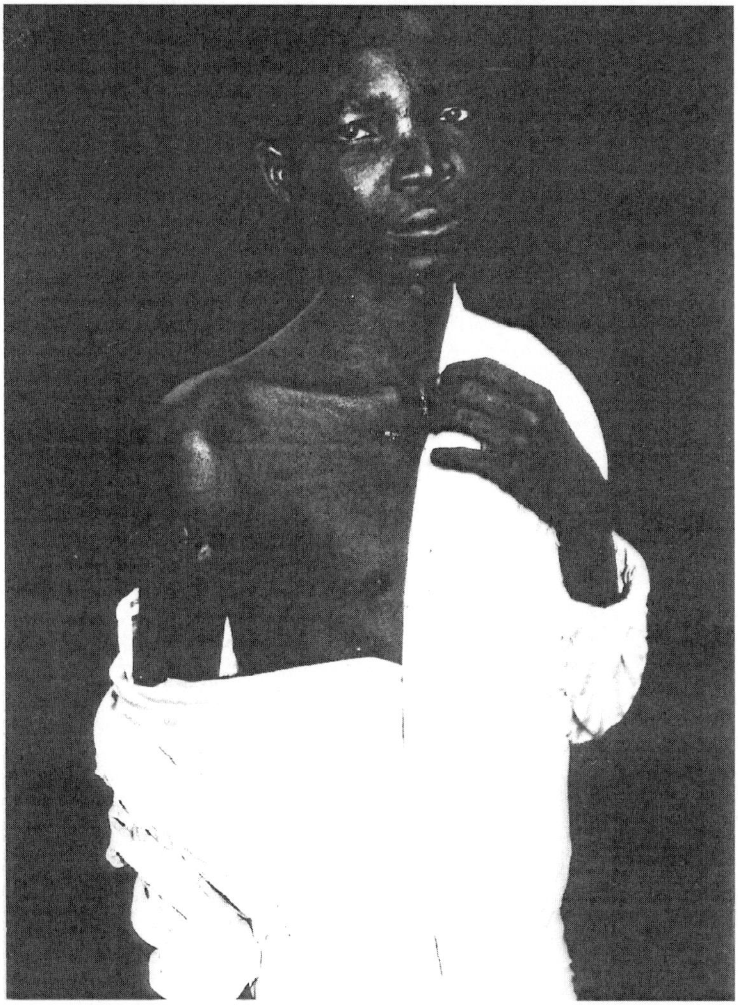

This is the boy who had been suffering for four years from a wound that did not heal. He is now rejoicing since he came to the *sing'anga* Mr. Banda finding that the wound would heal after three pieces of bone had been removed from it.

At Khumbirina village, T. A. Kunthembwe, Blantyre District,
December 17, 1993. Photo no. 93/5/9

The sick people in Mr. Banda's clinic. This is one of the wards in which the sick are accommodated.

At Khumbirina village, T.A. Kunthembwe, Blantyre District,
December 17, 1993. Photo no. 93/5/8

Mr. Banda is pointing to the building of his clinic and calling other patients who had been here for some time to tell him how they respond to the treatment he was giving them.

At Khumbirina village, T.A. Kunthembwe, Blantyre District,
December 17, 1993. Photo no. 93/5/6

The *sing'anga* Simon Banda is seen here together with his two wives, explaining various facts about his medical practice. The two women are also the ones whom he identified as his secretaries and who administer medicines to the patients.

At Khumbirina village, T.A. Kunthembwe, Blantyre District, December 17, 1993. Photo no. 93/5/4

Mr. Banda explains the shell of which he says that it functions like his "horn" (*nyanga*). It originates from the Indian Ocean and he makes it operate together with his medicines. He says that all his medical practice *(using'anga wawo)* depends on that "horn" and that the medicines inside cannot fail to be effective before any disease whatsoever.

At Khumbirina village, T.A. Kunthembwe, Blantyre District,
December 17, 1993. Photo no. 93/5/15

Jonasi Masangwi
(Mr.)

The day I heard reports about the *sing'anga* Jonasi Masangwi, was when the musician-composer Donald Kachamba and I were going the highland area of Thyolo, south of Limbe, on December 9, 1994, to see another *sing'anga* who was known in the area as CheChikwama, [92] and who had a reputation of being knowlegable in medicines to protect the body (*mankhwala wotsitikila thupi*)[93]. After we had arrived there, and finished our programme and were about to say good-bye, the wife of Mr. Chikwama suggested that we might want to have a look at the work of another *sing'anga* who had recently arrived here, and who claimed to be able to catch wizards and witches and take away their phials (*ndikuwalanda nsupa zawo*). She said that he was an itinerant *sing'anga* who would travel from village to village, perhaps he would also arrive here. She explained that right now he was at Nzuna village, T.A. Nchilamwela, in Thyolo District.

So we decided to start another journey traveling to that village. However, when we arrived we heard that on this day he would not dance (*tsikulo sanali kubvina*) pointing to the fact that all the work this *sing'anga* was doing to discover wizards and witches was through dancing. But people continuied to say that the next day he would begin to dance and thereby get hold of the weapons of everyone who was a *mfiti*. The show would begin at 2 o'clock in the afternoon. Since Donald Kachamba and I were concentrating at that time on research about *using'anga* and not any other subject, we had no choice but to return home.

Early in the morning we drove back to the village to find out what that *sing'anga* was doing. He was known in the area under the nickname Nkholo-Panja (the buttocks outside) [94]. This name was considered to be his work name, his professional name. His real name was Jonasi Masangwi. He was from the Khokola ethnic group as it is also clear from his pronunciation of Chichewa words in the recorded interview (see below). Jonasi Masangwi looked like a man of about 50 years. However, due to the absence of birth certificates and other records in the rural areas, he could not tell me his exact age. Probably he did not know.

The things he was doing on the day of our visit, the 10th of December 1994, were absolutely amazing. What I am writing now, I am copying from the field notes I took that day when we were on the spot. When we arrived he had actually arranged for his departure to the next village, so his drums were playing in anticipation of the last performance he would give here before leaving. It was at the open place (*bwalo*) in the middle of Nzuna village that he was expected to perform. The drums were played by his assistants in a style which they identified to me as a Khokola dance genre (*chamba*) called *kumbasa*. They used five drums. These were fastened to a stand composed of vertical poles and a long horizontal bar placed across (see photo).

---

[92] CheChikwama was from Zomba, and had married in Thyolo. The name indicates that his parents were -Yao and -Lomwe. Che- is a honorific prefix found in the Ciyao and Elomwe languages for addressing a man (see also: Sanderson 1954: 31)

[93] Protective medicines, medicines which protect a person against witchcraft.

[94] I have not been able to ascertain the meaning behind this epithet, but I believe, that it serves like the nicknames of many other *asing'anga* in southern Malawi to startle and even frighten the general public, underlining a *sing'anga*'s special power.

After the drums had been played for some time, an assistant appeared who said that he was the son of the *sing'anga*. He and two small children then began to dance together in an odd manner. The style of this dance drama, he explained, was to mirror the way wizards and witches were thought to dance inside the graveyard when they obtained meat from the corpses in the graves wich they dug up, and rejoiced.

Eventually, the *sing'anga* Jonasi Masangwi came out of the small house he had been given by the village people for staying together with his son who assisted him organizing his performances and some small children who were also with him. They all had put paint round their eyes, everywhere on the face. The *sing'anga* was dressed in a frightening style. As the leader of the group he proceeded to the dance ground ahead of the others to perform, his assistants following his steps. In his hands he carried certain objects, such as two small white bottles, a small axe (*kankhwangwa*)[95], a small spear and his "doctor's tail' (*nchila*). The aim of his performance would be to incapacitate the local wizards and witches and take away their weapons. When he arrived, he began to dance in a state of agitation, and those drums began to be played frantically, *kwa ntima bii* as is said in an idiomatic expression, meaning "with full strength of the heart"

The tools he carried with him were meant to help him find and deal with the wizards or witches. In the small bottle there was a liquid, about which I thought that it was not just water, but liquid medicines. From time to time he lifted the bottles up to his forehead like small cameras. And he held them up before his eyes, as if he wanted to take a photograph. No doubt, this was symbolic, indicating that he was able to identify and target the *amfiti* (wizards, witches), and therefore I came to the conclusion that it was not merely water inside those two bottles, but medicines whose nature their owner would know alone. The people who had arrived to submit their complaints about witchcraft to him were first sitting quietly on the ground. When the dancing reached a climax, the *sing'anga* Jonasi Masangwi began to point his bottles at individuals whom he thought *amfiti*. At such moments everybody in the audience cheered and the women made trills (*ndikululutila nthungululu*) expressing joy that he had indeed caught somebody. This went on for some time. The crowd then got ready to disperse and go to their houses, but those whom he had identified as wizards and witches were expected to proceed with him to their houses and have their witchcraft confiscated. The *sing'anga* put his bottles down on the ground, while continuing his dance.

Eventually the *sing'anga*'s whistle (*wenzulo*) was sounded. All of a sudden he snatched up his bottles from the ground with a quick movement of his right hand (*kukhwathula*), and began to run while singing, and with the bottles in his hand, in direction to a neighbouring village: Ndalama. The crowd began to follow the *sing'anga* with the songs on their mouths to that place which was quite distant, about 2km, and even we researchers ran along with him, tape-recorder, microphone and camera in our hands.

We were soon exhausted, since his journey was a marathon. Finally we arrived at the village, Ndalama, where he had intended to go and where he had perhaps already negotiated his arrival with the local headman (*nyakwawa*). Here then he began to take aim at each house, one by one, with his bottles held up to his forehead. While this was going on

---

95 *Nkhwangwa* is an aggressive tool. It symbolizes the weapon used by the *sing'anga* to incapacitate a *mfiti*. (Compare also the section on the *sing'anga* Akina Thomas and her conversations with her client)

he sang the songs together with his assistants, and the drums were played. Their performers, of course, had followed him to this place. While continuing to take aim at individual houses, the *sing'anga* then identified one house in which he suspected witchcraft by its owner and entered it. He then asked his assistants to bring him water and he began his work. After a while we saw him come out with a plate provided by the owner in which there was mud mixed with water *(madothi awisi*). Inside the house the *sing'anga* had dug up the mud from the floor in the middle of the house, digging a hole, at the exact place where he thought that the suspected wizard or witch were keeping their "horns" (*nyanga).* Those "horns" were hidden in the mud which he dug up and put on the plate, softening the mud with water.

Emerging from the house he handed the plate with its content over to the owner of the house who then had to carry it, following the *sing'anga*. He went from house to house and the same thing was repeated. After a while there were already five or six people following him with their plates in their hands. It also happened that he entered a house and found nothing, no evil magic. In that case he did not ask for water and just came out of the house and continued his search elsewhere. But it could also happen that he found that the owner of a certain house was forewarned and had already removed all the evil medicine, hiding it at the nearby river. In this case the *sing'anga* would run there to the river and take those weapons *(zida*) there. The "horns" (*nyanga*) were called weapons (*zida*) by him.

We also observed something frightening. While the drums were going on, people singing and making noise, the *sing'anga* arrived at a certain house, in order to take the "weapons", but the son of the owner of the house who was a woman, and who was himself about 35 years old did not want his mother to be exposed as a witch in public. When Jonasi Masangwi entered he also entered with a knife in his hand intending to stab the *sing'anga*. While the noise of the music and the onlookers outside was tumultuous, some people quickly overpowered the man and removed him from inside the house. After this incident, the *sing'anga* did not take anything out, because of the man's intervention, but he only said the following to the man: "All right. Your mother will not have a long life again; her "horns" are in there!"

All this happened to the backstaging of songs that were sung and the sound of a small drum *(kang'oma*) which is called *mbera*. When the *sing'ang*a had finished inspecting all the houses, he and the *amfiti* (witches) he had identified, as well as his assistants, those youngsters he used to call *mayufi* (from engl. Youth League), set out for the return journey to Nzuna village, leaving the village of Ndalama. The whole crowd followed them again. The *amfiti* he had identified were eight women and they too followed him, each of them holding the plate with the mud from their houses in their hands. The crowd was eager to hear about what sort of things the *sing'anga* had found with those witches. When we arrived at Nzuna village Jonasi Masangwi began to make public what he had found in possession of those eight women. His speech was declamatory, so that everyone should hear well. He said that these were the people who were spoiling relationships (*kusakaza*) in the village of Ndalama, but all that would end from today on. Then he ordered everyone to put their plates on the ground (*kukhazikila),* those which they had carried all the way from their homes with the softened mud in it that the *sing'anga* had dug up there. The *sing'anga* now told them that everbody stir the mixture in their plates using the index finger of their right hands. When the accused *amfiti* began to do so strange objects came to the surface from below the mud. Nobody could have identified those objects and their meanings. The *sing'anga* began to explain each and every device the *amfiti* had used to kill, and the audience became aware of the magnitude of this witchcraft practice. The manner in which the *sing'anga* identified each object and its purpose was by singing in his own language, Chikhokola, and thereafter one of his assistants explained his words in Chichewa.. Every object in the plates was explained. The crowd *(khamu la anthu)* was very surprised to hear what the *sing'anga* launched [96] without paying attention to social damage that might result from it. Others came up with the funny story that a certain *mfiti* was sucking off power from somebody's penis with the result that in the night when the latter would sleep with his wife, conception was impossible.

The manner Jomas Masangwi identified and denounced witchcraft practice was that one of his sons would begin a song to which some others responded. Similarly, the *sing'anga* also sang his own song, being answered by others, and in between the lines of the song he would identify those dangerous objects he had found with the witches.

His songs are in Chikhokola language and I was, unfortunately unable to understand everything in the original recordings on our tapes. But the *sing'anga*'s words in the songs were always translated a moment later, and this text is clear to me. The translator to the local people was also one in the group of Jonasi Masangwi, and he used to dance with him.

Recording of a performance by Jonasi Masangwi, aged about 50, and his assistant, with remarks by the witches (*amfiti*) he had identified. – At Nzuna village, T.A. Nchilamwela, Thyolo District, December 10, 1994. Original tape no. M 94/5

Mnyamata	(Mn.)	=	the assisistant
Mfiti	(Mf.)	=	a witch or wizard
Moya	(M.)	=	author

These recordings were made after the intervention at Ndalama village was completed and the *sing'anga* with his crew accompanied by the witches and wizards had returned to Nzuna village. The drama which deleloped now, had in a sense the character of a public trial, a show trial. The wizards and the witches did have an opportunity to respond to the *sing'anga*'s accusations as the text below clearly demonstrates. Nearly all of them denied being in possession of witchcraft, denied having done anything wrong. But the reaction of the public was always negative towards the accused persons, especially also concerning the case of the premature death of a secondary school student (see below my interview with the accuser, James Bernard). There was grief and an outcry of indignation.

[96] *kuulutsa*. Literally: to make fly. The implied meaning is *kunena mosasamala* (to say something without taking care about possible damage to anybody's reputation).

Case I (the couple accused of having killed a student)

Mn. Tinvesele kuno abale,abambo awa ali ndi chisimo,97) kwaoko ali ndi botolo, m'botolomu muli magazi 98) omwe amaphela munthu,ndiponso anapha kale munthu mnyamata wasukulu 99) kwaoko. [Nyimbo]	Mn. Let us listen brothers and sisters! This man here has a peculiar nature (*chisimo*) [97]. At his home he is in possession of a bottle, and in that bottle there is blood[98] which he uses to kill people. He has already killed one person at his home village, a Secondary School boy[99]. [Singing by Jonasi Masangwi in Chikhokhola]
Mn.Tinvesele kuno, amaiwa ali ndi chisimo, mavuto achitika zanawa apanga ndi amai omwewa, kulila komwe amalila kunali konama amangolila kuti nanga ndipange bwanji, akufuna kuti abweze ngongole.100) [Nyimbo]	Mn. Let us listen here! This woman has a peculiar nature (*chisimo*).The tragedy that happened the day before yesterday was caused by this woman! Her crying there at the funeral was all pretended. She was just crying, because she was worried about how she would pay back her debts. [100] [Singing by Jonas Masangwi in Chikhokhola]
Mf. Kodi ndimayesa munandichosanso ufitio kale ndiye pano ndautenga kuti? kuti ndiphere munthu ameneyo? [Anthu ena akuyamba kulila,omwe zinawakhudza kwambiri, chifukwa cha munthu yemwe anafayo. Zosanveka anthu ambiri akulankhula].	Mf. I seem to remember that you had previously removed witchcraft from me so where did I now take it from so that I should kill that person ? [The audience is not impressed by the witch's denial. Some people begin to cry. The event of the funeral has deeply touched them, because the boy died prematurely. On the tape many people can be heard talking and making comments].

Case II (the witch with the gourd)

Mn. Amai awa ali ndi bvuwo,101)lomwe amati anthu akapha nyama yawo, iwo ndikumanyamula, ndipo anthu ndikumagulila pamutu pawo.	Mn. This woman ,the *sing'anga* says is in possession of a broken gourd which, he says, she uses for carrying the meat obtained by other witches from killing a

97 *chisimo*, a term close to *khalidwe* (character), in this case with a negative by-meaning: "bad character".

98 The blood in the bottle of the wizard is not the one collected from his victim, but blood used as medicine (*mankhwala*) to kill.

99 See the story of this case in the interview with the accuser, James Bernard, transcribed below.

100 *Mfiti analira kwambili pa maliro a mwana, ngati ali ndi chisoni, koma nkonama* (The witch was crying excessively at the funeral of that boy, as if she were grief-stricken, but it was all pretended.) Jonas Masangwi accuses her – in the words translated by his assistant into Chichewa – that she really cried about her debts in the form of human flesh which she would have to pay back to her friends in the witches' group.

	person. She carries it on her head so that other witches buy the meat from her. [101]
Mf. Ine ndifuna kuti ndimudziwe yemwe amandinyamulitsa nyamayo kuti ali kwayani?	Mf. Myself I would like to know who the one Is who makes me carry this meat?

Case III (the witch who kills through bad talk)

Mn. Akuti amaiwa ntchito yawo amagwila amaiwa, kapena munthu atodwala ngati mnyumba ngati muja amachita miseche, 102)ndipo ndi misecheyo munthu	Mn. The *sing'anga* says, the work of this woman here is that after visiting a sick person at his/her home, she goes out and makes *miseche* [102] [talking bad

[101] *bvuwo*, according to my assessment, refers to a large gourd from which one part is broken off (*ntsuko waukulu, kusweka pang'ono, kutsala mbali imodzi*).

Atha kuikamo mankhwala adzitsamba ndi kutsilamo madzi nkumasamba
(She can keep medicines in the gourd and pour in water in order to wash her hands because of those medicines). *Chifukwa chinasweka mbali imodzi atha kupisamo manja nkumasamba kuti akhale ndi mphamvu ya ufiti (*Because it is broken on one side, she can put in her hands and wash them, so that she gets the power of witchcraft).

Ntchito ya bvuwo nkunyamulilamo nyama ya munthu. Ngati akunyamula choncho akupita kumagulitsa nyama yamunthuyo. (The use of the broken gourd is to carry human flesh inside. If she carries it, she walks along in order to sell the human flesh to her friends in the wizard/wiches group).

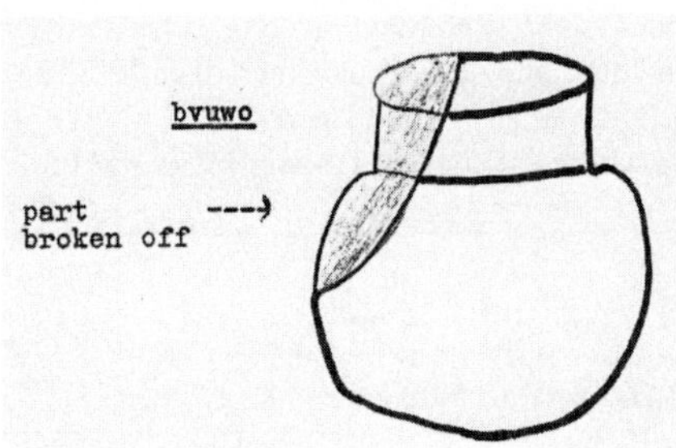

Flg.3 (drawing by Monika Malamusi)

[102] A person is ill. That witch visits him, but then she talks bad about that person. Through talk (*polankhula*) she "ends" the disease causing the person's death.

A person can also be hired to do that (*ganyu*). The hired killer visits the patient, talks to him or her, and then helps through *miseche* to "end" the disease with the patient's death.

Miseche (sing. *mseche*) is a key term in Cinyanja/Chichewa characterizing negative social relationships. The word is usually translated into English as "slander", "backbiting","scandal" etc. *Miseche* characterizes all the bad talk done by others behind somebody's back. The musician composer Daniel Kachamba (1947 – 1987) made many songs about the evil of *miseche*. *Miseche* can kill a person, push him into the grave, as he complains in a song about his own future funeral, composed in 1971 (cf. Kubik 1974: 48 – 50).

amamwalila. Akuwamaliza matendawo. [Nyimbo]	about that person] and it is through those *miseche* that the person dies. Through her action she ends the disease. [Singing by Jonas Masangwi]

Case IV (the wizard with the burial water

Mn. Tinve mbili ya abambowa, iwo ntchito yawo nkuti munthu uja akafa ndiye pomwe akumusambitsa paja, iwo amatenga madzi 103) akewo ndikumakatsitikila maminda yawo, kumachedwa kukawa.104)Kukhwimila munda kapena kukhwimila chimanga.	Mn .Let us listen to the report about this man here! His work is that when a person dies and the corpse is washed before burial, he diverts some of the water [103] and uses it to protect (*ndikumakatsitikila*) his gardens. This is called (*kuwawa*) [104] to strengthen one's crops, or to strengthen one's maize.
Mf. Ai,olo misimbenso ndinakhwimila?	Mf. And what about my sugar-cane? Am I also strengthening it that way?
[Uko ndikunena motsutsa kuti zomwe akunena sing'angayo ndi zabodza, poti iye amalima yekha. Ndipo abambowo akupitiliza kunena kuti " ine inde mwandigwila, koma ine zamankhwala sindidziwa koma alipo munthu yemwe wandisambilila ine kuti ine ndigwidwe."105)] [This person expressed himself in a sarcastic manner to denounce the accusations of the *sing'anga* as lies. He continued to say that because he used to work alone in his field and was successful, others were motivated by jealousy and now accused him of witchcraft. He said: "It is true that you have caught me, but in reality I don't know anything about witchcraft. There is someone who must have washed me with medicines so that I should be caught." [105])]	

[103] The burial water is used by the wizard as *chizimba,* as a catalyst, something that will propel a reaction. *Amakasakaniza ndi mankhwala* (when he mixes it with medicines) it becomes effective. He sprinkles it over his fields and the crops become very strong, at the expense of the crops of other people's fields. *Madzi a maliro ndi chizimba cha mankhwala amenewa* (the burial water is the "propellant" of those medicines). *Chizimba chili chooopsya, chovuta kupeza* (*chizimba* is something dangerous, something difficult to obtain). For example, it can be that a *sing'anga* gives a patient some medicines, but advises him to catch lightening in order to make the medicine work. A person is afraid of finding *chizimba.*

[104] *kukawa* = to attract the power of the neighbouring fields owned by others. All the good crops will move to the field of the wizard. He might even send small animals to the fields of his neighbours to collect the power and bring it to his field.

[105] The accused suggests this: m*unthu wina wapanga mankhwala kuti sing'anga atsimikize kuti nd'abambo amenewo ali ndi zoipa* (another person applied medicines, so that the *sing'anga* would testify against him that he possessed evil things).

Interview with a patient of *sing'anga* Jonasi Masangwi, Mr. James Bernard, about 35 years old. Recorded at Nzuna village, T.A. Nchilamwela, Thyolo District, December 10, 1994. Original Tape no. M 94/5

M. = Moya (author)

B. = James Bernard

M. Mwina muyambe mwafotokoza dzina lanu kaye, ndi mudzi umene mwachokela.	M. Perhaps you start by explaining to me your name and the village you come from.
B. Ine ndine James Benard,mudzi mwathu ndi mwa aNdalama,106) ine ndimagwila ntchito kuBlantyre, kwa Osiman,107) ntchito yanga ndimagwila ine ndi ya ugadi yaulonda.108)Zomwe zinachitika nkuti ndzukulu wanga109) yemwe amaimba sukulu ku Chileka Secondary sukulu mulungu wathau, omweu anandichitila phone kuti akudwala ndzukulu wanu, ndipo anali kuchipatala ku Queens ndiye ndinapita kukamuona ndipo kenaka anatuluka kuchipatalako kubwela kuno kunyumba, ndiye kuno matendawo analimbika kwabasi mpaka tinapita naye ku Malamulo ndipo kuMalamuloko wakhalako lolemba ndiye lachiwiri kuma 5 koloko kumanva kuti mwana uja wamwalila. Ndiye tinakatenga malirowo mpaka kuika,ndiye pambuyo pake ndipomwe timaganiza kuti aa apa ife tipite kwa sing'anga kuti atithandize ndiye ndizomwe mwanva zija kuti ndi mai wina yemwe anachita zimenezo. Ndiye chomwe tikulonjeza 110) pano nkuti ife tadziwa munthu yemwe anachita izo, ndiye sikuti tikapita kumudzi kwathu kuti nkhani ikakhala ili nkamwankamwa ai, koma malingana ife anuwake tadziwa chilombocho.111) Anthu	B. Myself I am James Bernard, our village is situated at Headman Ndalama's place[106]. I work in Blantyre with Osman, [107]. the type of work I am doing is that of a watchman (*ugadi ya ulonda*). [108] What happened was this: Last week I was phoned that my nephew [109] who frequented the Secondary School in Chileka was ill. He had been admitted to Queen Elisabeth Hospital in Blantyre and I went there to see him. Thereafter he was discharged and arrived here at home, but here his disease regained strength until I went with him to Malamulo Hospital in Thyolo District. He stayed there all Monday, until on Tuesday at 5 o'clock I heard that the child had died. So we took the body and arranged for burial, and it was after this had happened that I thought: Oh no, we should go to a *sing'anga*, so that he should help us to find out the person who killed our child, and as you have already heard, it is a certain woman who was doing it. Now what we promise[110] here is that we, since we now know the person who was doing this, will not just go to our village, so that this news should be in everybody's mouth, but perhaps only we the victims should know that animal[111]).

[106] Ndalama village is close to Nzuna where we found the man.

[107] Osman, an Indian shop owner in Blantyre.

[108] *ugadi ya ulonda* is "township" Chichewa spoken by people in the social environment of Mr. Bernard. *Ugadi* is a Chichewa corruption of the English word "guard". *Ulonda* is an abstract form describing the work of a *mulonda* (a guard, a watchman). It is Ciyao language.

[109] *mwana wa alongo wao* (the son of his sister). Mr. Bernard was the *malume* (maternal uncle) of the boy who had died. He is a figure of authority in the matrilineal society of the people in southern Malawi. As the group interacted I observed that the biological father of the deceased boy was very quiet. He hardly spoke anything. The whole case was conducted by Mr. Bernard, the maternal uncle.

[110] He says "we" because they arrived at the *sing'anga* as a group.

omwe agwidwa aja mamuna ndi nkazi amathawathawa kwambiri, kuno tinayamba kubwela dzulo, ndipo iwo osabwela kupita, kunyumba osawapeza, ndiye kenaka mpomwe tawapezano lero ndizomwe awagwila panozi.	The people who were identified (by the *sing'anga*) a man and a woman, they are constantly on the run. Yesterday we began to arrive here, and they did not come. Going to their house they could not be found. Eventually, after we found them, the *sing'anga* confirmed that they were *amfiti.*
M. Ndiye pamene awapeza chomwecho, chachiwiri chimene chichitike ndichiyani?	M. And now since he has identified them as wizard and witch what will be the next thing to happen?
B. Chachiwiri chimene chitachitike pamene pajapo, zimene zili ndi iwozo awachotsa konkuno, akuti amachita K27,00 munthu aliyense. Ife mwana yemwe anatisiyayo sikuti anadwala kwenikweni ai,china ndi chimenecho chomwe chiantidabwitsa,112) ndiye pano atiuza zonse zomwe anachita kumubaya ndi nthungo 113) pa mutu ndiye chifukwa chake anafa. Akutinso njila yakumandako akuti anaisilikanso, 114) kuti wasalanso mmodzi. Akuti afuna kubweza ngongole ya nyama ya wanthu kwa anzawo komwe anakongola. [Nyimbo ndikubvina]	B. What will happen next is that the *sing'anga* right here will remove the bad medicines which they have. He says it will cost 27 kwacha each person. The child who left us behind was not really ill, this death is something that has startled us. [112]) And now the *sing'anga* has told us everything the *amfiti* were doing, they pierced his head with a spear (*nthungo*) [113] and it is because of that that the boy died. The *sing'anga* also told us that the wizard and witch had also planted[114] more medicines on the path to the graveyard, because there was one more person left (to be killed by them). He said that they wanted to pay back the debt in human flesh (*ngongole za nyama ya wanthu*) to their comrades from whom they had borrowed. [Song and dancing]

[111] *chilombocho* (that animal) refers to the *mfiti* (who acts like an animal)

[112] He did not believe that the boy would die, but had thought that he would recover.

[113] An invisible spear as used by wizards.

[114] The correct Chichewa word is *kutsitika.* The *amfiti* planted other medicines on the graveyard, with various aims, for example, that the mourners should feel no concern with the loss of the child and not pursue the case, or – if they went to a *sing'anga* for consultation – that the *sing'anga* should experience a black–out and just see nothing; and also, in this particular case they owed their comrades, i.e. other wizards and witches one more kill (*watsala wina kuti afenso*). Wizards and witches are parts of groups, and they borrow from each other the flesh of people (*amfiti amakongozana nyama ya wanthu)* which they have killed by witchcraft. They share it and borrow. In this case, according to *sing'anga* Jonasi Masangwi, the man and the woman who killed that boy, had a lot of debts with other wizards and they were hard-pressed. So they first first killed the boy, and were hoping to target yet another person on the path to the graveyard, in order to pay up all their debts.

Interview with the sing'anga Jonasi Masangwi, 50 years old, at Nzuna village T.A. Ncil-amwela, Thyolo District, December 10, 1994. orig. tape No. M 94/6

J. Ine dzina langa ndine Jonasi Masangwi, sopano la ntchito yangayi ndine Nkholo-Panja.115)	J. My name is Jonasi Masangwi, and now, my professional name is *Nkholo-panja* [the buttocks-outside]. [115]
M. Eya dzina limeneli linabwela bwanji?	M. All right, how did you get this epithet?
J. Oho, zina limeneli linabwela, molingana kuti nditayamba kudwala,kudwala kokuja, ndinagwa mmazi, pofuna kugwa mmazi kokuja ndinachosamo supa, ndiye nditachosa supa ija,ndipo ndinayamba kumagwira afiti, ndiye ndipomwe ndinazicha Nkholo Panja, Dalaiva wa Amfiti.	J. Oho, This name came to me at the time when I [was not yet *sing'anga* and]began to fall ill, get sick over there in my village. I fell into water, and as I was about to drown I discovered a phial (*nsupa*) inside the water and picked it up. I picked up that phial and through it I began to catch wizards and witches. It is from that moment on that I call myself Buttocks Outside, Driver of the Wizards/Witches.
M. Aaa, monga mungakumbukile chaka chimene chinachitika zimenezo; kuti chinalii chaka chiti?	M. Aaa, perhaps you might remember the year when these things happened, which year?
J. Iii, koma sopano madeti ache sindingaziwe iyayi.	J. Iii! But now the date of this I wouldn't know.
M. Simungaziwe?	M. You wouldn't know?
J. Aaaa!	J. Aaaa!
M. Koma ndikalekale kwambiri?	M. But is it very long ago?
J. Iii, ndikale.	J. Iii! It is long ago.
M. Kodi ntchito imeneyi mwakhala mukugwila kwa nthawi yaitali bwanji?	M. You have been doing this work for a very long time, haven't you?
J. Iii, chaka chino cha teni.	J. Iii! This is the tenth year.
M. Mukugwira ntchito imeneyi?	M. That you have been engaged in this work?
J. Ndikugwilabe eee.	J. And continue to do so, yes.
M. Ndiyebe paja kumudzi simunanene paja village ija ndi chiyani?	M. Now, you have not yet told me where your home village is, which is it?
J. Oho, sopano village ndi Sabwe,Thyolo.	J. Oho! The village is called Sabwe, In Thyolo District.
M. Ndiyebe tsopano,poti zofuna kudziwa ndi zambiri,aaa inu zimatheka bwanji, chimachitika ndichiyani kuti mudziwe kuti uyu ndi mfiti? Chifukwa monga pali azising'anga osiyanasiyana, pali ena amachita za azimu, mwa azimu omwe amanena kuti ndiomwe amauza, tsopano monga inuyo muli mbali itiyo?	M. Sure, much remains to be known, aaa! How is it possible, for example, that you can identify this or that person as a *mfiti*? Which avenue do you pursue in your work? I am asking because there are several types of *asing'anga.* There are some who call the spirits (*azimu*)and they say that it is the spirits who tell them. To which side do you belong?

[115] Nkolo-Panja Dalaiva Wa Amfiti (Buttocks Outside, Driver of the Wizards/Witches). Jonasi Masangwi did not tell me exactly the meaning of this phrase in his personal history. Unfortunately I did not pursue this question. But many of these epithets serve the purpose of frightening others. Many of these names are fanciful and serve to underline the person's special power.

J. Sopano monga ineyo ndimapanga chochi, fesite wani kuti ndikupita ndikasake amfiti ndimayamba kuthila sembe,116) sopano ndikagona amfiti onse waja akumudzi omwe ndifuna kukasakawo amabela kwa ine pano,zinyanga zawo 117) zonse kubwela nawo, ndiye pomwe ndikuchoka kuno ndiye kuti ndikuziwa pomwe abisala iwo ndikuonamo.	J. As far as I am concerned I proceed as follows: The first thing to do before I go to hunt down the wizards/witches is to offer a sacrifice [*kuthila nsembe*] [116].Thereafter, when I sleep, all the wizards and witches of the village where I intend to go for hunting them, come by themselves to my place. They take all their "horns" (*zinyanga zawo*) [117]) with them to me, and so when I set out I already know where they are hiding and I can see them in their hiding places.
M. Ndiye kuti amfitiwo mumachita kuwaitana kuti abwele madzulowo?	M. Do you actually call the wizards and witches that they should come in the evening?
J. Sopano usiku paja amabwela kucheza nawo limodzi, kukambilana nawo limozi, ndikumanena malo omwe asiya zinthu zawo,kuti "ine changa ndasiya poti, ine changa ndasiya poti."	J. Now in such a night they do come for their conversations in order to exchange their news, and to tell each other the places where they leave their things, such as: "Myself I left my things in a such place, myself I left my things in such place" and so on.
M. Kumeneko kumakhala kuti ndi kumatsenga kapena kumizimu?	M. Is your method to discover witchcraft through *matsenga* (magic) or through *mizimu* (spirits)?
J. Koma kumizimu, zimabwela ngati mizimu.	J. But through the spirits; these things come like spirits.
M. Ndiye nthawi yomwe mukupita ija mumadziwa kuti ndikapita pakuti pakuti?	M. When you set out for your work, do you know exactly the place you will go?
J. Zonse zija timaziziwa,kaya athawisa apita nawo kumazi, tikafika mnyumba muja kuyang'ana kuyang'ana kuti oo basi apita kumazi, ngati kunapita ine kusidya kuja simunandiona ndikuthamangila kumazi kuja, nditalowa mmene muja ndaona kuti aa chinthu chija basi athawisa basi ine kumathamangila kumazi kuja.	J. I know it beforehand, and perhaps the wizards will try to run away and hide their medicines near the water. When we arrive at the house there and look round we have to say in resignation: "All right, they have gone to the water."Like myself, when I went to the other side of the river, didn't you see me how I was running to that water? When I had entered a certain house, I discovered that the (witchcraft) thing was gone, the owner had run away with it. I pursued her to the river.
M. Ndiye kumadziko munachipeza?	M. And did you find that thing at the water?
J. Ndinachipeza aa, ndinachichotsa eee.	J. Yes, I found it, and I removed it, yes.
M. Tsopano pajapa ndinaona kuti mumati mukalowa mnyumba mumaitanitsa madzi.	M. At that place I observed that when you enter a house, [as soon as you have found the horns] that you also call your assistants

[116] The *sing'anga* takes flour (*ufa*) and sprinkles it on a tree (*kuthila pantengo*) in order to secure the consent of the spirits.

[117] The "horns" (*zinyanga*) used by wizards/witches for killing.

	to bring you water.
J. Oho, eyaa, sopano ndikalowa mmene muja,ndikamenyapo ndi chila,118) kuti chinthu chija sichituluka iyayi, ndimati bwela naoni kuno mazii, ndikumenya kumenya sopano ndikukumbapo sopano chinthu chija basi chingoti phidiguku,119) basi ndikuchigwila.	J. Oh, yes, when I enter a house [in search of Evil magic] I strike in various directions with my tail (*nchila*) [118] but when the evil things does not come out, I call my assistant to bring water, I continue to strike the spot with my tail and I dig that thing out from the ground; it then erupts[119], comes to the surface and I catch it.
M. Kodi, ho, tsopano monga amfiti amenewawa zimakhalano bwanji kuti azikhala ndi zinthu ngati zimenezizi.	M. How do those wizards and witches get into the position to possess things like those?
J. Mhu, sopano zimakhala chochi, wina kolo lache amakhala nawo zida, sopano mwana uja pofuna kubadwa zimene zija amamupasa, sopano akamakula ndiye zinthu zomwe zili nkati mwamwana uja nazo zimakula ngati momwe akukulila mwanayo,120) ndiye zikakhwima kwambiri nthupi lamwanalo,ndiye amamupha munthu wina ndikumudyesa mwana uja. Ndiye zikatelo mwana uja sopano amayamba kugwila ntchito yokapha anthu munjila yomutuma,121) ndiye iye uja amapita kuyamba kupha munthu nyamayo akulu akulu 122) ndikugawana. Ndiye nthawi zina mumanva kuti "a iwe undibwezele	J. Mhu! Now it is like this: it can be that it started with a parent of that person who had such weapons (*zida*). Now when a child is born and still very small, it can be that the parent transmits the witchcraft to the child and when the child grows up, those witchcraft things inside the body of the child grow in the same way proportionally. [120] When the witchcraft power implanted into the child has gained strength in his body, the parent kills somebody [by witchcraft] and gives some of the dead body's parts the child to eat. When this stage is reached, that child begins to take up the work to kill people by the way of being sent out to do so by the parent (*munjila yomutuma*) [121]). So

---

118 *nchila* (pl. *michila*) = tail; here one of the tools of a *sing'anga* which he uses to detect where evil objects (containing witchcraft power) are hidden in a house belonging to a wizard or witch. If the witchcraft objects resist to come cut, because of their strong inherent power, he intensifies the process by striking the supposed spot repeatedly with his tail, ordering his assistant to bring water, and he begins to dig up the objects hidden in the ground.

119 The sudden eruption of the witchcraft objects from the ground after digging a bit, is described by Jonasi Masangwi here with an ideophone: *phidiguku*. It implies that something comes out, erupts with a strong force in a process of inversion: what was below comes to the surface. This can also be explained with a gesture, such as reversing one's hand position: the left hand comes up on top of the right hand.

120 The parent transmits his or her witchcraft to the child in one or another way. Perhaps he/she gives the child witchcraft to eat, so that it should reside in the child's abdomen, or perhaps the child receives a mark (*kachizindikiro)* on the forehead or elsewhere on the body. The term parent (*nkolo*) includes most of the adult persons in a household, besides father and mother there are several other relatives. Any of those can be a *mfiti* and transmit the witchcraft. This witchcraft then grows inside the body of the child, in the way the child grows up.

121 *munjila yomutuma.* It is common in village households that children are sent here and there by their parents, for example to fetch water, buy something quickly from a shop nearby. A grown–up person is not "sent" that way. The child is treated like an apprentice of witchcraft. It is important, hewever, that at that stage the child is totally unaware of his/her witchcraft, it kills by witchcraft without knowing that he/she has killed a person. (See also the story of Sowa, elsewhere in this book).

nyama yanga, unangongola nyama yanga", wina unva: "iyayi ndifuna mwendo", ndiye kuti pobweza ayenela kubweza mwendo omwewo.Kaya anatenga nyama ya mutu, unva "basi ndifuna nyama yanga, koma undigawire mutu" kaya nyama yomwe anatengayo inali munthu wamamuna, kuti anamupatsa mbolo, amatinso "ai, inenso ndifuna mbolo yemweyo",umo mumakhala muli muufiti 123) mwawomo.	the child embarks on missions to kill people and the flesh is shared with the adult members (*akuluakulu*) of the group[122]. Some time you can hear a *mfiti* say to another one:"You, you bring back my meat, you have taken credit, now you pay it back!"Or another one says :"No, but I want a leg!"and so his/her partner has to pay back exactly what he had borrowed, such as a leg. Or otherwise, someone borrowed meat from a head, then you can hear these words:"Sure, I want my meat back, but you should share the head (of the person killed) with me." And if, for example, the meat he/she had borrowed the other day was from a male victim, and what he borrowed was the penis then the other *mfiti* will say: "No I also want a penis!" You pay back a credit, with the same type of meat, that is the rule of *ufiti*. [123])
M. Koma monga ndi zoona kuti nyamayo amaidyadi, kapena amadya matsenga omwewo?124)	M. But now, is it true that the flesh[from a dead person] is actually eaten, or perhaps they eat the inherent magic? (*kapena amadya matsenga omwewo*)? [124])
J. Iiii, kwabasi, kwabasi amadya, poti kwakhala mfiti kuti iyo ndi mfitidi, pophika nsima 125) ija, woti ndiwodziwa bwino bwino, kuti walembela zosiyanasiyana, amabwela nawo mphika wawo pamalo omwe akudyela nsima anthu ndikumadya nawo pamodzi mbale	J. Iiii! They really eat the flesh. When a woman is a real witch, and it is well-known that various witchcraft things are written on her body, after cooking *nsima* (maize porridge[125]) she comes with it in a pot to the place where all the people in the household will eat. As she eats with them there is one pot containing the *nsima*

122 The child is now part of the group of adult *amfiti*.

123 The members of a group of *amfiti* regularly exchange "meat" from the corpses of their victims between themselves such as when one *mfiti* has killed someone and dug up the meat from the graveyard, then he or she shares it with the others. Those are now debtors. Next time he or she will ask from the partner those parts which were handed out to be replaced. There are lots of quarrels in the group of *amfiti* (*phokoso pakati pa amfiti*) because of *ngongole ya nyama* (credit taken in form of meat).

124 My question was motivated by what one can often hear from rumours (*mphekesera)* in the villages, namely that in some instances people seem to have found indications that *amfiti* were digging up the corpse in the graveyard of a person they had killed, but when the relatives decide to look for themselves and issue an exhumation order, they invariably find that the corpse is still there. So I asked the *sing'anga* whether his narrative about the *amfiti* eating the flesh of their dead victims was to be taken literally or perhaps in a symbolic manner.

125 The other people in the household are relatives (*anthu pa chibale*) who are not *amfiti*. The witch puts the pot of *nsima* from which everyone will eat, on the table. Each person is served his or her relish individually on a plate. But in addition she puts an invisible pot on the table, from which she eats alone. That pot contains the human flesh.

imodzi ya nsima, koma ndiwo iye ndikumadyela nyama ya munthu uwo yemwe ukudya naye uja osaona kapena osadziwa kuti iye akudya nyama ya munthu.	from which all eat, but there is also an invisible pot of relish (*ndiwo*) which contains the human meat from the corpses and she will eat from that pot alone. The other people who eat with her, eat the relish served on their plates, they don't see that special pot and have no idea that in their midst there is someone eating the meat from a person (*nyama ya munthu*).
M. Ndiyebe inuyo ndikuona kuti mumagwilitsila ntchito zida zosiyansyana, monga pali mabotolo aja ndipo pali michila, palinso nkhwangwa, inu zinthu zimene zija zimakuthandizani kuti mutani?	M. I am realizing that you perform your work using various kinds of weapons, such as those bottles [which you raise up in front of your eyes],then there are the medicine tails (*michila*), and there is also the axe (*nkhwangwa*). In which way do all these tools help you?
J. Oho, sapano nchila uja, ndikaona kuti sopano oo mfiti iyi ndiwamakani 126) kwambiri, oti ameneyu satheka iyayi ndimammenya nawo nchilawuja basi iye ndikufookelatu.	J. When I see that a *mfiti* turns out to be a person of severe resistance [126]) and I fail to finish him, I use this tail and beat him with it, then he begins to get weaker and weaker.
M. Kodi mumamumenya kweni kweni kapena mwamatsenga?	M. Do you beat him as a real person or perhaps by the way of magic(*matsenga*)?
J. Mwamasenga kungoti chochi basi afooka. Ndiye ine ndimapeza mphanvu yotengela chinthu chija.	J. By the way of magic, in that way he/she becomes weak. Then I find the power to take away that witchcraft thing.
M. Tibwelela pambuyo pang'ono,kodi inuyo mutagwa mmadzi muja, kodi podzuka munadziwa ndi mitengo 127) yomwe, kapena munangodziwa kuchotsa ufiti kwa anthu?	M. Let us return to an earlier topic: When you fell into the water, in the past, and you woke up again, did you wake up with knowledge of herbal medicines, [127]) perhaps you only woke up with the knowledge of removing witchcraft from the people?
J. Iyayi, zonse mitengo zinabwela kumizimu,128) sindinapite kwa munthu kugula iyayi, ndilikudwala, kumathamaga basi, kumakumba mitengo basi, kumabwela nawo, ndikumagwila anthu kuti "iwe ukudwala	J. No, all this knowledge of herbal medicine came to me from the spirits (*mizimu*) [128]. I did not go to anybody in order to buy this knowledge from him or her. I was ill and just ran to the trees, digging them out, came back with

[126] *wamakani* = a person who enjoys contest, challenges a person who is impertinent in his/her pursuit of power and superiority. In a group of *amfiti* a dispute can arise. Some members warn the others of trying to enter the house of a certain person, because they think it is dangerous, especially if that person has many protective medicines. But one among them, known as *wamakani* would boast and say: "No I am going, I'll do it all alone."

[127] The reference to herbal medicines is "*ndi mitengo*" (with trees) or "*kumakumba mitengo*" (digging out trees), because most herbal medicines of a *sing'anga* come from the wood, and quite often the roots of specific trees.

[128] When he was ill he was dreaming those trees. He did not obtain this knowledge through any instruction, he claims, or through purchase. Some other *asing'anga* pay for such instruction from their colleagues, but Jonasi Masangwi insists that the *mizimu* (spirits) revealed it all to him.

moti moti", munthu uja ndikumabvomla. "Ii iyayi mwana wakoyo amupasa chinthu chakuti chakuti chofunika kuchotsedwa". Munthu uja kumabvomela,kuti "eee zoona eee."Basi kuchokela pomwepo ine ndinayamba kumaitanidwa.	the herbal medicines, and identified people saying to them: "You are sick of such and such" and the person agreed. At another time someone came with a child and I said: "Ii! No, your child was given such and such witchcraft thing and it is necessary to remove it!" The person agreed, saying: "Yes, that is true, yes!" From that time I began to be invited.
M. Ndiyebe ifeyo tikufuna kudziwa kuti zinthu zimene mwazipeza zija inuyo mumazitani?	M. We would still like to know about those witchcraft things which you find, what are you doing with them?
J. Sopano ndikazipeza chonchija, pofuna kusamuka pano, zones zija ine ndimaziocha moto, pofuna kuocha moto amfumu ndi ma youth ligi akhalepo. Basi ndimati "bwelani kuno zinthu ndifuna ndizioche zonsezo" kuzigumulila mmenemo, ndi mbale zomwe zija kuzigumulila momwemo, poti kuli kanyumba kawo 129) kumeneko kuseliko, basi kuocha moto ndikuyamba kumazungulilapo basi kumawaza sopano mankhwala. Zina zimauluka momuja kuti buuu 130) kuti zithawe komanso zimagwela pamoto pomwepo basi ndikupsya. Basi kuli biii,131) ife wenzulo kwekekweke ndikunyamuka kupita mudzi wina. Nkusiya moto ukuyaka ife ulendo.	J. Now if I find them in that way and when I want to leave the place, I burn them up in the fire. In order to do that it is necessary that the chiefs and the Youth League are present. I am saying: "You all come here, I want to burn all those things, throw them all into the fire (*kuzigumulila*), including those plates [of the wiards/witches]. There is [here at Nzuna village] a small hut[129]) there behind. I kindle the fire and begin to dance round the place and sprinkle my medicines. Some witchcraft objects then come out from the fire with a sound: *buuu*! trying to flee, [130]) but they fall back into the fire and burn up. Then it is dark there, *biii*! [131]) I sound my whistle, *kweke kweke* and start out for another village. Leaving the fire to catch everything, we are on our journey.
M. Kusonyeza kuti zonse mphamvu yake yathela pomwepo. Tsopano munthu amene wa ufiti uja amatani?	M. Which means that the power of all those things is finished right there. Now what are the wizards and witches doing?
J. Sopano kutero kuja mawa pano ndikuwachosa, mawa ndili kuwachosano sapano ufiti wawo.	J. As promised, tomorrow I will remove from them their witchcraft.
M. Tsopano lero pano agona pompano?	M. Will they sleep here today?
J. Lero afuna awomboledwe, akaomboledwa azipita, sopano mmawamawa abwele ndi abale wawo ndiziwachosa sapano ufiti wawo uja. Kuti asabweleze,sopano anuwake wodandaula aja akanena kuti ameneyu sindifuna kuti akhale	J. Today it necessary that they pay ransom [*awomboledwe*], when they have done that they are free to go. Now tomorrow morning they should come back here with their relatives, so that I remove their

[129] This was not exactly a hut, but a kind of enclosure (*mpanda*).

[130] *Nyanga zina zomwe zili ndi mphamvu zimafuna kuthawa ndiye zimauluka* (some "horns" which are very powerful want to flee and they fly up).

[131] biii, ideophone, suggests something black.

masiku ambiri, sopano ndimachosa kumalizila, ndiye ndikamalizila ndiye amangotha 3 months basi ndikumwalila pokuwachotsa kwamwetsa mankhwala, iyayi sindifuna kuti ndiwapange chipongwe, ndimangomuchotsa ndimusiyire pang'ono basi aziyenda.	witchcraft. To avoid that they relapse and do it again, if the person who had complained, says: "that one I don't want him or her to stay alive for many days", then I remove the witchcraft to the finish; if I finish their witchcraft totally, he or she will stay alive just for another three months and then die. To remove the witchcraft I make him or her drink certain medicines. But when the victim says: "No, I don't want to exer upon him/her any Insolence (*chipongwe*)", then I remove that person's witchcraft only to the extent that a little bit of it remains and he or she should go.
M. Ndiye kuti mukangomaliza kumuchotsa ufiti wonsewo, ndiye samakhala nthawi yaitali?	M. So this means when you remove all the witchcraft from that person, he or she will not survive for a long time?
J. Ufiti uja ndikangoumaliza wonse ndithu kumumwetsa mankhwala sipangathe 3 months, basi wayamba nyonswe nyonswe.	J. Indeed, if I finish all the witchcraft and make the person drink certain medicines, within three months he or she will begin to become a wreck [*nyonswenyonswe*] [132].
M. Tsopano mumachotsa munjila yotani?	M. Which is your method to remove it?
J. Kale makolo akale, akapanga chochi, kungomulembela lembela ndikumumwesa mankhwala, basi apange chochi kaya ndi nkazi azivindikile chochi bwino bwino, ndikulowesa chochi zanjali133) uwona ufiti uja ukubwela chochi thaa 134), sopano boma zimenezo analesa. Masiku ano sichomwecho iyayi, kungomulembela-lembela basi ndikumumwesa mankhwala ,basi nkumuuza kuti akhale pamalo ena, koma asakhale ndi panti iyayi. Ndiye ine ndimayamba kunenelela kwambiri kuti ufitiwo utuluke, ndiye khale khale amaunya ufiti uja unvekeni yolo pansi. Nthawi zina mpaka kunyelanso mphika omwe amausunga mmimbamo. Dzulo wina wanyela mphika pamodzi ndi manyi omwe phiii! mmenemo. Izi ndi zooonadi ngakhale mufunse mfumu yapano.	J. At the time of our ancestors, when they were doing this, they were writing on his/her skin and making him/her drink medicines. They would also do something else, if it was a woman, she is told to sit down and the hand is entered into her, [133]) then you see that the witchcraft comes out like this *thaa*!, [134]) but now the government has prohibited this. Nowadays it is no longer like that. We are only writing on his/her skin and make him/her drink medicines, and tell him/her that he/she should sit down at another place, but without underpants. And myself I begin to declaim that the witchcraft should come out, and indeed after some time, the person craps the witchcraft from his bowels, and it drops down. At another time it can happen that the person even excretes a pot which he has kept in his abdomen. Yesterday someone excreted a

[132] *nyonswe nyonswe*, ideophone, derived from the word *kunyonzoloka* = to become thin, to shrink etc. *Chimanga kumenyedwa ndi dzuwa kwambiri opanda mvula kubwela, nde chimayamba kunyonzoloka* (if maize is hit by the sun very much without any rain to come, then the maize begins to become slim).

[133] I have not seen myself what exactly is done in that case.

[134] <u>*thaa!*</u> = finished.

[Tonse tikuseka pankhani yakunyayi]	cooking-pot together with shit, phiii! This is true, you may ask the chief of here. [Everybody laughing]

The *sing'anga* Jonasi Masangwi (in front) is leading the crowd on his marathon to Ndalama village, T.A. Nchilamwela, in Thyolo District with the intention to expropriate the wizards and witches in that place and take their "horns" (*nyanga*). – December 10, 1994. – Photo no 94/4/3, author.

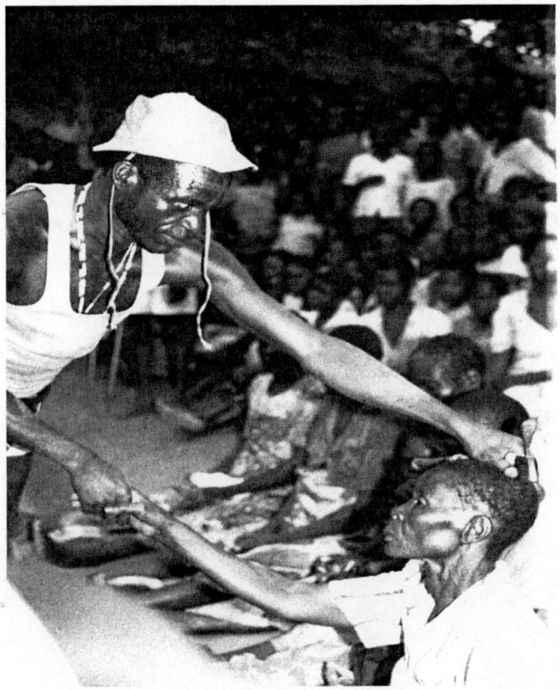

Here, the *sing'anga* shakes the hand with the captain (*kaputeni*) who steers the nocturnal aeroplane (*ndege yausiku)* of the group of witches and who also sells the meat to her partners. He urges her to confess where she has left her plane, but she denies being in possession of any such plane. But she keeps other things, such as phials *(nsupa)* and owls (*akadzidzi)* for making people sick.

At Nzuna village, T.A. Nchilamwela, Thyolo District, December 10, 1994.- Photo no. 94/4/30

The axe (*nkhwangwa)* in his left hand, the *sing'anga* Jonasi Masangwi shakes the head of an elderly woman while holding her right hand with his own right hand. He speaks out what he has found in her house. He denounces her, saying that she was keeping the testicles of a man in her house for the purpose of beating small children during their sleep. The child would then develop fever, the gentials would get sick, and the abdomen would get swollen until it dies.

Same place, same date. Photo no 94/4/29, author.

This is the group of drummers who performed while the *sing'anga* Jonasi Masangwi was getting ready for his work of catching wizards and witches. There were always four drums in action and they were struck with thin bamboo sticks (*tinsungwi).*

Same place, same date. – Photo no. 94/11/35, author.

The *sing'anga* Masangwi (centre) is seen dancing as if in a frenzy together with his assistant and the two children in his care, before starting his trip to Ndalama village for " hunting" the wizards and witches (*kukasaka amfiti).* He is doing this to develop his power (*kudzipatsa mphamvu)* of recognizing *amfiti* and where they keep their witchcraft medicines.

Same place, same date. Photo no. 94/11/33, author.

The *sing'anga* Jonasi Masangwi in his white short and white hat, seen here during the last dance performance before setting out to the neighbouring village Ndalama. His style of dance movement is considered to be identical to that carried out by wizards and witches in the graveyard. In the background, left, of this photograph, there is my companion Donald Kachamba recording the event.

Same place, same date. Photo no. 94/4/1, author.

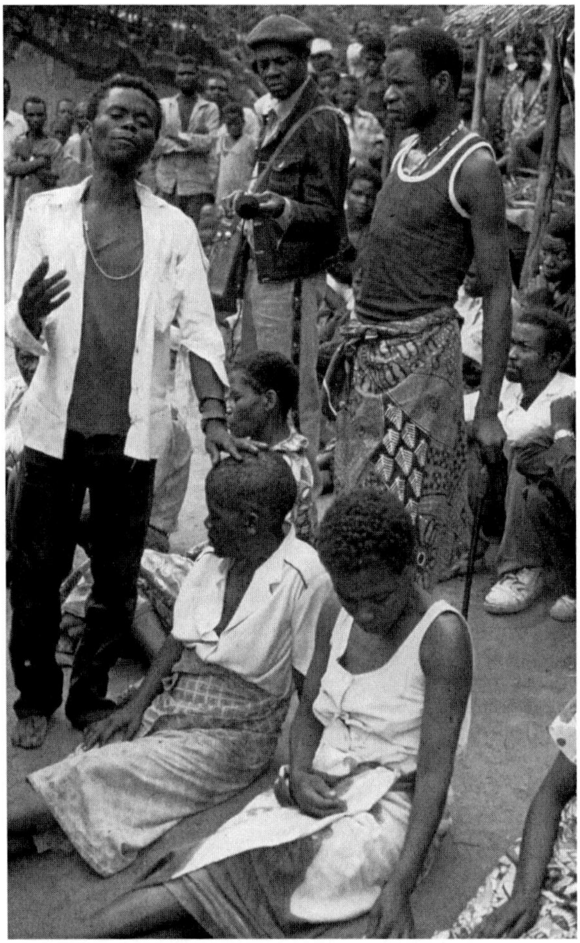

The *sing'anga*'s assistant touches the head of an elderly woman who was identified as a *mfiti* eating people. He is explaining what exactly the *sing'anga* has found concerning that person's witchcraft.
Donald Kachamba with microphone is seen in the background.
Same place, same date. Photo no. 94/11/31, author.

The women who are seen here sitting on the ground are those whom the *sing'anga* found in possession of various objects used by them for carrying out witchcraft. In the pots seen between their legs are those witchcraft medicines and "horns" (*nyanga*) they had used. The person standing is the *sing'anga* Jonasi Masangwi. He is in the process of sprinkling anti-witchcraft medicines over their heads.

Same place, same date. Photo no. 94/4/26, author.

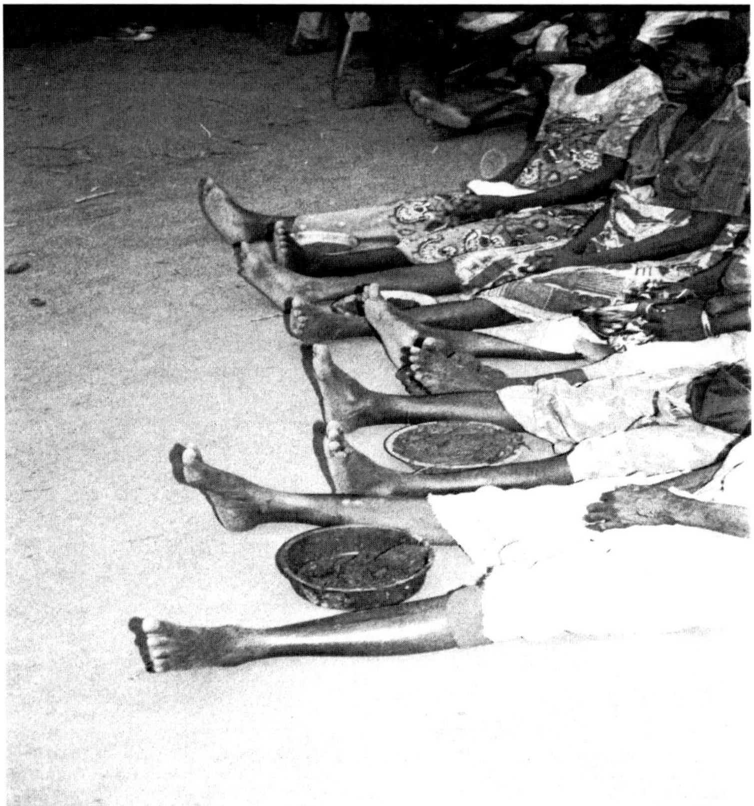

This photograph shows what is found in the pots and plates of the women identified by the *sing'anga* as witches. The witchcraft medicines are mixed with mud which the *sing'anga* has dug up in their houses. As soon as the *sing'anga* has identified someone as wizard or witch, he digs up the hidden "horns" (*nyanga)* inside a lot of clay.

Same place, same date. Photo no. 94/4/27, author.

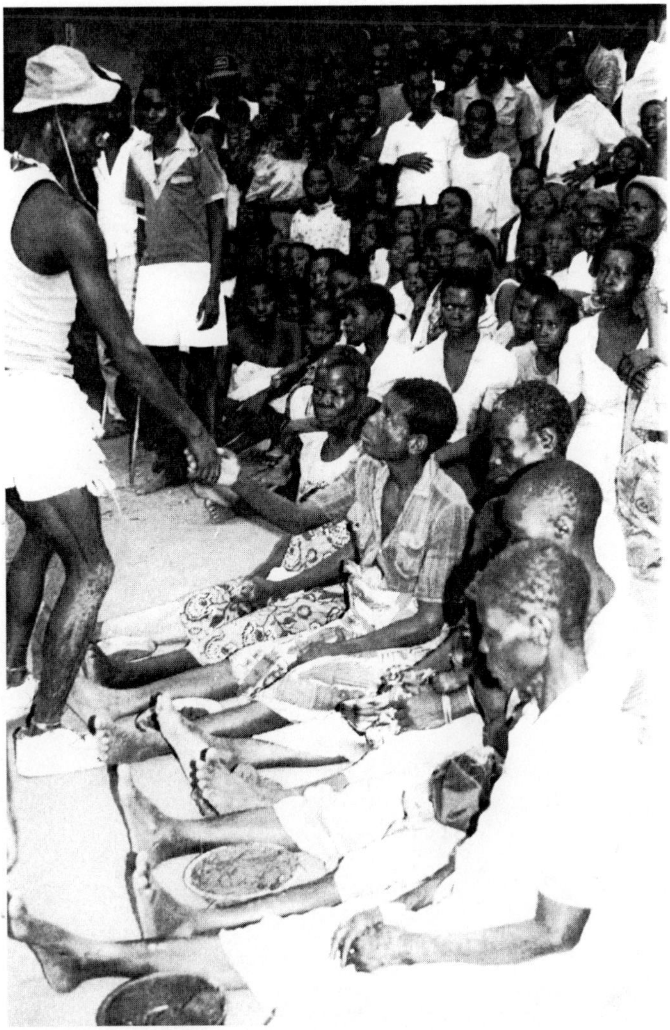

Another view of the same scene with many people in the background watching: the *sing'anga* is standing before the row of the witches sitting on the ground. He greets one woman, touching her hand in a certain manner (see also photo 94/4/30 shot from the other side) this is called *akugwilana chanza* (friendly hand-shaking), and it is the moment he touches her hand this way that he discovers the witchcraft things she possesses. At that stage the woman began to tremble *(kunjenjemela)* because of fear.

Same place, same date. - Photo no. 94/4/31, author.

Paulo Luka

(Mr.)

Reports about the *sing'anga* Paulo Luka began to circulate in 1985. The news that was heard across the entire country of Malawi was that a certain *singanga* had appeared in the area of Ntcheu (in south-central Malawi, see MAP) able to find persons believed to have died and who had been buried, while in reality they had not died at all. Instead they were leading a kind of shadow existence somewhere else in the service of a wizard or witch who had got hold of them. As a matter of fact, the funeral of the person in his or her home village was a fake, and what had been buried was banana stalks or a mortar (*ntondo*) [135] instead of a corpse. The real person, unable to communicate with his or her relatives or even remember his or her origins due to the effect of the witchcraft drug, had been kidnapped by the wizard, and sometimes sold to another wizard in another area to work for him.

As such reports circulated, many people in their personal grief for having lost a relative, suspecting that the cause was witchcraft, would flock to Paulo Luka in order to find out whether their beloved one was perhaps not dead at all. One of the reports that surfaced was about a certain boy named Antonyo (Port.: António) from Mozambique who had been buried, but was later found working in a maize mill in Malawi! Everyone had thought that the boy was dead and that he had been buried in Mozambique; but through the power of his medicines, Paulo Luka discovered that Antonyo had actually been "buried" in a maize mill owned by a certain man in Malawi. Antonyo and his parents were from Tsangano, not far from Ncheu, across the border in Mozambique.

In 1985, this story was heard over and over with its sinister background. It was said that Antonyo's maternal uncle *(malume)*[136] had been asked by that rich person who was the owner of many maize mills in the administrative area of Ntcheu, to recruit for him, by magic (*matsenga*), a boy who would then always work for him in serfdom. The uncle was told to bring the "corpse" of the boy (who was not dead at all) to that rich man and put it down next to the bag where the rich man used to keep his money which he was collecting daily from the revenue of his maize mills. The work of the boy would be to look after the money, and sometimes collect the revenue himself in the various places and bring it there.

He would then always sit next to the bag of money (*pathumba la ndalama*) as a guard. After the uncle had received the proposal from the man, he signed the contract obliging him to kidnap his nephew *(mdzikulu wake)* for the purpose of selling him into serfdom. Thereafter the uncle went back to their village and began to apply his magic (*matsenga*

---

135 *Ntondo* is always carved from the wood of a tree known by the same name. *Ntengo wa matondo kupangira ntondo* (the tree which gives the *matondo* fruits is used for making a mortar). *Ntondo* in Chiyao and Chichewa, also in the spelling *mtondo* is described as a "deciduous tree up to 24m. with a branched bush crown and rough reddish brown bark, leaves alternate, pinnate, flowers small golden-yellow in numerous racemes of 6 – 12 flowers, fruits fleshy, yellow, the size of a lemon, usually containing two reddish-brown seeds...The fruits are edible; they have an unpleasant smell and are only eaten by old people except in times of hunger... The timber is said to be somewhat coarse-grained but very durable and is useful for rough constructional work, and is used in the making of mortars, hence the name, *mtondo*" (Williamson 1975:80).

136 The maternal uncle (*malume*) has much power in the matrilineal societies of southern Malawi, and uncle/nephew relationships are often tense and a playground of witchcraft activities from either side. On the importance of the *malume* see also Kubik/Malamusi 1987: 8 – 9.

awo) until Antonyo fell ill and suddenly seemed to have died. Public knowledge was that the boy was dead and had been buried in the local graveyard; but in reality what had been buried was a useless object, while the person had been drugged and taken away to be sold in Ntcheu to stay at the maize mill of the man there. The uncle began to spend the money he had received for the deal. However, it happened that Antonyo's mother was unable to come to terms with the loss of her child, realizing that Antonyo had died without having been seriously ill. In her grief the matter aroused her suspicions, and within a short time, she went to Paulo Luka explaining everything that had happened to her child. The *sing'anga* Paulo Luka comforted her, saying that she should not worry; her child would be found (!). But he warned that such an investigation would take time; so the mother stayed there at the *sing'anga's* place for several days, waiting for anything to come up that might lead to finding her son. After a week had passed she was called by the *sing'anga* who told her bluntly that her child had been found, and that he was arranging for the day that she would fetch him; but he added that the place where he was spotted was far from their village, and that it was in Malawi and not in Mozambique where they stayed. He said that the boy had been found at a maize mill in Malawi. In order to bring him back, however, she would not have to go to the maize mill personally; instead, he the *sing'anga* would escort her to their home village and arrange that the boy would reappear out of the graveyard!

The report by people then goes on to say that the day the *sing'anga* went there to resurrect Antonyo was a Saturday. Paulo Luka and his assistants started their journey to that village together with the mother. Many people were gathering there to see what would happen. Then, they say, Paulo Luka was waiting until it became dark, and then set out alone to go to the cemetery. There he met with the boy by the power of his medicines, after he had made an invocation to him (*atamuchita muitano)* that he should come back from where he was staying. They say that Paulo Luka remained inside the cemetery until the boy arrived. Shortly before dawn, the people of the village were seeing Luka as he emerged with that boy, but the boy had no clothes on, and he was unable to speak the way he used to speak long ago, and his appearance was not like that of a real person. Thereafter, he was dressed up in good clothes and Paulo Luka set out with him to the place where he used to carry out his work of *using'anga*. That very day the big news began to spread across Malawi that *sing'anga* Luka had been waking up a person from the grave who had died long ago. In his clinic, Luka began to give the boy some of his medicines so that he would transform back into a normal human being and that he would start to talk again in the manner he used to do in the past.

But the bad luck (*tsoka)* was, according to these reports, that this endeavour did not succeed. Some people are convinced that it was indeed the same boy who had been found, but that it was difficult to induce him to talk again like before and act like a normal human being. His behaviour had changed into that of a mad persom (*munthu wamisala)*.[137]

[137] *misala* (madness) is classified as a disease (*nthenda*). However, there are distinctions between individuals displaying "mad" behaviour, according to whether their behaviour is destructive and threatening to other people in the community or not. Either a person can be called *wamisala* or *wopenga,* or just *wozungulira mutu.* Someone known as *wamisala* exhibits a specific behavioural syndrome. He or she is considered to be an individual capable of doing anything considered destructive or dangerous (*munthu amene kuchita chili chonse choononga, kapena choopsya)* for example, any time he meets with somebody on the path he picks up a stone and throws it at that person (*akutenga mwala akumana ndi munthu akumugenda*), or he puts off his clothes and walks naked (*kubvula dzobvala nkuyenda maliseche*). The term *wopenga* often refers to a violent form of madness. Sometimes it is necessary for the community to bind the person to prevent him/her from destroying things (*amumanga mwonse kuti*

He tried to run away repeatedly, and so his mother decided to take him home to Mozambique without delay, getting increasingly tired of staying at Paulo Luka's place. Moreover, Luka had committed the woman to work for him, and help him in various ways in his *using'anga*. The mother of the boy did not like that at all. Eventually she left the place with her son, and returned to their village. However, there within a short time, the boy ran away, disappearing to destinations unknown.

It was reports of this kind which filled people with awe of the power of *sing'anga* Paulo Luka. Everybody now expected from him to perform more miracles such as he had retrieved that teenager from magic captivity in a maize mill. But nobody except Paulo Luka himself will probably know the secrets (*zinsinsi*) behind the matter. Even for me it is difficult to patch together an accurate picture of what really happened at that time. It would be an enormous task to continue the investigation of these reports.

People also claimed that it was not the only instance of Paulo Luka retrieving a person considered dead. They said there was a certain girl known by the name of Magi (engl. Maggie) whom people had thought to be dead in her village, while in fact she was found working in captivity in somebody's shop.

It was because of reports such as these that I became interested in meeting with the *sing'anga* Paulo Luka. So I began to organize a trip. From time to time reports of this kind were even heard on the radio (Malawi Broadcasting Corporation) to inform puzzled audiences about what Luka was doing. He was considered to be a great expert in *using'anga*. For me it was important to get a direct field assessment of his work. So on October 29, 1994, I set out for Ntcheu in the company of one assistant from my center, Watson Mtekesa.

Actually we were on the way to Lilongwe, the capital of Malawi to fetch a DAT recorder that had been bought for my Oral Literature Research Programme, as part of a cultural aid package provided by the Ministry of External Affairs (Auswärtiges Amt), Germany. Arriving in Ntcheu, however, I decided to stop for inquiries. We had started our journey in Chileka about 9 a.m. and arrived at the *boma* (administrative post) of Ntcheu about 11 a.m., when I began to inquire about the place we could find Paulo Luka. People at the *boma* explained to us that he was working at a certain village called Chipula, close to the Tsangano turnoff, about 2 km further on from Ntcheu to Lilongwe. Arriving there we found some young men who were assistants of the *sing'anga*. They appeared to be rather high-handed in their talk when I requested to meet with Paulo Luka. One of the boys said to me that I should state my problems for coming here so that he himself would take care of the matter! I replied that what I wanted was beyond his competence, because we had come to conduct an interview with the *sing'anga* to learn about his life and his work. The boy then countered: "What are your credentials that you should know something about the life of *sing'anga* Paulo?" While this interrogation was continuing I simply began to unpack my tape-recorder and camera for the purpose of recording the very insolence that came out of the mouth of this boy. All of a sudden, however, to the bad luck of the assistant, the *sing'anga* Paulo Luka appeared. When he noticed that we had a

asaononge zinthu). Conversely, if a person only displays obsessional ideas and strange behaviour without harming anybody, he or she is referred to as *wozungulira mutu* (literally: "someone whose head is turning").

tape recorder, he realized that we had come to learn something about his work. He said: "Welcome!" and to the boy: "These are my guests!"

This was my first encounter with Paulo Luka. We followed his lead and entered a small house where he received us formally. Luka turned out to be an extremely polite and hospitable person who also knew to deliver a discourse. We soon began to ask him many questions concerning the matters we wanted to know. With politeness he answered each and every question. At one stage he invited us to the large waiting room for people who had come to see him with their problems. But when the consultations were over, Paulo Luka suddenly rose up and told us good-bye (*akutitsazika*). He said that he did not live here, but was staying at the Ntcheu administrative center; that his house was there and that we were requested to visit him there in order to talk to him again! Shortly thereafter we then also left the place, following him to Ntcheu. Since it was now about 5 p.m., it was clear that our original plan of traveling to Lilongwe would not materialize that day. So we went to seek accommodation in the local resthouse in Ntcheu. After checking in we proceeded immediately to the *sing'anga*'s residence for further talks. However, to our dismay we met him already on the way; he said that he had just been called back to his clinic as Chipula village, because people had arrived who needed him urgently. To our surprise he suddenly put his hand into his pocket, pulled out a 50. – Malawi Kwacha note [138] and gave it to us with the words that regrettably we would not meet again today, since he was unable to anticipate the time of his return. He said, he was wishing us all the best for our journey.

With this gift he wanted to reassure us that he was very happy about our coming to his place. Instead of demanding money from us for allowing us to record him, taking pains to explain to us so many aspects of his work, he honoured us – in the local tradition – by offering money to the departing guests! I could, of course, not refuse the gift.

This was our first journey to see Paulo Luka. The interviews trancribed below were made on October 29, 1994, before our continuation to Lilongwe.

A year later, I would come back, this time together with the musician-composer Donald Kachamba who would help me to record the sessions. So my hands were free to photograph. The only purpose of this journey was to see Paulo Luka and talk to him again. When we arrived he received us as usually, taking us to his clinic. Then he called together all his clients who had arrived that day for consultation. We stayed for a few days with him.

During this second visit, in October 1995. the news was in everybody's mind that in the Ntcheu area a hyena (*fisi*) was rampant, attacking and eating people. Almost every day new reports were heard about yet another person having been killed and eaten by the hyena. The matter was brought to the attention of Paulo Luka and it was considered to be his task to find out what was behind it. The very day we arrived, groups of people had entered his clinic, all of them with the same complaint about having lost to the man-eating hyena a young brother or sister, or a child. When the *sing'anga* noticed the urgency of the complaints and their frequency he told his clients to enter the room where he kept his divination "video" (*vidiyo*), in groups of four, because there was no need for

---

[138] About 17 US-Dollar at that time.

giving each of them individual treatment. They were told to look at the *vidiyo* and discover by themselves what they would have to do.

This turned out to be a main theme of our second journey. Reports about the man-eating hyena had already surfaced in 1993. In August 1993 the news was heard on the M.B.C (Malawi Broadcasting Corporation) programme called 5 Moba[139] that Paulo Luka had identified a certain person as a wizard and compelled him to transform into a hyena. After the funeral of a certain victim, people had come to Paulo Luka with their complaints. A certain man from that village was subjected to a test. Since the man denied being a wizard, Luka made him jump over a certain object to discover his true identity, and indeed – so claimed the radio report – the man transformed into a hyena in front of the people assembled. With the fact of his witchcraft established, a brother was asked to pay a fine in order to bring him back to human existence. A reporter from the M.B.C. went to Paulo Luka to obtain information about what had happened and what had come out of it. The person who had transformed into a hyena was also interviewed, and he admitted that he had exerted witchcraft upon his brother. This matter came up because, to the surprise of everybody, there had been nothing but funerals in that village for weeks. This alarmed the community to go and see Paulo Luka for advice. All the people of that village set out for Chipula. Only one person refused to go: a certain man who was staying alone, without having a family. When the people of the village arrived at Luka's place, Luka told them immediately: "Even if you have all come, I am seeing that there is still one person who has remained behind. It is that person's presence I want!" A letter was written to the chief *(mfumu)* of that village requesting that the man who had stayed behind should be summoned to appear before the *sing'anga*. Eventually he arrived in the company of some others. Paulo Luka then declared in front of everybody that all the funerals which had taken place recently were in fact caused by the witchcraft of that man. The man, however, denied the accusations categorically. Eventually, the power struggle *(mpikisano)* between the forces of the *sing'anga* and those of the wizard *(mfiti)* ended with the latter's defeat.

Paulo Luka had disappeared inside a room where he was keeping his medicines. He reemerged with a very short pestle (*munsi waufupi*). He put it on the ground outside the house and said: "All right! Since you deny that you are *mfiti* who has killed all those people, then jump over that pestle (*mudumphe munsi umeneu*) to the other side! If you are innocent you will remain as you are, a person, but if you are that wizard then you will metamorphose into a hyena!" To convince the crowd of his innocence the man agreed to jump over the pestle. What then happened, however, was startling. He transformed immediately into a hyena with his hands placed on the ground, and hair beginning to grow everywhere on his legs. In order to avoid remaining a hyna for the rest of his life and eat rotten meat, he finally complied: "Please let me free! I will say that I am the wizard, indeed!" But Paulo Luka did not release him immediately. He told all the brothers of this man, as they had assembled, to pay the sum of 1,000.- Malawi Kwacha for him to be absolved. If they were unable to produce this money, he would remain in his present condition until the money finally came from somewhere.

At that juncture the police of the administrative area of Ntcheu was notified and in turn they informed the M.B.C. to send a reporter. Eventually the police and the radio people

---

139 Name of a fictitious aeroplane. This popular programme brings local news, often of curious or humorous content. It is imagined that the journalists go to the spots with the "5 Moba" plane.

arrived jointly on the spot, and they verified what had happened to that man. Under the eyes of the police and other people, *sing'anga* Paulo Luka then decided to forgive the man, and he removed him from his identity as a hyena, without insisting on any king of remuneration. Thereafter, many questions were posed to that man who had been turned into a hyena. He was requested to explain all the details about what he had done by the power of his witchcraft (*afotokoze zonse zomwe amachita pa ufiti wawo).* In many people this information created vivid interest (*chidwi*) and compassion (*chisoni*).

The *sing'anga* Paulo Luka was very much feared by people who practise witchcraft (*ufiti*) and magic (*matsenga*). What he used to accomplish in his clinic from time to time puzzled many people. From my own observations I have obtained the following picture of his daily routine. Beginning his consultations of the people who had brought to him their complaints on a certain day, he would first enter a small room inside his building, next to the large room where his clients were waiting. Returning, he would call the patients to come closer and begin singing various songs with Christian religious texts (*ya mau a Mulungu* = with God's words) in chorus (*kubvomereza*); some residents in the village would help them learn those songs. The start of the singing was his signal (*chizindikilo chake*) for the people who had arrived that day that they should now enter the consultation room so that their troubles could be identified and explained to them (*kukaonedwa ndikuuzidwa mabvuto awo*).

The *sing'anga* participated in the songs as a leader (*ntsogoleli*). While the singing was going on, we noticed that he repeatedly produced noises similar to giving a belch (*kugeya*). This meant that the spirits had entered his mind. He was also talking between the textlines of the songs, requesting everybody found wearing a watch to leave it outside the building; everybody who had coins in their pocket to deposit them outside; and also those who were wearing beads (*mikanda*) were told to leave them outside; in fact any objects of metal had to be removed. We made recordings of the session. But some of the words he spoke in between the songs cannot be heard clearly on the tape. He talked about a variety of things.

While the performance was going on, Paulo Luka then proceeded to put on his white robe (*nkanjo*) with a red cross in front and on the back. On his head he put a hood (*kapusi*) that was white like the robe. As soon as he was dressed for his job he seized his ceremonial staff with the right hand, and in his left he held a red cloth. At that juncture his wife helped him a lot with the songs, besides some long-term residents in his clinic who were still undergoing treatment and getting better.

In his work the *sing'anga* paid attention to each patient individually. He seized the hand of the first person whose problems he wanted to investigate, and began to ask him many questions, usually in Chichewa. People who had come across the border from Mozambique were asked by him in Portuguese. It appears that Paulo Luka himself was born in Mozambique and had grown up there.

A patient would normally reply: *eee!* (yes) to each statement by the *sing'anga.* Paulo Luka amazed everybody by being able to tell a person right away where he or she had come from, where their house was build, which objects could be found on the veranda (*pakhomo pake*) etc. After this demonstration of his visionary power, he then started to discuss the causes of the person's problems. Paulo Luka claimed that he was able to actually see things that took place far away. But he warned his clients that in the event he was mistaken, they should immediately contradict him (*ayenera kutsutsa),* before he would resume his discourse. Everybody agreed that they would raise objections. However, what surprised us was that in practice nobody was doing that, but everyone just replied: eee! to any of the *sing'anga'*s statements. I think people were afraid to contradict him. When we wanted to participate in the process, knowing that we had no "problem" he said smilingly "Do you want to test me?" On two occasions we also observed that he would even beat someone slightly with his right hand, if they delayed their reply to his statements, with *eee* (yes) or *ai* (no). That might have been one more reason why many people quickly quoted his statements with a loud *eee.*

During the process of consulting his patients in order to help them find solutions and cure, he periodically struck the ground with his saff (*ndodo)* and he shook the red cloth (*nsalu yofiira).* Obviously, these paraphernalia were his tools (*dzida).* People were sure that there was some powerful medicine inside the cloth enabling him to discover instantly why a certain person had come.

Some people were theorizing that he had scarified himself with medicines (*mwina iye anachekela mankhwala)* whose catalytic power (*chizimba chake*) was obtained from a certain bird by the name of *gonkho*, a rare bird found more often in northern Malawi than in the south. This is a bird of prey about which people say that it can dream where to find meat (*mbalame imalota kumene kupeza nyama*). The name *gònkhó* suggests the sequence *gò* (with a low tone) expressing that the bird is asleep, followed by *nkho* with a high tone which symbolizes that the bird suddenly wakes up in the tree, and gets excited (*akudzidzimuka*) because in its dream it has spotted the place and direction where it will find meat. People believed that *sing'anga* Paulo Luka had killed such a bird, cut off its head, cut it to pieces, then cut off some bark (*kutemera*) from trees of pharmaceutical usage, ground it all together and finally rubbed the paste into incisions he made in his own skin.

In analogy to the bird, this medicine would then enable the *sing'anga* to "see" and spot the "meat" (i. e. the wizards and witches) like the bird in its dreams. Normally he would give attention to each client individually, and walk out after each consultation before attending to the next person. However, what sometimes happened during the divination (*pakati pakuombeza)* was that some people whom he had already screened were walking out of the room, beginning to report details about the manner they were investigated. In such instances – by the power of the bird whose substance he had rubbed upon his forehead, he would immediately know that a certain person was talking bad about him (*munthu wina alikumunena).* He would then stop his divination and begin to look as if he was weeping, stammering words such as: "please my brothers/sisters who are outside, stop talking bad about me! When you do so, I cannot be in tune with my spirits (*mizimu yanga sindikugwilizana nayo).*[140] If you have something to say, then just come in here!"

This happened when we were there. A certain man was not satisfied with what Luka had told him during the time he had examined him (*panthawi yokwapimayo).* As soon as he got out of the room he began to talk bad, but with a whispering voice. Suddenly we

---

[140] Since it is the *mizimu* (spirits) who tell him everything, so he must be in tune with them. The bad remarks by the person outside are perceived as an interference with his spiritual communication. He can then no longer call the spirits *(kuitana mizimu*).

heard these words coming from the *sing'anga*: "Please my brother, you are hurting me by talking bad about me outside! If you have something to say, then say it right here!"

Recordings transcribed from the original tapes and translated:

I. Conversation with the *sing'anga* Paulo Luka. Place: Chipula village, T.A. Njolomole, Ntcheu District, October 29, 1994. Original tape no. 94/2/side 2

M. = Moya

L. = Paulo Luka

M. Eya, tsopano ine monga ndimafuna choyamba mundifotokozele dzina lanu, ndikumene munachokela, kapenanso munabadwilanso mbali zina zake, choyamba tisanayambe kudziwana zambiri .	M. Before I am asking you many things which we would like to know, could you kindly say your name , and tell us where you have come from, and perhaps also where exactly you were born, so that we become acqauinted with each other.
L. O dzina langa ndine Paulo Luka, kumene ndimakhala ndi mmudzi mwa Chipula m'boma la Ntcheu, Tsangano turn off.Tsopana kumene ndinabadwila ndi kuMozambique, m'mudzi mwa Ntengula, boma la Ntengo wa Mbalame. 141)	L. Oh! My name is Paulo Luka. The place where I am staying is the village of Chipula, within the administrative area of Ntcheu, at theTsangano turn off. But where I was born , that was in Mozambique, in the village of Ntengula, the administrative area of Ntengo wa Mbalame. [141]
M. Inuyo pali panopo muli ndi dzaka dzingati?	M. How old are you by now?
L. Ndili ndi dzaka 30	L. I am thirty years old.
M. 30 eti?	M. Thirty, is that so?
L. Eeee.	L. Yes.
M. Eyaa tsopano mungatifotokozele motani pantchito yanu imene mumagwila pano?	M. Eyaa! Now you might explain a bit about the kind of work which you are doing here?
L. Ntchito imene ndimagwila pano, ndimagwila ntchito zosiyanasiyana koma zokhudzana ndi using'anga . Ntchito yomwe ndimagwila pano ndiyoti ena amadwala nthenda ya mtima timachilitsa, mutu timachilitsa, azimai apakati timachilitsa, akakhala amisala openga timachilitsa, nthenda yakugwa 142) timachilitsa ndi zina zotero zosiyana siyana bwana	L. I am engaging in various types of activities all connected with medical practice (*using'anga*). The work I am doing here is to cure those who suffer from cardiac problems (*nthenda ya mtima*), from chronic headaches, and I also help women in pregnancy. If there are people with mental problems (*amisala openga*) I cure them; I treat cases of epilepsy (*nthenda yakugwa*) [142]

[141] The place is on the road from Ntcheu to Gago Coutinho.

[142] Epilepsy is usually called *mfayi* or *khunyu* in Chichewa/Cinyanja. *Nthenda yakugwa* (literally: "the disease of falling down") is a descriptive term.

timachilitsa	and many other ailments, Sir!
M. Oho tsopano monga inuyo, ntchito imeneyi munayamba motani kutino mupezeke mukudziwa zonsenzi?	M. Oho! Now someone like you, how did you start this kind of work so that in the end you would have become experienced?
L. Kuyamba kwa using'anga kuti ndiyambe using'anga sindinaphunzile kwamunthu iyayi, koma poyamba ndimagwila ntchito yodikila anyani ku Bwanje mmudzi mwa Nkhwani ndi wena wake asing'anga amati Apadatani. Tsopano nditagwila ntchito imene ija, ndinakhala nawo dzaka dzitatu. Ndinachoka kumeneko ndili wankulu ndithu pang'ono kudzayamba using'anga, kuyamba kwake mphwanga dzina lake Antonyo adamwalila mpakana kudzafika poti masiku atatu ali chimwalilileni, ndiye ndinapsya mtima ine mpakana kupita kumanda kukakwela mwamba, 143) kuchoka kwake mwambamo ndinangozindikila mulibe mwambamo koma adakandiyika kuphanga. Anthu ena akusaka ndiomwe anakandipeza kuphanga kuja, ndiye mmamawa adapita amalume ndi anthu ena kudzachotsa mwala umene unali kumenekowo kukandichotsa ineyo, koma nditatha masiku ndili kuphanga kuja.	L. As concerns the start of my medical practice, I did not learn *using'anga* from any particular person. It all began with my working in the field of a certain *sing'anga* whose name was Apadatani, at Nkhwani village in the area of Bwanje (Mozambique) watching out for baboons (who would destroy the crops). I stayed three years with him. When I left him I had already grown up a bit indeed. That I should start *using'anga* really began with the death of my young brother whose name was Antonyo. After he had been dead (*chimwalilileni*) for three days I lost my patience (*ndinapsya mtima*), and went myself to graveyard, climbing up something (to see what was going on)[143]. About what happened thereafter, all I am aware of (*ndi mangozindikilabe*) is that suddenly I was no longer there, but they (the wizards) had put me into a cave (*phanga*) inside a big rock. It was hunters who eventually found me in that cave. The following morning, my maternal uncle (*malume*) and some other people went there to remove the rock and get me out. But it was days that I had been under the rock there.
M. Eya mwafotokoza kuti choyamba chenicheni munali ku Bwanje, kodi ku Bwanje ndiye kuti?	M. Eya, you have explained that at the very beginning you were in the Bwanje area, where exactly is that?
L. KuBwanje ndi boma la Ntcheu lomwelino, koma kuChigwa uko.144)	L. Bwanje is within the administrative area of Ntcheu, but there at the slope [144]
M. Ndiye choyamba munali ndi sing'anga?	M. First you stayed with a *sing'anga*?!
L. Eee sing'angayo ankachita zake, ine ndimagwila ntchito yodikilila anyani	L. Yes, but he only pursued his own work, while

[143] The young Paulo Luka was sure that his young brother had been a victim of witchcraft (*ufiti*). After three days had passed he couldn't stand it any longer, went to the graveyard and climbed up a tree, hiding in there, to observe the activities of the alledged wizards who would come to dig up the remains of his brother. Apparently, however, the struggle *(mpikisano)* between him and the wizards ended with his defeat. The *amfiti* discovered him in the tree and knocked him out. When he regained consciousness he was found under a heavy rock *(phanga)* somewhere else in the area.

[144] Bwanje is the name of a river in the Ntcheu District; Chigwa (the name comes from *kugwa* = to fall) refers to the escarpment or slope from Ntcheu down to Lake Malawi.

ku munda	my work was to watch out for baboons in the fields.
M. Kudikila anyani, zausing'angazo sizinakukhudzeni?	M. While you were watching out for baboons, the things of *using'anga* did not concern you?
L. Ayi, sizinandikhudzeyi.	L. No, they did not touch me at all.
M. Choo, ndiye mutachoka kumene kuja kubwelela kumudzi?	M. Oho! And after you left there you returned to your village ?
L. Nditachoka kumene kuja , kubwelela kumudzi ndipamene ndinkakumana ndi zimenezi mabvuto amphwangayu.	L. It was after I had left there and returned home that I encountered the troubles of my young brother.
M. Mphwanu nkumwalila?	M. That your brother died.
L. Mphwanga nkumwalila eee, tinalipo anthu 11 mmimba mwa amayi wanga. Mai wanga ndiamene ali panjawo.	L. That my brother died, yes. We had been eleven children born from my mother. She is the one who is sitting outside here.
M. Mhu!	M. Mhu!
L. Pa anthu 11 onse aja nkumwalila nkutsala ndekha ine Paulo Luka, ndinanyamuka kumene kuja popysa mtima mpaka kumene anapita iwo kumandako, kumafikizana mphwanga uja kumatuluka panthumbila paja, mmene ankachita zawozo ankatenga phale 145) kumawaza panthumbila paja, ndiye panthumbila paja mphwanga uja anatuluka mmenemomo kufikizana panja, atakhala panja, ineyo ndinangoyang'ana koma unali usiku kumapast 9 yausiku, ndiye kunali mdima wa mvula ine ndinkangoyang'ana, ndiye aja adanyamuka anali gogo146) wanga wa mkazi amene adabeleka mayi anga . Ndiye atamunyamula mwana ameneyo kumukhazika panja koma ali moyo ndinkangoyag'ana ndili mwambamo. Ndiye ndinayamba kukodza ndili mwamba momuja, ndiye atadabwa anthu aja kuti kukubwela mvula bwanji, ndiye ndinangowona kwabwela mdima , kuyela komwe ndinali kuwona kuja kwatha chifuka kudadzayela nthawi imeneyo, ndiye	L. Of those eleven people all have died; it is only myself, Paulo Luka, who has remained. When I finally lost my patience (*popsya ntima*), I set out for the graveyard where my brother was buried, because I knew they (wizards and witches) would be there. I wanted to intercept them when they would lure my brother out of the grave, in the manner they usually do their things: taking broken pieces (*phale*) of a water jar[145] (prepared with medicines) and spray the medicines on the mound (*panthumbila*). And there at the mound (grave) my young brother really emerged from inside, to meet them. When I saw him outside I only stared at the scene in amazement, but it was past 9 o'clock in the night , and there was darkness of rain clouds in the sky (*mdima wa mvula*). Gazing at the scene I suddenly noticed that the one who had also appeared was no one else but my grandmother[146] who had once given birth to my mother. After she

[145] *phale* = *chinthu chosweka cha pantsuko* (a piece of a broken water-jar.) The *amfiti* (wizards/witches) put medicines (*mankhwala)* on the pieces and then spray (*kumawaza)* them on the grave in order to make the dead person come out whose meat they want to share.

[146] Paulo Luka was hiding in a tree, and discovered to his surprise that the witch who had killed his young brother was his own grandmother. A struggle (*mpikisano*) ensued between him and the witches and wizards. He urinated from the top, startling them because his urine dropped like rain and extinguished the luminosity with which the wizards had surrounded their scene.

nditadzachoka malo amenewo, anadzangondichotsa kutangobwela chimphepo, ndipo machokedwe ake sindinadziwe bwino kuchoka kumandako. Kukafikizana ndili ku phanga, ndiye kuphanga kujanso ndinakhala sabata zitatu ndili kuphanga komweko, ndiye anthu osaka atafunafuna kundilephela, makolo anga, anthu osaka adanyamuka kunka ndasaka ndiye patatuluka kanyama kalulu adakalowa kuphanga kuja ndiye anthu pokafufuza kanyama kaja ndipamene adakapeza ineyo. Ndiye atandipeza kuphanga kuja, adapita kukauza amalume anga kuti mwana wanu uja ndamupeza ali ku phanga. Ndipamene ndinkanyamuka kumeneko kukanditenga kubwela kumudzi, ndiye kunyumba kuja anandichotsa kupita kwa aSimbazako 147) mmudzi mwa aKasakula komwe ku Ntchisi 148) kukayamba kundipatsa mankhwala. Mankhwala ake anali bembelezi 149 amene ankandidyetsa kuchokela nthawi imeneyo ndidayambanso kuyankhula 150) mpaka kubwelanso kunyumba , ndiye kunyumba kuja ndinkati ndikangogona nkumalota mankhwala munthu akadwala nkumupatsa mpakana kuchila, kuyambila momwemo ndidayamba using'anga bwana.!

got hold of that child (my brother) she placed him outside, and he was alive! I was watching everything from above (where I was hiding). And o began to urinate from up there! Those people (the witches and wizards) wondered: "How come that the rain is now falling?" Myself I noticed that it was getting very dark! The strange luminosity which had surrounded the witchcraft scene began to disappear. They tried to restore the luminosity as soon as I had changed position up there. Eventually they noticed me and just removed me with a terrible storm (*chimphepo*). I don't know well how I was removed from that cemetery. When I regained consciousness I found myself inside a cave and I stayed in there for three weeks. After my parents had failed to find me anywhere, some hunters who had set out for hunting were chasing a small animal, a hare (*kalulu*) and it happened to enter that cave.
The people searching inside for the animal discovered me! When they found me they went to notify my maternal uncle (*malume*): " We have found your child! He is inside a cave" At that time I came out from there, and they took me back to the village. But soon thereafter they removed me from home, sending me to Simbazako[147]) in the village of Kasakula in Ntchisi [148]) for treatment. The medicine he gave me was an insect, Bembelezi[149]. He was feeding me with it, and from that time on I began to speak again[150] until I was able to return home for good. When I was back home I was dreaming in my sleep about medicines,

---

147 Simbazako is a famous *sing'anga* who practises until now in the Central Region of Malawi. (See the articles in *Moni*, 34 (388), 1997 and *Moni*, 34 (390), 1997, page 22.

148 Ntchisi is a small town north of Lilongwe in the Central Region. It is the capital of a district of the same name.

149 Bemberezi (also written Mbembereze) is a small flying insect (*kachirombo kena kake kamauluka*). Scott and Hetherwick (1929: 279) identify it as "the ichneumon-fly" and say "the fly takes caterpillars and turns them into children".

150 Paulo had lost his speech in the cave, due to the trauma inflicted upon him by the witches and wizards.

	and that it was feasible to administer medicines to a sick person until the person would recover. That was the start of my medical expertise (*using'anga*), Sir!
M. Eya tsopano mwanena kuti nthawi imeneyi, chimene chinakunyamutsani kunyumba kwanu kuti mukapezeke kumanda mumtengo chinali chiyani? Munkadziwa anuwakenu kapena anali matsenga?	M. Eya! What was it really that instigated you to set out from your home that you should be found in a tree in the graveyard? Was it your own decision or were you lured there by magic (of the wizards)?
L. Ndinkadziwa koma unali ntima woti aaa koma ineyo anthu onsewa amwalila ndiye akuti kuli mfiti kumeneko kumanda amaika anthuko, ndiye mfitizo ndi zomwe zikadye mphwanga uja, ndiye ine ndidapita kumeneko kuti ndikawone mmene amadyela ndi ntima mmene unkandiwawila, ndiye posowa pokhala ndidakwela pamwamba.	L. I knew in my heart that since all those people (in our family) had died, there were most certainly wizards and witches in the graveyard where all my relatives had been buried, and those wizards/witches were the ones who would now "eat" my young brother. So I went there in order to see for myself how they would consume the flesh. My heart was paining and lacking a place to position myself, I climbed up [a tree].
M. Eya, tsopano inuyo, monga munthu mmene ndimadziwila kumanda kumaopysa kwambiri, sungangoti kunyamuka kunyumba nkupita popanda kanthu kokulimbitsa iwe ntima? Ndiyeno inu tandifotokozeleni munalimba mtima bwanji kapena kanalipobetu kanthu kamene munali nako kuti mukaonane nazo mfiti pakutinso mfiti munthu siungazione ndi maso?	M. Eya! In view of the fact that the graveyard is known to be a very dangerous place, how could you as an ordinary person have set out from the house without any special preparation that would give you the courage (*kukulimbitsa iwe mtima*?) Explain to us how you had the heart to do so: perhaps there was some device in your possession to enable you to meet with the wizards/witches, considering that *mfiti* is a person whom one cannot see with the [naked] eye?
L. Ai bwana ndinalibe chilichonse, ndinangonyamuka ndisanayambenso kudziwa ntchito ya using'anga ai kupita kumanda kuja kukakwela mmamba chifukwa cha mtima kuti ngati akufuna kumaliza akamalize ndi ine ndemwe pakutha pa abale anga eleven, ndichifukwa chake ndinakakwela mwamba, tsopano kumene kujako mmalo iwo wajawo sadya munthu amene ali wa moyo amadikila ayambe amudwalitse kuti munthu uja afe, akafa adye bwino. Ndiye kuja nditakakwela mmwamba sadakaputenso andidya, koma adakangondizunza nkukandiyika kupanga,	L. No, Sir, I did not have any medicines at all, I set out at a time when I had not yet started to know the work of *using'anga*. I was going there to the graveyard, and I climbed up there, because my heart had told me that, if they [those *amfiti*] intended to proceed with their work, then let them finish me after the loss of my eleven siblings! It is because of such thoughts that I was climbing up there. Now at that place, however, those wizards and witches do not eat a person who is alive; they wait until they can make him sick first, so that he would die. After he has died then they rejoice eating him! So after I had climbed up

mpakana kukachoka kuphangako kupita kwa aSimbazako, ndiye kwa aSimbazako ndinakayamba kulankhula lero nkudzayamba using'anga. Koma kuti ndidapita ndi ntengo uliwonse kumanda iyayi koma ndidakangokwela mmwamba mwana ndithu wopanda chilichonse.	[the tree] there [in the graveyard] they could not have provoked me until they would eat me up! Instead they would only treat me cruelly (*adakangondizunza*) by putting me into a cave. So when I got out there after all, I had to go to Simbazako. There at Simbazako's place I would regain my speech. Thereafter I would start *using'anga*.But that I should have proceeded to the graveyard in possession of any herbal medicines (*ndi mtengo uliwonse*) that was not the case. I just climbed up the tree like a innocent child without anything at all.
M. Tsopano mutakalandila chithandizo kwa aSimbazako, nkupeza bwino chimeneno chinakuchitikilani kwa inuyo ndi chiyani?	M. Now after you had received help from Simbazako, and recovered, what happened to you later?
L. Nditapita kwa aSimbazako kukapanga zimenezo, nditachoka kwa aSimbazako kudzafika kunyumba ndinadzayamba kumakhala ndikugwidwa nthenda ya mtima, ndiye anthu ankamati muntu uja wapenga 151) Kuchokela nthawi imeneyo koma inali nthenda ya mtima zimene ndinkaziwona nkamagona ndinkawona anthu aja amene ndidawakapeza kumandawo nkumadziwa kuti awa ndi auje abwela akupita kukatamba lero, awa ndi auje abwela akupita kukatamba, koma opanda mtengo uliwonse. Ndiye iwo waja akapita ndiye kukacha mmawa amangofikila kundilundila152) ndi mmene ndimawaonela muja, ndinayamba kuti ndikalota nkumalota mankhwala , ndiye ndikatenga mankhwala aja nkuwapanga iwo, wajawo ndiwona zathekadi, mpakana amai wawo wa amai wangawa analowa mmanda chifukwa cha zofuna zawo, nditapita kumene kujako nditakawapanikiza ndinayambano zanga 153) nditayamba kudziwa mankhwala wobwezelela kumalota mankhwalawo, ndid wabwezela amaiwo mpaka adafika pomwalila.	L. After I had gone to Simbazako for treatment and returned to our home I began to suffer from heart problems (*ndikugwidwa nthenda ya ntima*). The people [in the village] were saying about me: "This person has run mad (*wapenga*) [151]!" But it was heart problem due to the trauma I had suffered. In my sleep I began to <u>see</u> the witchcraft activities of others, I would see those very people I had found in the graveyard, and would recognize them, knowing that such and such person had gone there today for the witch dance. But I was able to do everything without using any herbal medicines (*opanda ntengo uliwonse*). And when those witches and wizards who were there retreated from the graveyard at dawn and arrived in the villages, those very ones I had spotted there in my sleep then used to behave in an extremely violet manner against me (*kundilundila*)[152]. It was at that juncture that I began to dream about medicines (*nkumalota mankhwala*). And back in my waking life, I began to apply those medicines against those individuals and discovered

[151] Paulo's heart problems were probably of psychological origin. He probably experienced an accelerated heartbeat (*kugunda*) and perhaps pain (*kapena kupweteka*). His complaints in front of others, perhaps his cries: "Mayo mayo mayo!" under intensive pain, were taken by his social environment as a sign that he had run mad.

[152] Apparently those witches and wizards knew that Paulo had spotted them in his dreams. Arriving in the village, they took revenge calling him bad names, such as *chitsiru iwe* (you fool!) etc.

Kuyambila momo ndidayamba using'anga. Mai wanga adwala nthenda ya mtima ine nkuwapatsa mankhwala ndaona achila. Ndiye ine lero ndimapangadi mankhwala osiyanasiyana, kuti kaya wina sakuyenda kuyambila matendawo kuukulu ine ndimamuyendetsa.	that it worked; until the mother of my mother ended by herself in the graveyard because of her witchcraft urges. After I had pursued her and caught her redhanded (*nditawapanikiza*) I began to apply my own medicines immediately.[153] As soon as I had learned about medicines of revenge (*mankhwala obwezelela*) by dreaming those medicines, I took revenge on that woman, until she met her own death. It was from that moment that I began medical practice (*using'anga*). Once when my mother had developed heart problems I gave her medicines to the effect that she recovered. Today I am producing many types of medicines indeed, so if for example, someone cannot walk having developed this ailment as an adult, I would make him or her walk again.
M. Oho! tsopano nthawi imeneyo mukukumbukila chinali chaka chiti?	M. Oho! Now the time as you remember it, which year was that?
L. Inali 89	L. It was in 1989.
M. 89, muli wochepelako ndithu.	M. 89, you must have been very young indeed!
L. Eee ndili mwana wochepa, ndili ndi zaka 20 154)	L. Yes, I was a minor, I was twenty years old [154].
M. Tsapano kuti muzolowele kuti apa ine ndafika podziwano zinthu izi ndi izi zinayambika liti?	M. Now that you were getting used to say of yourself "finally I have attained knowledge of such and such things", which year did you start off?
L. Nditadziwa zonse zimene kuti izi ndazikhozadi kuti izi zimakhala mwakuti ndidadzayambano 1984, ndinadzayamba kudziwa zonse kuti izi zili mwakati izi zili mwakati mpakana kudzafika uno 1994.	L. After I had come to know the uses and effects of all the medicines, I felt capable of applying my knowledge beginning in 1984. From that time on until now, in 1994, I have kept in mind the uses of various substances.
M. Tsopana chimachitika choncho munthu pachikhalidwe pake osalephela pantchito imene amagwila, kuti pantchito imene ndimagwilayi ichi chakuti chakuti ndichimene ndimachikumbukila pano, ndichimene chidandipangitsa kuti	M. Now, it is in people's nature, and it occurs to everyone, that a person would say about his or her work "what really motivated me in the first place was such and such"[155] As you recall the year 1984, what was it exactly that

[153] *zanga* (my things) here means "my medicines" to fight the wizards and witches (*zomenya amfiti*).

[154] As often in personal memories, the years must have been confused. If Paulo Luka, according to his own earlier statement was thirty at the time of the interview (October 29, 1994), and if reports about him had already circulated in 1985, he could not have been a "minor" (*mwana wochepa*) in 1989.

[155] I am trying to ask Paulo to reveal to me what really pushed him to become a *sing'anga*, according to what he remembered. But I am asking him in an indirect way to avoid posing any leading questions (*ndimafunsa mozemba kuti ndisawapatse yankho*).

ndidzichita izi.155) Ndiye pa 1984yo chimene mungachikumbukile kuti chidakupatsani mphamvu zeni zeni kuti ineyo panopo nditha kuchita chakuti chakuti chinali chotani?	gave you the inner force that you could say about yourself: "from now on I am able to accomplish such and such things?"
L. Nditayamba ineyo kuti ndiyambe kufika poti mutu wanga wayamba kutseguka 156) kuti kunja kuno kuli mfiti 1981 imeneyo ndinachoka kwa aSimbazako kupita kunyumba kuchoka uko ndinapita kwa asing'anga aBwanali 157) nthawi imeneyo ali ku Nkulumadzi,158) ndiye ine ndimawafunsa kuti ine zinandichitikila zakuti zakuti , ndiye ine ndingachite bwanji?, 159) ndiye kuchoke-la nthawi imene ija anayamba kundiweluza kuti "aa zimakhala mwakati mwakati mwana iwe." Kuchoka pamenepo ndinapita kuBalaka kwa asing'anga aKademo, aKademo nkukandiuza kuti "aa kupanga kwake izi amatele" basi kuchokela pomwepo kufikilana lero kudzakhala sing'anga.	L. Actually, it was in 1981 that I began to reach the stage when my head started to be opened up[156] and I would be able to identify a *mfiti*. That was after I had returned from Simbazako to my village. From there I set out again to see another *sing'anga*, Bwanali [157] who at that time used to stay in Nkulumadzi[158]. I told him everything that had happened to me in the village, asking for his advice[159]. And from that time on he began to instruct me saying "aaa! These things are contained in such and such substances, you child!" From there I went to Balaka to see another *sing'anga* whose name was Kademo. And he told me: "If you want to use these substances then do such and such!" So from that time until today I have been a *sing'anga*.
M. Mhu, tsopano pali panopo anthu mumawathandiza motani?	M. Mhu, in which way do you help people nowdays?
L. Mathandizidwe ake akabwela kuti akudwala, amabwela kunoko kudzanena kuti akudwala, tsopano nthenda imene akudwala iwowo samanena amati ndiwauze ndekha ngati ndili sing'angadi, ndiye ineyo ndimapita kujaku kukanyumba kaja 160) ndikubvala inifolomu 161) nkuyamba kumaimba anthu aja, tsopano akamayimba ine ndimagwa mizimu ya Mulungu basi ndiye	L. As concerns various the forms of help I am giving people, they just come and tell me that they are ill. They do not name the disease from which they suffer. I alone in my capacity as *sing'anga* diagnose it and inform them. And I proceed to the little house[160] to wear my ceremonial dress[161] and begin to sing with the people who have assembled. Now as the songs go on, I become possessed by the spirit

[156] *nzeru zatseguka (* the mind has been opened up) is a common expression in Chichewa, for example if a school child has always had bad test results, but all of a sudden good ones. *Kutseguka* = to be opened up in these cases stands for *kudziwa zinthu zambiri* (to know many things).

[157] Bwanali was a *sing'anga* who was very famous, even more than Simbazako (*wotchuka kwambiri kuposa aSimbazako*). He is no longer alive.

[158] Nkulumadzi is the name of a river, an affluent of the Shire, between Blantyre and Mwanza.

[159] He asked Bwanali for wisdom about witchcraft and magic (*akupempha nzeru za ufiti ndi matsenga*), although at that stage he already knew very much. In that sense his earlier statement that he was nobody's apprentice in *using'anga* is probably true, but by visiting other *asing'anga* he wanted to get their advice and increase his knowledge. He was not yet sure of the things he already knew.

[160] The clinic, or consulting room which could also be called the "chapel" (*kachalichi kwao*) because of the Christian imagery employed by him.

[161] He used the term *inifolomu* (from engl. "uniform").

ndimadziwa chimene chikumuwawa munthu uja kuti "iwe uli ndi matenda akuti akuti". Ndiye iye uja ngati ndikunama ayenela kukana kuti ai ukundinamizila , koma ngati ndizoona ndimawauza kuti mudzibvomeleza kuti ndi zoona, kuti ndidziwe mtengo wokupatsani. Ndiye ndikadziwa kuti ndimomwe zomwe ndanenazo ndiye timapeza mankhwala ndikuwapatsa, nthendayo ngati kuti tiyikwanitsa, timaikwanitsa162) nkumupatsa zones nkumachila.	of God (*ndimagwidwa ndi mzimu wamulungu*) and I know what has hurt that particular person. Then I say: "You! you are suffering from such and such ailment!" But in the event that I am wrong, they must disprove of my words immediately, by saying "no! you are cheating us!" and if it is correct what I say then they must reply that it is true, so that I can decide which kind of herbal medicine to give them. As soon as I have my diagnosis reconfirmed by the client, I find the right medicine to give to them. As long as it is a disease which I am able to treat,[162] the patients receive everything they need to recover.
M. Mhu, mwafotokoza kuti amayimbanso nyimbo, kodi limeneli limatokhala lake lake tsiku lapadela kapena nthawi iliyonse pangabwele munthu?	M. Mhu, you have explained that the people sing songs. Does this happen only on a certain day, or every time someone comes seeking advice?
L. Nthawi iliyonse imene angafike, basi timachita zimenezo, ndiye pakakhala kuti pali zina zoti ndi zamuufiti kaya munthu wamwalila ndiye mamwalilidwe ake sakudziwika bwino tidakhoma chipepela 163) mnyumbamo timaonetsa kuti onani apapa, ndiye amayamba kuona nyumba yawo kwawo kumene achokela, kaya ndi ku Blantyre kaya ndi kuLilongwe akaiwona nyumba yawo ija pavidiyo paja kaya ndi muofesi yawo momwe ilili zonse zija ayamba kudziwa kuti munthuyu akuchoka nyumba iyi akubwela nyumba iyi akudzatamba. Ndiye apo amadziwa kuti awo ndi auje, kaya wamwalila ayamba kuona bokosi madwalidwe ake amunthuyo mpaka momwe akupita kumanda ndipo akatha kumandako ndiye nkudziwanso kuti munthuyo ali panyumba yakutiyakuti ndiye ife timakadzutsa.164)	L. Any time when people arrive, we do these perfomances. In the events of complaints about witchcraft, for example that a person has died without the circumsta-nces of his or her death being known well, then we take the client to a big screen of paper which we nailed on the wall (*tidakhoma chipepala*[163]) inside the house and tell them: "Look here and watch!" And the clients begin to see how their house appears on that paper, in their home village where they come from; no matter whether in Blantyre or Lilongwe, they will see their house on the video (*pavidiyo paja*); or they will see their office where it is and begin to know everything such as that a certain person [the wizard/witch] has left one house and entered another one in order to dance the witch dance (*akudzatamba*). And thereby my clie nts get to know that a certain person is a wizard or a witch. They also begin to see the coffin (*bokosi*) of the one who died and discover the

[162] With this statement Paulo hinted at the one disease he could not treat, and nobody could: AIDS (*edzi* in Chichewa). *Edzi saikwanitsa* (the medicines are not applicable to aids). But he did not want to mention the name AIDS.

[163] This is a large brown paper which the *sing'anga* nails on a wall inside the clinic and which he calls video, because it serves as a kind of screen. The client actually receives a (probably hallucinogenic) drug and begins to see things in the paper, including the witches or wizards who are supposed to have killed his or her relative.

	circumstances of his or her illness up to the point when people proceed to the graveyard [for the funeral]. And my clients find out that [the burial was a sham and that] the real person is alive somewhere at the house of such and such [wizard or witch]. Then it is my work to resurrect him or her (*timakadzutsa*) [164]
M. Amaona papepala paja, munthu wabwela odandaula uja amaona yekha?	M. Concerning those who look at that screen, does a client who comes to you with complaints watch it alone?
L. Eya, pali anthu ena akuona panopo	L. There are others who are also watching it at the same time.
M. Ena akuona!	M. Others also watch it?
L. Eee, mnyumbamo	L. Yes, inside the house.
M. Tikondwanso kuti ifenso tikaone zimene zimachitika kumenekoko, komabe tsopano mankhwala munthu osalephela kuti amayamba kutha mphamvu,165) inuyo zimakukhalilani bwanji mukaona kuti mankhwala awa simukuwa-khulupilila kweni kweni kuti mupeze ena mankhwala?	M. We would be pleased if we were allowed to have a glance at that room and see what is going on. Now another issue: it is well known that medicines may lose their power in their application to people. [165] How do you cope with that possibility, if you discover that you can no longer rely upon a certain medicine, and that it is necessary to find an alternative?
L. Timapanga chonchi, ndikadziwa kuti mankhwala amene ndikupangawa munthu sakusintha, ndimachoka kupita kukapemphela kumene ine ndimakapempha zangazo, 166) ndiye kujako ndikagona dzimandiuza kuti kayende malo akuti akuti ukapeza mtengo wakuti ntchito yake ndiyakuti. Ndiye ndimanyamuka mmawa ndi khasu langa ndakazi wangawa ulendo wopita kumeneko. Ndiye tikakapeza mtengowo tiyambe kupemphela ndiye tikapemphela tiona ndi zomwezo ndipo nkunyamula mtengo uja nkudzamupatsa ngati momwe anatiuzila kutulo kwathuko, timachita choncho.	L. We proceed in the following way: if I know that a client's condition does not change through certain medicines I produce, I go away to the place[166] where I normally pray and ask for many things. When I sleep there, the spirits tell me: "if you go to such and such spot, you will find such and such medical tree, whose medical usage will be such and such." Next morning I set out with my axe (*khasu*) in my hand, together with my wife on a journey going there. When we find the tree, we begin to pray (*kupemphela*) and as we pray we see that we are on the right track, and we carry the herbal medicine home and give it to the sick person; if that was what we

[164] Paulo wants to say that the wizards or witches arranged for a sham burial. What is buried is something else, not the person; they put some other object into the coffin, while the real person is alive, and they keep him somewhere as their captive. Then it is Paulo's work to bring the real person back to a normal life.

[165] I am alluding here to resistance against antibiotics and other medicines, e.g. the rise of chloroquine-resistant malaria parasites.

[166] This could be a place on a mountain (*ku phiri*) or in the graveyard (*ku manda*) or at the water-course (*ku madzi*). Its exact location is the *sing'anga*'s secret.

	were told during our sleep at home, we carry it out.
M. Ehe, kodi tsapano azising'anga ena amathandiza kuchiza anthu, komanso amadziwa zina ndi zina 167)inunso monga muli chimodzimodzi?	M. Ehe! Other *asing'anga* also help to cure people, but they have a wide range of knowledge, [167] are you on a par with them?
L. Eee, timati zimenezo zikuchitika, kaya munthu uja amwalila timamuuza kuti umwalila siuchila, koma kuchokela muulosi 168) omwe tikunena uja kuti amaimbilidwa mpakana kugwa mzimu mpakana kumanena , kaya inuyo penapake mwaononga timakuuzani kuti inunso ndinu woononga ndiye kuli bwino muleke, kaya inuyo mwadya mwana wanzanu timakuuzani kuti inuyo munadya mwana wanzanu ndiye nzanuyonso wakudyelani wanu,mukaleke basi zimakhala choncho.	L. Yes. We can say what happens is this: If, for example, we find that the person will die, then we simply tell him/her: " you will die, you will not recover!" but we are giving such a statement on the basis of prophecy (*kuchokela muulosi*);[168] when the people [in my clinic] are subject to singing, until someone gets possessed by the spirits and talks. For example if you [Moya] are spoilt somewhere, we will tell you that "you too, you are already spoilt; it would be good if you stopped it [the *ufiti*]" or, if you have eaten the child of your neigbour [through witchcraft] we would tell you: " You have eaten the child of your neighbor, and your neighbor will eat yours, you had better stop it, otherwise things will be like that!"
M. Tsopano panopo mumalandila odwala angati patsiku?	M. At this stage , how many sick people do you receive every day?
L. Amakwana mwina 50 mwina 60 patsiku, leroli mmene munabwela muja anali kale 46 wodwala.	L. They come up to 50 or 60 per day; today, the moment when you arrived, there were already 46 patients
M. Ena monga alipo amene amagonela pompano?	M. Are there perhaps some who also sleep in your clinic?
L. Ndi ambiri, mukuwawonawo ndi-wodwala okha okha amenewo, eeee	L. There are very many; you can see them, they are all patients.
M. Ndiyebe mwina ndilankhulebe ndi bambo anu aja, monga zimawakhudza zimenezizi? 196)	M. [Pointing to an elderly person standing nearby]: Could I also speak to your father there, who seems to be involved in your medical practice! [169]
L. Ai, amangolemba matikiti, koma zikuwankhudza ndi awa.	L. No, he only writes tickets, medical practice does not concern him, but it concerns this person

[167] Such as knowing about witchcraft (*za ufiti*) or magic (*za matsenga*) etc.

[168] The noun *ulosi* comes from the verb *kulosa* (to predict, to prophesize), in its applied verbal form: *kulo-sela. Zolosela* = things predicted about the future.

[169] It is unlikely that the elderly man was Luka's biological father, although he referred to him as such. His work was to register the patients and issue tickets of admission.

	here [pointing to the young man who had received us first]!
[I am turning to that young man who was Paulo Luka's assistant . He was the very person who had received us with insolence. Now in the presence of his mentor, he tried to be very nice.]	
M. Ndiyebe ndilankhuleko ndi inuyo mundifotokozele dzina lanu!	M. Let me then talk to you. First tell me your name!
Ny. Inde, ine ndikuthilila ndemanga, padziko pano anthu akufika kwambiri amatenda kwalandiladi, kwasamala bwinobwino. Ndipo wochila nkumachila onse amatenda osiyanasiyana.	Ny. [he does not reply to my question, apparently wishing to remain anonymous] Indeed I can only corroborate what has been said (*ndikuthilila ndemanga*); many sick people arrive here to be received well and taken care of. They all get a cure for their various diseases.
M. Kodi monga inuyo munthu mukamupatsa mankhwala chonchi, pali china chilichonse chimene amapeleka kapena mumangokwauza kuti pitani choncho?	M. After you have given treatment and medicines to a person, will he or she offer you something in return or are you just allowing the person to go home without any fee?
Ny. Palibe chomwe amapeleka, koma munthu uja akakachila ndiye amadzatili-pila.	Ny. At first the patients do not pay any fees, only if the treatment turns out to be successful, that is if they recover are they required to pay a fee.
M. Oho, mumamuuza mtengo kuti aa chitani mwakuti mwakuti, kapena iye yekha mmene angaonele kuti thupi lake lili bwino?	M. Oho! Are you telling them what amount they will have to pay [after recovery] or perhaps do your patients decide for themselves what they will offer when the body is alright?
Ny. Timamuuza mtengo wake umakhala K 2.00	Ny. We tell them that the fee is K 2,-.
M. Kwa munthu aliyense amene angabwele wodwala?	M. Is it the same fee for every patient who comes?
Ny. Eee!	Ny. Yes.
M. Makamaka matenda amene amabwela wochulukila ndiye ati?	M. Which kinds of disease are particularly frequent among your patients
Ny. Amabwela matenda ambiri ndithu, makamaka akufa dziwalowa, ndiwotupa ena amatenda akugwa, amabwela ambiri ambiri osiyanasiyana.	Ny. Many different diseases are brought to our attention, such as when some bodyparts have died (*akufa dziwalo*) and are swollen, or the illness of epilepsy, and so on.
M. Kodi pali nthawi zina zimene mukamuona munthu wodwala mumadziwa kuti munthuyu sanalodzedwe, koma nkungodwala chabe?	M. Does it happen from time to time that you see a patient and you know that the person was not bewitched (*sanalodzedwe*), but is just ill with an ordinary sickness?

<table>
<tr><td>Ny. Nkhani imeneyi ndi ija akamba kale achikulile,170) kuti amayamba apima, akapima ndiye amadziwa chochita.</td><td>Ny. This is the the kind of information which my superior (achikulile)[170] has given you already , that he would first examine (apima) the person before deciding what to do.</td></tr>
<tr><td>M. Ndiye monga inuyo ntchito imeneyi mukuphunzila kapenabe mukungothandizila choncho?</td><td>M. Now you yourself, are you an apprentice of this work, or are you simply assisting in it?</td></tr>
<tr><td>Ny. Ine akundiphunzitsa achikulile angawa.</td><td>Ny. My superior here teaches me.</td></tr>
<tr><td>M. Akukuphunzitsani, tsopano pali panopo mwafika pati?</td><td>M. Since he is teaching you, what level have you reached by now?</td></tr>
<tr><td>Ny. Pakali panopa zina ndi zina ndikudziwa ndithu, koma zakutsogolo sanandimalizile.</td><td>Ny. Up to now there are certain things which I know, indeed, but there are many other things of the future which have not yet been completed.</td></tr>
<tr><td>M. Sanakumalizileni eti? Kodi pamatenga dzaka zingati kuti munthu aziwe zonse zimene?</td><td>M. Other things not yet completed? How many years does it take until someone knows the whole programme?</td></tr>
<tr><td>Ny. Iii ndi dzaka zambiri, dzaka five.</td><td>Ny. Iii, it takes five years</td></tr>
<tr><td>M. Tsopano monga inuyo panopa mwakhalapo dzaka dzingati?</td><td>M. Now someone like you, how many years have you been here?</td></tr>
<tr><td>Ny. Chino chachitatu.</td><td>Ny. This is the third year.</td></tr>
<tr><td>M. Chachitatu mwatsala dzaka dziwiri.</td><td>M. The third! So there are two years remaining</td></tr>
<tr><td>Ny. Mhu.</td><td>Ny. Mhu.</td></tr>
<tr><td>M. Mukadzamaliza, akadzakuuzani kuti apa ndiye mwaphela cholinga chanu ndichiyani?</td><td>M. When you will have finished, and he perhaps tells you “now you are an expert” (mwaphela) what are your further aims?</td></tr>
<tr><td>Ny. Ndicholinga chochilitsa anthu wodwala.</td><td>Ny. My intentions are to cure people who are ill.</td></tr>
<tr><td>M. Mudzamasuka malo ano kapenabe mudzakhala pompano?</td><td>M. Will you then leave this place or will you stay?</td></tr>
<tr><td>Ny. Zonse adzandilamula ndi achikulile, pakuti ndine ng’ono wawo koma ndidzasamukapo.</td><td>Ny. The one who will decide is my superior, because I am the junior, but [in fact] I will leave here.</td></tr>
<tr><td colspan="2">[I am now turning back to the sing’anga Paulo Luka, asking him one question about a certain person seen in the group, about whom we had heard the news that he had <u>died</u> and was resurrected by Paulo Luka]</td></tr>
<tr><td>M. Kujakunso munadzafotokoza kuti awawa anamwalila.</td><td>M. Over there you explained that this person here once died.</td></tr>
<tr><td>L. Anamwalila mpakana masiku atatu, ndipo ulendo wa aLita anali mugulu la amenewowo. 171)</td><td>L. He died and was dead for three days, the girl Lita and her companions was also among those [whom I brought back life][171]</td></tr>
</table>

[170] Referring to his mentor, Paulo Luka.

[171] Paulo Luka points to a girl named Lita about whom he claims that he also resurrected her from death. (*Paulo anamudzutsa aLita).* The phrase *ulendo wa aLita* is idiomatic Chichewa. It is not to be translated as “the journey of Lita”, but the *ulendo* is an abstraction meaning “company”, “companions”. *Ulendo wa aLita”* is *Lita ndi anzake (*Lita and her friends, her company, her companions). The phrase is

<table>
<tr><td colspan="2">[I am now turning to that person whom Paul Luka claims to have resurrected. His name is António Luka, the brother of Paulo, and the only one of all his siblings whom Paulo was able to save from death.)
A.= António]</td></tr>
<tr><td>M. Tsopano monga inuyo mukukumbulila chimene chinakuchitikilani panthawi imene munamwalilayo, choyamba munenanso dzina lanu!
[phokoso kuchokela pa wanthu]</td><td>M. Now someone like you, do you remember the experiences you had at the time when you died? But first also pronounce your name! .....[Someone else is talking between. unrelated, not transcribed].</td></tr>
<tr><td>A. Ine ndine António Luka, m'bale wawo wa aPaulo Luka. Poyamba mabvuto anandipezekela, ndiye mwai umenewo utapezeka kuti ndikhalenso bwino 172) anakhala akumandipitilizila ntchito yawo. Ndiye pano amandiphunzitsabe 173) mpaka tinapita kwa Juwawu,174) mpaka monse amakachita zimenezo inenso nkuti ndili pompo ndipo ndinawonelapo kufikila nthawi inoyo ndimathanso kumaunika nkumudziwa munthu kuti amachita zakuti zakuti, kapena uyu akudwala chakuti chakuti, kuchokela mwaiwowo achimwene angawo</td><td>A. Myself, I am António Luka, the brother of Paulo, at first I had encountered troubles, then it was my luck that when I found that I would lead a normal life again, [172] he [my brother Paulo Luka] made me progress through his work. Until now he still teaches me; [173] we even went together for João[174] and indeed I have been sharing in all his activities. At that time I realized that I was reaching a stage of being able to throw light upon and identify a person who was doing such and such [witchcraft] things; or to realize that a person was suffering from such and such illness; all this luck comes from my brother.</td></tr>
<tr><td>M. Kodi tsapano kwa Juwawu ameneyu anachuka kwambiri Juwawuyu chinachitika kweni kweni ndi chi-yani?175)</td><td>M. What exactly happened there with that João who has became so famous from the reports? [175]</td></tr>
<tr><td>A. Chinachitika kwa Juwawu ndiye kuti anamwalila, ndikutha chaka ndi miyezi inanso, ndiye atabwelela amayi wake a Juwawu nthawi ina anabwelela, nkuwauza kuti mukatenge mboni zanu. Ndiye atapita nkukatenga mwana wawo, nthawi inanso nkudzabwelelanso</td><td>A. What happened to João was that he died, and that he had been dead for a year and some months. When his mother came to seek advice [from Paulo Luka] at first she was returned to her village, because Paulo demanded from her more evidence. Then she went and came with</td></tr>
</table>

used in public discourse when there are many people and it is difficult to mention everybody. It is something like "Lita et al." The girl Lita was in the group of those Paulo Luka claims to have brought back to life (*mu gulu la anthu anadzutsidwa ndi Paulo Luka*).

172 He refers to the miracle that his brother Paulo Luka brought him back to life after he had died.

173 After resurrecting him from death, Paulo began to teach his brother *using'anga.*

174 In the process of his training Paulo took his brother everywhere he went, even on a trip to a graveyard to try and resurrect a certain João who had died through witchcraft. António was able to watch his brother at work.

175 The reports about that João's resurrection were heard everywhere (*mbiri inanveka kwambiri*) in the region.

nkukatenga mwana wawo wina, nkukwana ndithu kagulu ndiye nthawi imeneyo ndithu anadzatitenga kupita komweko tinakagona mmanda momo, basi anadzamuona Juwawu wakufayo atabwela tinadzangoona phazi lokha kenaka atabwela anadzachita odi Juwawu, koma osamuona176), ndiye achimwenewa anabwelanso kuno kudzatenga mankhwala ena kuti tsopano akamuone. Ndiye pamenepo anamuona mpaka kumugwila ndiye nthawi yomweyo tinafika ku Sharpevale 177) kukakumana ndi apolice nkuona momwe zinalili, mpakana pano. 178)	her child; at another time she came again bringing another one of her children. Until they were a small group (*kagulu*) to present their complaints. At that juncture my brother took us all to that spot. When we slept there inside the graveyard, what happened was that Paulo should really see the dead João; but after he had come out, we only saw his foot (*phazi lokha*); thereafter he came out again, João, and he was saying; "Odi! " (Can I enter ?), but without seeing him. [176] So my brother decided to return here [to our place] in order to procure himself other medicines so that he would finally be able to see him. This time then he really saw him, until he caught him (*mpaka kumugwila*)! We then proceeded to Sharpevale [177] to meet the police and report the matter to them so that they should see themselves.Until now [it has remained like that] [178]
[Ndikutembenukila kwa Paulo Luka kuti ndilankhule nayenso]	[I am now turning back to Paulo Luka to talk to him]
M. Koma Juwawuyo pali pano ali moyo?	M. But, João, is he alive at the present time?
L. Eeee, ali moyo.	L. Yes, he is alive
M. Ali kutino?	M. Where is he now?
L. Ali ndi mayi ake, Juwawu atatulutsidwa mmanda kudzafika kunoko mai wake tinawauza kuti asadye nkhumba asasute fodya, asadye mbewa, ndiye mai wake china chilichonse tanenachi atapita kwao ku Mozambique ankakampatsa chilichonse, ndiye Juwawu anapenga pakali pano. Pano kunjakuno watsala Lita, Bwiza, Antonyo. Juwawuyo alipo koma mutu wake siukugwila bwino bwino, ndiye ndikufuna kuti ndiuchape bwino bwino.	L. He is with his mother, After he was made to come out of that graveyard and to arrive here, we told his mother, that he should not eat pig meat, that he should not smoke, that he should not eat a mouse! But everything we had forbidden her to do, his mother gave him after they had gone to Mozambique, so João ran mad, and that has remained so until now. The ones who have remained [in good condition] are Lita, Bwiza and Antonio. João is there, but his head does not function well, and I want that I

[176] Paulo Luka first had problems to make the dead João come out of his grave. Only his foot was seen, and at the second attempt only his voice was heard, saying "Odi!" This is the standard call in Chichewa by anyone seekingto enter somebody's house. Instead of knocking at the door one can say "Odi!" Only after he applied more powerful medicines did the *sing'anga* manage to get the person out of his grave and grab him, thereby bringing him back to life.

[177] Sharpvale is a place on the railway line from Limbe to Salima, northeast of Ntcheu.

[178] He wants to say, that João is alive, until now.

	wash it well.
M. Akumakhalabe konkuno kapena ali komwe ku Mozambique?	M. Does he still stay here or perhaps he is there in Mozambique?
L. Anali konkuno ndiye anapita ku Mozambique.	L. He was here, and he went to Mozambique.
M. Oho, tsopano inuyo nthawi imene munamuchotsa kumandayo, nkuti ali bwino bwino kapena zina zake zitasokonekela nthupi mwake?179)	M. Oho! At the time when you got him out of the graveyard, was he in good condition, or perhaps were there already confusions (*zina zake zitasokonekela*) in the body? [179]
L. Ai, anali bwino bwino, koma sankabvala chifukwa titamufunsa bwanji wabwela maliseche watani? Anandiuza kuti ife 180) timagwila maliseche ntchito yathu ndipo timagwila ndiusiku. Anali kwa Pengapenga 181) muchigayo cha munthu wina,182) munthu ameneyo angamudziwe ndi amai wake a Juwawuyo, koma nchigayomo tidakafikako	L. No, he was absolutely fine, but he was undressed. When we asked him "what's wrong, why have you come naked?" he replied: "We[180] do our work naked, and also during the night." He had been at Pengapenga [181], working at the maize mill of....[182],, the person who knows that big man is João's mother, but we did arrive at the maize mill.
M. Mhu!	M. Mhu!
L. Eee!	L. Yes!
M. Iyeyo ankagwila ntchito muchigayomo?	M. He worked in that maize mill?
L. Kumakatunga madzi kudzayika mnyumba mwawo ndi usiku basi akatelo kumutu-ma, kuti chitani chakuti kumakalima zina ndi zina, koma mogonela amagonela muchigayocho.	L. Drawing water from the well, putting it into their house; only in the night, was he sent to do the work. He was told "do such and such" for example plant in the fields such and such crops, but as concerns his sleeping arrangement, he slept in that maize mill.
M. Kodi ndiye kuti mwachitsanzo, munthu akalodzedwa akamwalila ndiye kuti amakasungidwa kwina kwake kapena amakadyedwa kapena amakatani?	M. If, for example, a person was bewitched and has died, is it that he or she is being kept [by the *mfiti*] somewhere, or perhaps is he or she eaten, or what else might happen?
L. Pali wena akamwalila amawadya, akawaphela ndiwo, pali wena akamwalila amawawaza mankhwala kuti asanduke ng'ombe, kaya ndi wamphon-go amati asanduke mfule,183) kaya ndi wankazi amati nthandi basi pakudya pa-	L. There are some, when they are dead, the wizards or witches eat them, because they killed them for relish (*ndiwo*). There are others when they have died, they sprinkle medicines upon their bodies, so that they metamorphose into cows. If it is a male person, they say that

[179] I am thinking of the possibility that the wizards/witches had already treated him in a way that he should no longer have human thoughts (*asakhale ngati ali ndi maganizo a umunthu*) when they got hold of him. So some "things" in his body would have been "confused" (- *sokonekela)* at that time.

[180] ife (we) refers to *anthu ophedwa* (the people who had been killed). Their work was to help their master, the wizard.

[181] Pengapenga is a place in Ntcheu District, on the railyway line, east of Ntcheu boma.

[182] Paulo Luka did not reveal the name of the owner of the maize mill; I believe he knew it, but was afraid of being sued for libel.

ja amati ndikudya nyama ya ng'ombe,184) koma lúdzu 185) la munthuyo amalichotsa. Ndiye wena akafa sawasandutsa chilichonse, amakangowagwilitsa ntchito kuti akhale munthu wa ntchito ndithu koma za usiku.186)	he should turn into an ox (*mfule*)[183] and if it is a female person they order her to turn into a heifer (*nthandi*). When they finally eat them, they say [to themselves] " I am eating beef (*nyama ya ng'ombe*),[184] but that person's ability of speech (*lúdzu*)[185] they first remove. Others still, when they have died, the wizards and witches do not turn them into anything at all, but they let them work for them, so that they should become [slave] workers, but of nocturnal activities (*za usiku*)[186]
M. Zausiku ntchito zake monga kumalima?	M. A specific work of the night, such as in the fields?
L. Ee, bwana monga kumalima, kumawatuma zina ndi zina, kumukhazika pa thumba la ndalama, iyeyo ndalamazo asanjike iyeyo basi, choncho koma pakutha pa mwezi salipidwa amalipidwa pakutha pa chaka 20 Tambala. Monga mnyamata uja Juwawu ankalipidwa pa chaka 20 Tambala.	L. Yes, Sir, such as working in the fields on contracts, or placing him on top of a bag of money to watch it. But at the end of the month he is not paid. He is paid at the end of a year, only 20 tambala. Such as that young man João, he was paid 20 tambala per year.
M. 20 Tambala, tsopano iyeyo amaigula chiyani?	M. 20 tambala. So what did he buy with it?
L. Amangosunga osagula kanthuyi.	L. He was just keeping it without buying anything
M. Mhu!	M. Mhu!
L. Eee bwana.	L. Yes sir.
(I am now turning to the mother of João who happened to sit nearby to ask her a few questions. Her name is Elite (=E.)	
M. Iyayi pakuti zofuna kudziwa ndi zambirimbiri, ndiye mwina kapena mai muli ndi zina zofuna kukambapo? Ehe	M. Well, since the things in need of being known are so many, perhaps I might ask you, mother, if you have something else you might like to relate? Ehe! You might

183 *mfule* is "an animal 'cut', an ox, capon, goat thus treated, also *mfulene, mbuzi ya mfulene yosapita mwa akazi;* also a eunuch"(Scott/Hetherwick 1929:295).

184 While eating they imagine to eat beef and not human flesh.They repress any sort of idea of eating a person, but think of their act as eating cows' meat (*maganizo awo onse amachotsa kuti akudya munthu koma akuganiza kuti akudya nyama ya ng'ombe).* Why should that be so? The answer is that if a wizard thought of himself eating human flesh, then he would have to think of this act as analogous to devouring himself, the owner [of the bewitched] because he considers himself also to be a person (*ngati akuganiza kuti akudya nyama ya munthu angaganize akudzidya iye mwini wache chifukwa iyeyonso ndi munthu).* Paulo Luka's account is an interesting testimony to the process of removing something unpleasant, unacceptable from ones's consciousness, termed repression in psychoanalytic theory (cf. Moore/Fine eds. 1990:166 168).

185 *Lúdzu (*speech, words, tone of voice) is to be distinguished from *lùdzu* (thirst).

186 An example of such nocturnal workers is those little people (*anthu tifupi tifupi choncho)* called *ndondocha* (see also the section on Simon Banda in this book)

munakakambako pang'ono.	tell us a little bit.
E. Ai ndilibe	E. No, I have nothing (to say).
M. = Moya E. = Elite, mai wa mwana yemwe anamwalila ndi kudzuka	(After my first attempt failed, I am trying again to get her to speak)
M. Kodi eti mai tinamva kuti ndinu mai wawo wa Juwawu?	M. We have heard that you are the mother of João?
E. Eee!	E. Yes!
M. Ndiye paja dzina lanu ndi ndani?	M. So then, what is your name?
E. Elita	E. Elite.
M. Labambo ndani?	M. And of your father?
E. Eneya.	E. Eneya.
M. Ndiye inu tandifotokozelani, zinachitika bwanji ndi mwana wanu Juwawu?	M. Would you kindly explain to us how those things happened to your son, João?
E. Zoona, adati atadwala akangoti "basi ine mai ndikupita kumanda, kumandako, koma akakandigulitsa 187) ku chigayo, ndikupita kuchigayo anzanga ali komweko, mphasa andiyalila kale, bulangetenso andiyikila." Ine ndimati "aa matenda 188) ake ndi amene ukupita nawo kumandawo?" Ndiye akuti "ee ndi amenewawa" ndiye basi mmene likatele dzuwalo basi nkumwalila. Basino atamwalila chomwecho, basi masiku awiri tinaona akumabwela pakhomopo kumadzachita "odi odi"!	E. The truth is that after he had fallen ill, he was just saying: "Myself, mother, I am going to the graveyard, to the grave yard there, but in reality they [my uncle] [187] are going to sell me to the maize mill; I am going to the maize mill, my companions [who have died] are there; a sleeping mat (*mphasa*) has already been spread out for me, a blanket to cover me has also been put there!" Myself I was wondering because of those words and said: " Is this minor illness[188] the one that will bring you to the grave?" He replied : "Yes, it is this illness". And really, the same day at sunset he died. He died just like that; then for two days I noticed that he was coming to the veranda of our house demanding entrance: "Odi! Odi!"
M. Usiku umenewo?	M. During the same night?
E. Eee, usiku, ndiye basino kutuluka osamuona, mwana kumangoona mapazi ndi mmeneno tinabwela kuno kwa Paulo Luka, ndimati : "ine mwana adamwalila mnyamata, 189) ndiye atamwalila mwanayo ndiye akumabwela ndiye ndimafuna kuti mundithandize" Ndiye tidanyamuka pano ndi aPaulo Luka basino nkukawaza mankhwala Juwawu	E. Yes, in the same night. But whenever I went outside to look, I did not see him; only the next morning I discovered his foot prints outside. It was at that stage that we came here to Paulo Luka. I said: "I have come because my child, a young boy[189]) died, but after his death he has continued to come [to the house] and I am asking you

[187] João did not specifically mention his *malume* (maternal uncle) in the sentences reproduced here by his mother; but the story I heard was that his uncle had sold João to the owner of the maize mill in Malawi.

[188] The implication is that João had suffered just from a minor ailment such as headache or the like.

[189] At that time João was perhaps twelve or thirteen years old.

nkutuluka, adatulukila pasukulu, akuti mnyamata uja wabwela, ndiye basi nkupita ine kukanfufuza ndakapeza ndamupezadi. Ndiye titakhala kumenekoko ndiye tidanyamuka kubwela kuno kwa Paulo Luka nkudzamula-nkhulitsa.	to help me!" So we set out from here and Paulo Luka sprinkled medicines on João's grave. As he was coming out, he actually appeared from near the school [in our village], Paulo notified me: "That boy has come!" So I set out to search for him until I eventually found him. After some time in our village, we returned here to Paulo Luka's place in order to make the boy talk again *(nkudzamulankhulitsa)*
M. Mhu!	M. Mhu!
E. Eee	E. Eee
M. Tsopano ndiye mutachoka nayenso kupi-ta naye kumudzi chinakachitikano ndi chiyani?	M. Now, after you had left again here and gone back to your village with your son, what happened then?
E. Basi mmene tinachoka pano kupita naye kumudziko akangokhala m'bwalo190) ndi anzake kumacheza, ndiye kenaka ndikumva akuti "ndikumanka ndiyenda" ndiye ndikuti "kumanka nduyenda kuti? " Ndiye basi nkumanka nayenda191) ndiye ine nkumanka ndimulondola. Mpakana kuyamba kuthawa, ndiye basino kenaka nkunyamuka , ndiye basino kenaka nkuyamba kubwela naye konkuno. Nkudzampatsa mankhwala nkupeza bwino ndiye ali "mumusiye musamute-ngenso, taonani bvuto limene lidakachitikalo." Anati koma mudzibwela mudzidzamuona," Ndiye basi m'bale wake anabwela mwezi wa May ndiye nkumati "ndakamupeza ali bwino, koma akuti tidzipita tidzikaona, tsopano pakuti kunabvuta kwathuku, kumabwela dzigawenga amanka afuna anthu kumawakhalilila, ndiye ine ndimasowa dela loti ndidzele ndibwele kuno ndidzamuone. Tsopano mmene ndinabwela ndidamva kuti Juwawu palibe adachoka.	E. All right, when we left here and I took him to the village, he just stayed in the meeting place (*m'bwalo*)[190] with his friends for conversation (*kumacheza*), and thereafter I heard the words "I will go out for a walk" I said: "Go out for a walk to where?" And he just set out walking[191] and myself I followed him to watch him (*ndimulonda*), until eventually he began to run away. So I went with him back here to the *sing'anga*. Paulo Luka gave him medicines, until he got better, but he said: "Leave him here, don't take him with you again. You can see yourself the origin of this problem." And he added: "But you should visit him from time to time!" In the month of May, his brother then visited him (in Paulo's clinic) and he reported "I have found him in good condition". But he suggested that we should all go there and I would see for myself. Now, because of troubles in our country [Mozambique] and the fact that guerrillas (*dzigawenga*) had come, intending to ambush people, I

[190] The term *bwalo* in Chichewa refers to open, public places, such as in the middle of a village, a court, a football ground, or a dance place where the masks perform, or specifically an air-field (*bwalo landege)* etc.In the present case she seems to refer to the *gowelo* (the house of male youths) found in some villages, where male adolescents stay together. On the institution of *gowelo* see also: Kubik/Malamusi 1987: 41-42.

[191] The boy began to display strange behaviour. He consistently attempted to run away, leave the place and go somewhere.

	was lacking a possible passage (*dela loti ndidzele*) to come here in order to see my child. When I eventually arrived here, I heard that João had left with an unknown destination.
M. Koma pa nthawi imene anakupezelani Juwawuyo inu mumtima mwanu munanvamo bwanji?	M. But when João had found back to you [from the graveyard] how did you feel in your heart at that time?
E. Chinali chisangalalo kuthokoza kwa Mulungu mphamvu zimene anawapatsa aLuka	E. It was a great joy, and I was thanking God for the strength he had conferred upon Luka.
M. Pamenepotu ngakhale panobe. Tsonobe panopo pakuti iyeyo wasowa ndiye mukuganiza kuti ali mbali iti?	M. That is it, even until now. But now, in the view of the fact that your child is missing again, where do you think he is?
E. Atandiunikano,192) mmene ndinabwelelamo, ananena kuti " tamupeza kuDedza."193)	E. When I came here, Paulo enlightened[192] me about that, he said "I have spotted him in Dedza". [193]
M. Akungoyendayenda paliponse?	M. Is he just walking everywhere?
E. Eee akungoyendayenda mmisika.194)	E. Yes, he is walking round in the various markets[194]
M. Ndiye mwina pali zinanso zomwe mungafotokoze?	M. Are there other things you would like to explain?
E. Ayi, koma kuti mphamvu yawo iwowa andithandize, kuti akantenge mnyamatayo.	E. No, but only that the strength of Paulo will help me in my need, so that I sjould take that boy back home.
M. Iyayi ife tathokoza kwambiri mai	M. No doubt, as far as we are concerned, we thank you very much, mother.

I am now continuing my interview with the *sing'anga* Paulo Luka asking him specifically to explain what concerns the "horns" (*nyanga*) which are used by the wizards and witches and which Paulo regularly takes away from them after their identification (see also the photographs taken a year later). In an unrecorded part of our conversations on the same day, Paulo Luka had told me that among the many dangerous things which he confiscated from the *amfiti*, he also confiscated lightening (*chiphaliwali*) from a certain man, Mr. Ncherewatha, who had killed with it many people. Curious about these stories, I committed him to another round of conversations, since he had also promised me to show me the various types of *nyanga* (horns).

M. Ndiyenso pakuti pali nkhani zina, monga ya chiphaliwali zinatani?	M. Since there are more reports, would you explain to me the one about the lightning (*chiphaliwali*)?
L. A Ncherewatha195) poyamba amaponya	L. The wizard Ncherewatha[195] who lives at

[192] Paulo was finding out João's whereabouts through divination *(maula)*.

[193] Town in central Malawi, to the northwest of Ntcheu.

[194] Like the kind of mad person, called *wamisala* in Chichewa, picking the remains of food in public markets.

chiphaliwali kumapha ana wanzawo, ku Tsangano paKaphiribunje. Ndiye anabwela kuno anzawonso atawadyera mwana, amayi wena wake atawadyera mwana ndiye adabwela pano. Ndiye podzafotokoza za mwana wawo wamwalilayu nkugwidwanso nda aNcherewatha amene ndi chiphaliwali chomwe. Ndiye aNcherewatha chiphaliwalicho anabwela nacho mpakana anadzachisiya konkuno, chili konkuno chiphaliwali chawocho.	Kaphiribunje, in the area of Tsangano, Mozambique, used to throw lightning (*amaponya chiphaliwali*) in order to kill the children of his acquaintances, before he was exposed by me. And it happened that he came here to seek my advice after his own child had been eaten by his wizard-acquaintances in return. Eventually, a certain woman came also here after her child had been eaten [by Ncherewatha]. When Ncherewatha explained about the loss of his child who died, he was caught by me as a wizard, as the one in possession of that very lightning. Ncherewatha had actually come here with his lightning, but ended up leaving the device here with me. His lightning (*chiphaliwali)* is right here.
M. Kodi munthu amachiona ndi maso?	M. This means that a person can see it with the eyes?
L. Eee,196) timaonetsa panthawiyo tisanechizizilitse, timaonetsa anthu amadzaona gulu ndithu.	L. Yes[196], we were showing it to people at the time we had not yet cooled it down; a crowd of people was watching the performance.
M. Eee.	M. Ehe!
L. Imafikano nthawi yochiphano kuchizizilitsa, ndiyeno chimasanduka mipeni, koma poyambapo chimakhala ngati chimbalame, amachisula chitsulo ngati chimbalame chibakha, nkumangilila dziboda za bakha weniweni, kukhosi kwakeku amaikako chinsalu cha khwiriti 197) ndichimene amaikamo mpeni mmenemo basi nkutumizano kukapha munthuyo. ANcherewathawo anapha anthu ten adanena okha.198)	L. The moment I deactivated the device, cooling it down, it metamorphosed into knives (*chimasanduka mipeni*), but first it had appeared like a big bird. He [Ncherewatha] hammers the red-hot iron on the anvil to assume the shape of a big duck (*chibakha*) and fastens a real duck's webbed feet (*dziboda*) to it. At the neck of the device he attaches a *khwiriti*-cloth[197] and inside that cloth he puts a knife which is designed to be sent for killing the victim. Ncherewatha killed ten people in this manner; he himself told me.[198]

[195] whom Paulo had disarmed in his clinic.

[196] In spite of his statement Paulo Luka did not show me the lightning (*chiphaliwali).* He said, it had "cooled down". However as I understand the matter, in order to activate lightning for killing a person, the *mfiti* takes a special knife, holds it into the fire, until the steel becomes red-hot; thereafter he takes an object representing his victim, the person who resides far away, pronounces the person's name, and stabs the object. That moment lightning comes out of the knife, travels to the victim at the speed of light and kills him or her. To reproduce this experimentally Paulo Luka probably deemed too dangerous to show me.

[197] It is a duck-green, very ugly type of cloth.

M. Mhu, ndiye ho pakuti zofuna kudziwa ndi zambirimbiri, kodi mungandipatse mwayi watsiku lina uti tidzawone mmene mumaimbila nyimbozo, ndi mmene mumaombezela kuti mwauze anthu zimene abwelela mabvuto awo.	M. Mhu! Since there are so many things that are worthwhile to be known , will you perhaps give us the luck of a certain day to watch how you perform your songs and how you cast lots to tell people the cause of the troubles with which they come to you?
L. Tsiku lililonse limene mungabwele, lerolo mukadakhala kuti siinu wofulumila mukadaonela, chifukwa mwa ena mwa iwo alipo.	L. Any day which you come here,even today, if it is not you who are in hurry, you could see it, because by chance there are some others already here.
M. Alipo oti aombeze?	M. There are some for whom you would do the divination?
L. Ochokela ku Tete.	L. There are some who have come from Tete (Mozambique).
M. Moti zingayambike nthawi yanji?	M. What time will this performance start?
L. Timayamba 6 koloko mpaka pasiti 11, ndiye nkudula kuyamba kulemba matikiti ndi mankhwala. Ndipo timayambanso chakuma 2 koloko nkulekeza 4 koloko.	L. We are starting at 6 o'clock [in the morning] and continue up to after 11 o'clock, with an interruption for writing tickets and prescriptions. At 2 o'clock in the afternoon we start again and end the session at 4 o'clock.
M. Ndiye pano ndi kumathwelofu.	M. Now it is about 12 o'clock.
L. Ndiye tiyambeno kupeleka mankhwala, kwa anthu amene apimidwa mmamawa.	L. At this time we are beginning to distribute medicines to those people who are examined in the morning.
M. Inu muli mpingo wanji?	M. Which confession (*mpingo*) do you belong to?
L. Ine ndili mu mpingo wa akatolika.	L. I am in the Catholic denomination.
M. Tsopano katolika ndi zitchito zimene mukugwilazi zimalowelana ngati?	M. Now, the Catholic creed and the work you are doing, how do these things fit into each other?

[198] Among his devices, he also had an "aeroplane" which I photographed a year later (see photo no. 95/2/28). It was by chance that Paulo Luka had caught this dangerous wizard. Ncherewatha had come to the *sing'anga* to complain about the loss of his own child. But a woman had come at the same time who complained about the loss of her child and Ncherewatha was soon implicated by Paulo Luka. Ncherewatha, however, denied any wrongdoings. He said: "I am not a *mfiti,* I am crying for my own child". He did not want his devices to be confiscated by Paulo Luka.

L. Ayi, iwowo amakaniza, koma pakuti Mulungu sindiwo ndiye ine ndimangopitabe199), kuti pazintchito Mulungu akasankha yekha koma bola ndikudziwa kuti ufiti wopha munthu kuti nkadye sindinachite. Eya ndiye nchifukwa chake ndimapita mwandekha podziwa chimo langa kukamupemphelela Mulungu kuti andikondenso mbali imodzi.	L. No, those [Catholics] reject my work, but since God is not them, so I continue to go there [to church][199]. As concerns the deeds of someone, God chooses by himself, giving his own judgement. But I know that I myself did not commit the crime of killing a person by witchcraft so that I would eat him/her. Because of that I go to church out of my own free will, knowing that in view of my sins, I pray yo God that he should love me at least with my good side.
M. Apa ife tathokoza kwambiri!	M. Here we would like to express our thank to you!
L. Zikomo kwambiri	L. Thank you very much!

II. Documentation of the screening of people (*kuwunika anthu*) by Paulo Luka. Place: Chipula Village, T.A. Njolomole, Ntcheu District, October 29, 1994, afternoon. Original tape no. 94/3, side 2.

The session in which Paulo Luka is examining his patients, through his visionary power, in order to find out something about the causes of their illnesses, begins with songs in which he—sometimes replaced by others— functions as the lead singer (*ntsogoleli*). The songs are already known by those patients who have stayed in his clinic for a long time. They know the chorus phrase with which they should reply to each line sung by the leader. The form of the song is the call-and-response form. While the songs go on, the *sing'anga* begins to talk, enlightening those people who have come to him for consultation about their problems (*kuwunika anthu ena mabvuto omwe abwelela*). He also tells them where they have come from (*ndikuwauza kwawo komwe iwo achokela*) without getting this information from them.

Song (nyimbo)

N. = *Ntsogoleli* (leader)

O. = *Onse* (all), the community singing the chorus part

N. Kadzidzi wabangula a!	N. The owl is hooting
O. Kadzidzi wabangula pakati pausiku padenga wathetsa nzeru tipite kwa sing'anga (2x)	O. The owl is hooting in the middle of the night, on the rooftop. it has brought to an end our wisdom. Let us go to see a *sing'anga*! (2 x)
N. Ine ninapita a!	N. I went there, aa!
O. Nnapita kwa sing'anga, nsupa inayankhula, pakhomo panupo	O. I went there to the *sing'anga*, the phial was talking and it said: "There

[199] Paulo Luka frequented the catholic service in spite of his work as *sing'anga* to which the local catholic authorities did not agree.

nonse simugwilizana.	at your veranda, you people don't get on well with each other!"
N. Ngati pali mau amachita chokambilana	N. If there are problems, one had better talk to each other!
O. Musamakankhile nnzanu kumanda a! (2x)	O. Don't push your neighbour into the grave! Aaa!(2x)

Through the medium of song, messages such as these are composed by the *sing'anga* himself in his desire to demonstrate to the people the witchcraft acts which the *amfiti* carry out in a village, when they want that a funeral should take place soon. Many people in Malawi think that an owl incorporates a powerful wizard or witch, because what regularly happens when such an owl comes in the night, sitting down near the house of a certain person, and hooting, is that a funeral will take place in the villagewithout delay. This is what everbody in the village believes, because people say that the owl announces troubles (*amalosa zobvuta*) such as a funeral. In this way people maintain that the owl is a wizard or witch, because when it hoots at the veranda of somebody, a funeral will happen.

Here the *sing'anga* takes recourse to people's ideas about the owl, working them into a song. This is why the present song is found among many others of *sing'anga* Paulo Luka to corroborate people's belief that an owl is indeed a wizard or witch.

Kubangula in Chichewa means: cry out (*kulila kwambiri*) such as a lion roars or an owl hoots. *Wathetsa nzeru* refers to the emotional state of the people in the village when they discover an owl on somebody's roof top. It really is *kadzidzi wathetsa nzeru* i.e.the presence of the owl has brought people's wisdom to an end. They have no means to remove the evil magic symbolized by the owl. They are unable to do something so that the owl would not come again. All they can do is go to the *sing'anga* for advice.

At the *sing'anga's* place, the phial (*nsupa*) of the *sing'anga* begins to talk. Interestingly, it says that " there at your veranda, you people don't agree with one another!" The veranda (*pakhonde)* in front of the entrance to a house, is the place where people sit down, where they meet and discuss. It is a symbol of community life. In his statement, the *sing'anga* through his phial identifies the root of the people's problems, that they are not in harmony with one another, and therefore some community members, dissatisfied, begin to carry out their aggressions through witchcraft (*ufiti*). In the song, the *sing'anga* advises people to speak out, and if there are problems to discuss them instead of pushing someone into the grave.

Songs such as these are sung for some time during a session, and the *sing'anga* also sings together with the rest of the people for long periods. In the middle of one or another song, he begins to produce noises like a belch (*kugeya)*, and people say that he is calling the spirits (*mizimu*) so that they should help him with the things he wants to perform, and indeed, all of a sudden he begins to whirl his head (*kuzunguza mutu*) and to belch very much. He begins to talk things which an ordinary person will not understand, as to myself, there was nothing I understood! But those who are close to him understand what he wants to say, and they are the ones who translate his words to his clients.

Transcripition and translation of the session

L. = Paulo Luka

Ny. = *Mnyamata*, a young man of about 26 years who is the one who complains about his illness (*wodandaula*)

Ag. = *Agogo wao*. His grandfather who was once a *sing'anga* himself and has accompanied the young man to see Paulo Luka.

M. = Moya.

L. Imva tsono, chiyambi chache, choyamba ndafika kwanuko m'bale wanga 200)	L. Listen now, to start with, I am beginning to arrive at your place, my brother! [200]
Ny. Eee	Ny. Yes
L. Koma tili panjila paja tiyambe tapeza asilikali choyamba ledibuloko, tsutsa iwe ngati ndikunama! Kwanu kumeneko koma sitinafike. Tili munjila titangochoka ledibuloko tiyenda pang'ono tipeza gulaye, tachokatu mmagomo muno tili paulendo titangochoka mgomo tipeza siteji yoyamba pali nsika pamenepo, tikachoka pansikapo tiyenda tichoke pamene paja pali buliji ledibuloko ya asilikali, koma alipo awiri, waimva? Tichoka pamenepo pa roadblock tiyendabe, pang'ono munsewu wa tala pano tayang'ana kumeneko chakummwela kumeneko, dzanja la manzele tipeza pali khola lalikulu koma lokhudzana ndi boma.201)-- Unditsutse iwe ngati ndibodza zomwe ndikunenazi!– Khola limenelo anadzaliba anthu ena mpakana anthu ena anapha munthu pamenepo. Mlonda wapamenepo namucha kuti ndamene anapha munthuyo, tsutsa ngati ndikunama! Boma limenelo, kwanu kumeneko, dela la kuChikwawa tichoke pamenepo dzanja la kumanja kumadzulo kumeneko tipeza masitolo, pamenepo inayo yalembedwa Dziko lakunja, muli munthu	L. But we are still on the road there, first we are encountering soldiers (*asilikali*), a roadblock—contradict me, if I am telling lies—your home is right there, but we have not yet arrived. We are on the way; after we have left the roadblock and walked for a short while we find a corner (*gulaye*) then we pass a granite hill (*gomo*), we are on our journey; after we have left behind the granite hill we encounter a first bus station; there is a market at that place; after we have left the market and go on, leaving that spot behind there is a bridge with another roadblock by soidiers, but only two men are there—have you understood? If we leave that roadblock and still go on for a while on the tarmac road, we look there facing the south, and find that to our left is a large cattle kraal, but it is on the premises of the government[201]. —You should contradict me if it is a lie what I am saying!—Other people eventually stole this cattle kraal, even certain people killed a person there. One of the guards is suspected having killed that person [another guard]. Contradict me, if I am telling lies!—Near that place of the government there is your home, in the

[200] Paulo Luka concentrates and <u>travels</u> in his thoughts to the area where his client has come from. He describes his spiritual journey there in every detail, indicating directions, places etc. as if he were actually walking through all these places, or driving. From time to time he interrupts himself, seeking feedback from his client, whether it was still true what he was perceiving in his vision.

[201] Obviously, he refers to the large cattle kraal in Chikwawa which once belonged to Dr. Kamuzu Banda, former president of Malawi.

wakuda wankulu thupi pang'ono wainvi pang'ono wochedwa Fatchi, yandani imeneyo?	area of Chikwawa. If we leave that spot in direction of our right hand, and to the west, we are finding stores. One one of the stores it is written *Dziko lakunja*. Inside there is a black person, with a big body, a bit of grey hair, who is called Fatchi. Whose store is it?
Ny. Ya! aFatchi.	Ny. The store of Fatchi.
L. Yalembedwa Dziko lakunja, pali nyumba pano yaikulu koma ili sitolo pomwepo pali mtengo wankolobwi,202) patsogolo pang'ono pali filling station yopeleka mafuta. Chapatsogolo pang'ono pali famu ya mzimbe, tiyende pang'ono tikhote pang'ono kulowela dzanja la madzulo pang'ono tipeza nyumba yalibanda yoyamba, tsutsa iwe kwanu ku Chikwawa! Ndili kumeneko pano, tsopano tikachoka panyumba ya libandayo tipeza manda, ndapeza manda wainva? Ndi mmudzi mwandani manda amene ali kunjilawo?	L. Near the store with the writing Dziko lakunja there is a big house which is also a store, and there stands aNkolobwi tree [202]; a bit further on there is a filling station for petrol. A bit more further on there is a sugarcane farm; let us go on and turn a bit in direction west, we will find a first gable roof house (*nyumba ya libanda*)— contradict me!—at your home in Chikwawa I am now there [in my vision]; if we then leave that gable roofed house, we are getting to a graveyard. I have found the graveyard, do you hear? In whose village is that graveyard on the way?
Ny. Mwathu mmenemo.	Ny. It is in our village.
L. Wamva tafikatu lero, nanga ine ndinabwela kwanu? Udandiuza manda amenewo? 203)	L. You understand, we have arrived there today. Did I ever before go to your village? Did you tell me that graveyard's place? [203]
Ny. Iyayi.	Ny. No.
L. Ima unve lero, no no no no no,204) tichoke pamenepo mpakana tiyende pang'ono pali nyumba ina yalibandanso. Chauko kuli nazale ya mitengo yochepa, patsogolo pali mzimbe pang'ono, mbali ya dzanja linali kuli mitengo yaikulu ya boma, tiyende pang'ono tipeza nyumba yaikulu, yandani imeneyi?	L. Wait a bit, so that you hear something today no no no no no! [204] Let us now leave that place; should we walk on just a bit, then there is another house with a gable roof. As concerns that place there is a tree nursery (*nazale yamitengo yochepa*), further on there is some sugarcane, at the side of the other hand there are big trees [planted] by the administration; let us continue a bit, and we find a big house. Whose house is it?
Ny. Ya agogo wanga.	Ny. It is the house of my grandfather.
L. Mwini wake wa mmenemoyo wankulu thupi, wanfupi,wainvi pang'ono, koma muli nsupa, nayenso ndi sing'anga nzanga,	L. The owner of this house is a fat person, he is short, has some grey hair; but inside the house there is a phial (*nsupa*) because he also is a *sing'anga*, of my

[202] I have been unable to identify this type of tree. It is neither mentioned in Williamson 1975, nor in Scott/ Hetherwick 1929 (1970).

[203] *Sing'anga* Paulo Luka is stressing his power as a seer, but his clients are already convinced.

[204] He begins to whirl his head before he continues the visionary journey.

koma zidafa no no no no no ndikufuna yankho koma	profession, but his medicines have died. No no no no no ! I want an answer! But….
Ny. Adali sing'anga awa ali apawa.205)	Ny. He was a *sing'anga*. Actually he is right here![205] [words by many people, incomprehensible on the tape]
L. Mwanva madala? 206) Tikufuna tiwone zomwe akuchita anthu akwanu lero limenelo, ndapeza nyumba mwako, ndapeza nsupa m'bale wanga za nkazi wako, koma nawenso unali mugulu lomwelo, koma zidafa.	L. [Turning to me and my companion]. Have you understood, elders? (*madala*) [206] [turning to the young man] We want to know what the people in your village are doing today! [then turning to the grandfather] I have found your house, I have found the phial, my brother, of your wife, but you also were in that same group [of wizards and witches], but your medicines have died.
Ny. Zoona analidi asing'anga koma zafa.	Ny. It is true, he [my grandfather] was a *sing'anga* but his medicines have died.
Ag. Zoona ine nditsutsa bwanji?	Ag. How will I contradict this statement! It is true!
L. Zitatha zimenezo ndapeza mphwirikiti woyamba, maliro, maliro amenewa atatha, ndapeza wena maliro. Maliro amenewa atatha panali mphwirikiti ndipo ankagwila iyeyo kuti ndaamene amatamba uyu ameneyo.	L. After those medicines have died—I am now finding [in my vision] the initial disagreements (*mphwirikiti woyamba*), a funeral. After that funeral, I am finding another funeral. When that funeral ended there was more disagreement (*mphwirikiti*) and they caught him [the grandfather] accusing him that he was the one who was dancing the witch dance. (*amatamba uyu ameneyo*).
Ny. Zoonadi zinkatelo	Ny. It is true, it was like that.
L. Koma ndakana ine,ndakana ine pano nyama ya munthu sanaioneyoo, koma iyeyu ndi mtima wake amati tionana, ukaleke m'bale wanga dzina lakuti tionana, limathetsa anthu m'bale wanga. Ukangoti tiona amati wotambayo ndiye amadya anthuwo kuti adziti ndiwe yemwe wanena kuti tionawe. Ukaleke, koma iweyo ntchito zathu ngati zathu zomwe za using'anga, koma	L. But myself I disagree with those accusations, he [your grandfather] did not consume any human flesh. But during the quarrels he was saying to the other people: "we shall see what will happen!" My brother you should stop ever using again that phrase: "We shall see!..." It is this phrase which decimates the population, my brother! If you say to someone "We shall see...!

205 The young man is pointing at his grandfather who has come along with him to see Paulo Luka.

206 *ndala* (also written as: *mdala*) = *munthu wankulu kapena wachikulile* (an important person, or elderly person). It is a polite way of addressing someone.

dzidafa udaleka, tikuzifunatu zimenezo nsupa tikuzifuna. 207)	then those who dance the witch dance take advantage; they kill and eat those people and point to you saying that it was you who did it, because you had threatened them in the first place. You should stop that! But as concerns our common work of medical practice (*using'anga*), even if your medicines have expired and you have stopped that work, we still want that you hand over to us those dangerous phials! [207]
M. Koma zomwe anenazo ndi zoonadi?	M. [I am asking the grandfather]; But what he says [Paulo Luka] is it true?
Ag. Za nsupatu, eya ndili nazo koma sizanga ayi.208)	Ag. As concerns those phials, I am in possession of them, but they are not mine. [208]
L. Adamukonzela ndi nkazi wake nsupazo, koma maliro amene amachitika pamudzipo amati amadya ndi iyeyo, koma ndakana pano. Adangokula m'bale wanga koma ali ndi mwano, wolankhula ndi pakamwa kuti tiona. Kodi ine nditati tiona, ndiye inu popita kunjilako wina nkukuphani kunjilako, anthu angati wakuphani ndi ndani? Tsonotu ukaleke chalengi, umathetsa ana pakhomo.209)	L. His wife prepared them for him! But as concerns the funerals which took place in his village, when people say that he was the one who ate the victims, that is where I disagree! He was getting old, my brother, and yet he was full of insolence in his mouth, the way he used to talk, saying "we shall see what will happen!" What about me, if I said "we shall see!" and you, when you go your way and somebody kills you on that journey, the people will ask: "Who was it that killed you?" From now on you should stop challenging people, you are only decimating the children at the veranda! (*umathetsa ana pakhomo*) [209]
Munve tsono achikulile tapeza nyamata uyo ali apoyo ali ndi matenda, nanga inu mungadziwe pamene alipo? Munvetsele chimene chikumuwawa, tsiku loyamba ndapeza maliro, kachiwirinso ndapeza maliro, mpakana mwini wake 210) wa mwanayo adakana kumeta malirowo atakaikidwa, kuti sindimeta ine kulibwino angokudya maliro awowo. 211) "Ndiye kuyambila pamenepo panali kudana mpakana	[Now talking to me, the interviewer;] You understand now, my elder! We have found this young man here to be afflicted with venereal disease (*ali ndi matenda*). Would you as a non-professional have suspected anything like that [from such a good looking young man]? Listen to my explanations of what really hurt him! I found out that

[207] The *sing'anga* Paulo Luka is insisting upon confiscating the phials of the young man's grandfather, because he is convinced that the old man and his wife have used some of them also for witchcraft.

[208] He wants to indicate that those dangerous phials belong to his wife! But it became more and more likely that they were cooperating in witchcraft.

[209] With this metaphor Paulo wanted to emphasize that the old man's insolence and threatening talk encouraged the real killers to act, because thereafter they could point at him suggesting that he was the killer because of his earlier verbal threats.

kusiyana ntundu mpakana nawenso udayamba kudwala, matenda aiweyo anayamba pang'ono pang'ono. Udayamba ngati malungo, mpakana adadula chinthu chako kumasoko, mwanva pamenepo.	initially there was a funeral, and then again there was a funeral, until the owner[210] of a certain child (*mwini wake wa mwanayo*) who had suddenly died became suspicious and refused to do the head-shaving rite after the funeral (*ada-kana_kumeta malirowo atakaikidwa*). She said: "I will not agree to have my head shaved like those other people, they can ingest that funeral by themselves!" [211] After that incident intensive hate devel oped between the relatives, to the point that they even renounced their blood relationships (*kusiyana ntundu*). [Now talking to the young man again]: "And you also began to fall ill; your disease started gradually, it all began like malaria fever (*malungo*), but it ended with the fact that they amputated your penis. [212]. [Now turning back to me:] Have you under-stood? This is what I found out.
Ny. Zoonadi.	Ny. It is true indeed.
L. Mpakana udayenda muzipatala, mpaka aboma kudabwa mpaka anakuika paipi kumaso kwakoko.213) Koma zitatelo unalephela kuchila. Tsona anthu akwanuko ankati ungobvutika iweyo,214)	L. First you had gone to various hospitals with your problem; even the nurses at the government hospital wondered and they eventually inserted a catheter into your penis. [213] But even after they had

[210] Probably the child's mother or some other parent who took care of the child.

[211] To understand the desperate remark by the child's mother, it is necessary to know a few details about Nyanja /Chewa/ Mang'anja funeral rites. *Kumeta maliro* (to shave the funeral) is a phrase that refers to the custom that the relatives of the deceased, after having spent the night outside, and when the funeral is over, next morning will shave their heads. However, people believe that if a person was killed by witchcraft, the head-shaving ceremony which symbolizes the irreversibility of the fact that their be-loved person has died, and that he/ she will not come back and that the community has to accept this fact, can serve the *amfiti* (wizards / witches) as a signal to go ahead with their nocturnal intentions. It is believed that the *amfiti* keep the corpse somewhere else. The head-shaving is something like a catalyst (*kumeta ndi ngati chizimba cha amfiti*) opening up for them the avenue to continue with the next step of their witchcraft work (*kuti apitirize ntchito yao)* namely to divide the corpse among themselves and eat it. In the present case the mother of the child refused to be shaved, because she intended to go and seek a *sing'anga*'s advice (*cholinga ckake chofuna kupita kwa sing'anga*). But others had already fin-ished the rite. When they came to her she refused and said "eat the funeral yourself!" suggesting that some *amfiti* were perhaps among those people who seemed to be so quick saying: "Oh, let us shave, what happened has happened, it is finished now !"

[212] In the original Chichewa text (see above) the fact that eventually the young man had his penis ampu-tated in a local hospital, is expressed by Luka with a polite circumscription. He says: "*mpakana adadu-la chinthu chako kumaso*", literally: "until they cut your thing there at the eyes". Reference to the geni-tals in public discourse is always indirect. One way of reference is to say *kumpheto* (between the legs); another way of reference is to say *kumaso* (at the eyes) which is the most polite way, because of the displacement i.e. the focal shift from one idea to another "that is associatively related but more ac-ceptable to the ego" (cf. Moore / Fine, eds. 1990: 48 for terminology).

[213] Here again, he says: *kumaso* (into the eyes). *Paipi* (from engl. pipe) refers to the catheter as used by urologists.

mpakana bambo wako ankati usapite kwa sing'anga ndiye iwe pakuti wabwela kuno, ndiye choyamba tiyambe taphwanya nyanga za mbuyakoyu.215) "Mwana wako umusunge bwino ukumva?"	done that, you failed to recover. Now the people at your home were saying that your disease was merely unpleasant [but not dangerous] [214] and even your father said you should not go to see a *sing'anga.* But now, since you have come here, let us first smash (*kuphwanya*) the horns of your grandfather! [215] (Turning now to the old man); "Your child you should keep him well, do you hear?"
Ag. Eee bwana	Ag. Yes, sir
At this point, Paulo Luka concluded the session with the young man and his grandfather, and the latter walked out. He began to join the people inside his clinic in their singing, and the following song was started:	

Nyimbo (song)

N. = *Ntsogoleli* (leader)
O. = *Onse* (all)

N. Mneneli 216) amaona nthenda	N. The prophet[216] discovers the disease.
O. Mneneli amaonaa	O. The prophet discovers, aa!
N. Khomo latseguka mmwambamo	N. The veranda of heaven has opened.
O. Khomo latseguka. (3x)	O. The veranda has opened. (3x)
N. Tiyimbe aleluya mmwambamo. (3x)	N. Let us sing hallelujah in heaven. (3x)
While the singing was going on, some other clients came to be screened by Paulo Luka. But all of a sudden Paulo begins to call out and recite what those two people whom he had just released—the young man and his grandfather—were telling others about him outside. We all had not heard a word; Paulo alone seemed to hear even the whispering. He became very angry and shouted: "You outside are talking bad about me!" And he called those two people to come back to him, and tell him their true thoughts and what they were telling their companions outside with a whispering voice (*monong'ona*). Then Paulo seems to get possessed again by the spirits and he reprimands the young man and his grandfather.	
L. Wainva m'bale wanga, no no no no no, sipamenepo pamene ukuganiza ndikufuna yankho lomveka, invatu tsono ndapeza	L. Have you understood, my brother, no no no no no! things are not what you think they are! I want a clear answer from

[214] Paulo Luka says that village people were suggesting that those who had bewitched the young man did not, in fact, want to kill him , just let him suffer.

[215] With this statement, Paulo Luka openly accuses the young man's grandfather of being the wizard, and the origin of his problem. This is what gradually comes to the surface. In medical terms, Paulo Luka does not deny that the primary cause of the young man's problems with his urinary tract could have been venereal disease. But since at that time such infections were easily treated with penicillin, Paulo Luka suspects witchcraft involvement. "It was like venereal disease, but the disease had been thrown at him through magic!" (*ngati matenda azimai koma ali ochita kuponyeledwa pa matsenga*). The involvement of *matsenga*, according to Paulo Luka, was evidence, because all the treatments the young man had received in public hospitals proved ineffective, and eventually his penis was amputated.

[216] *mneneli* is a prophet, apostle, one who speaks from visionary insights. Paulo Luka seems to think of himself as a kind of prophet.

iweyo mmoyo mwako panjapo pamenepo umalingalila zochuluka, tsopano ine ndikusemphana ndi anzanga kumeneko217) chifukwa cha moyo wako. Zinthu zako ziyenda, koma iweyo wayambila patali kuyendako, ndiye unayamba kukaika , wainva iyo, kuti asing'anga amanama chifukwa chotopa, mpakana unkatinena kuti asing'anga ngabodza. Asing'anga ndi mafano, ndipo amaba. Uleke zimenezo ndiyesetsa zimene ukufuna.	you! Just listen! I have found by myself alone that in your life outside you are having fanciful thoughts (*umalingalila*) in abundance, but now because of this interference from your life my friends [the spirits] and I are missing each other! [217] There is progress in your undertakings, but you yourself started to go to remote places and thereby you developed doubts (*kukaika*)—do you hear my message?—so you started thinking that the *asing'anga* are just telling lies, because you got tired! Until you talked bad about me, that *asing'anga* are liars (*ngabodza*), that they are only producing images (*mafano*) and that they steal money (from their clients). You should stop such behavior, I am trying to respond positively to your needs!

III. Investigating a group of young men from Mozambique seeking advice from Paulo Luka. (*Kufufuza nkhani za anyamata ena omwe anachokera kutsidya la Mozambique kubwela kwa a Paulo Luka ndi mabvuto awo.*) Place: Chipula village, T.A. Njolomole, Ntcheu District, October 29,1994, late afternoon. Original tape no 94/3 side 2.

The story behind this record is that a group of people, mostly young men aged from 25 to 30 years, and one woman had arrived from Mozambique. But Paulo Luka already knew through his visionary power that those people had been talking bad about him, on their way from their home village to his clinic. They had accused Paulo, even before they had arrived, to be a money monger, that he was very expensive, and that they could never satisfy him. Paulo Luka considered that to be an affront, insisting that his fees were fair and reflected the quality of his treatments. An embarrassing conversation ensued. I am transcribing the text of their conversation to show yet another facet of the kinds of interaction that took place between Paulo Luka and his clients.

L. = Paul Luka
O1 = *Obwela oyamba* (First visitor), a young man
O2 = *Obwela wachiwiri* (second visitor),young man

L. M'bale wanga ndapeza nkhani yochititsa manyazi pakati pa iwe ndi ine. Kuchokela pamenepo unayamba kulongosola	L. My brother, I have become aware of an incident that only creates havoc between you and me! When you left your home

[217] Obviously, Paulo Luka is able to detect through extrasensory perception (ESP) what some of his clients are talking about him outside after finishing the consultation, especially if they denounce his work. The interesting point here is, that he experiences those negative thoughts by others outside as an interference with his communication with the spirits; similar to the effect of the noises caused in radio or television reception, if another transmitter near to its wave-length is near.

mpakana mau ako, unati "kupita tipita koma makobiri wokapeleka kumeneko?" ankatero uja ndani?	village you began to make various statements, saying things like :"as concerns going there, we will go, but the money he is expecting from us there is... Who made that statement?
O1. Ineyo.	O1. Myself.
L. Unkati makobiri atani?	L. And you said "the money we have" is what?
O1. Apelewela.	O1. It is not enough.
L. Poti amatani kumeneko?	L. Because of what sort is that *sing'anga* There?
O1. Amadula.	O1. He is too expensive.
L. Pita kosadula m'bale wanga, uyende ndi ntendere wako.	L. So then, go to where it is cheap, my brother go in peace!
Nyimbo	Song (nyimbo)
N. Mneneli amaona nthenda (2x)	N. The prophet discovers the disease (2x)
O. Mneneli amaona (3x)	O. The prophet discovers. (3x)
N. Khomo latseguka mmwambamo	N. The veranda of heaven has opened.
O. Khomo latseguka.	O. The veranda has opened.
The second visitor (O2) within the same group and his wife (who is silent) are now engaged in conversation by the *sing'anga*. They are part of the same group that came from Mozambique.	
L. Ndani akumva za awa, anandiuza nanga?	L. [Talking to me]: Who is able to understand the affairs of these people? Who has told me anything, after all?
O2. Ayiii	O2. Oh nobody
L. Mufunseni kuti anandiuza kuti pakundiwawa ndipakuti, funsoo?	L. [still talking to me]: Ask that man whether he told me "what hurts me comes from such and such"--- question!
O2. Ayi.	O2. Oh no!
L. Nanga ananena kumene ankandinenako?	L. [Now turning to the larger audience]: Did this group of people inform me about the place where they were talking bad about me?
O2. Ayi sindinanene.	O2. No, I did not say anything.
L. Nanga sindinakugwile?	L. And yet, didn't I catch you red-handed?
O2. Mwandigwila.	O2. You have caught me.
L. Wagwidwa m'bele wanga.	L. You have been convicted, my brother!
O2. Zoonadi.	O2. It is true.
L. Wagwidwa ndi nkhani yanji paja?	L. For which kind of statement are you guilty?
O2. Kuti kumeneko kumadula, ndalama mwina sizikakwanila.	O2. For saying that it is expensive here [at your place] and perhaps our money will not be enough.
L. Kuli bwino tingotani?	L. And you said "we had better do what?"
O2. Kwabwino tiyambe tapeza ndalama ina kuti tipite 218)	O2. We had better first find some other money before going there[218]

[218] In his replies during the interrogation by the *sing'anga*, the young man tries to weaken his earlier remarks while they had been extremely impolite and insolent (*za chipongwe*), virtually accusing Paulo

<table>
<tr><td>L. Chafukwa kumeneko nkodula, ndiye lero pita kuchipatala cha boma, osati cha private, koma upite chosalipila. Sindine ndi mtima wako, chafukwa ine ndikukuuza mochipa mwaimo, ndiye uko ukanena kuti ndapeleka ndalama zanga.</td><td>L. You were saying "because there it is unjustifiably expensive," so then, go to the government hospital, don't come to a private clinic, but go to where treatment is free of charge! My heart is not of your kind [full of insolence], because I have told you the best possible price for my quality services, and there you will say that "I have lost all my money".</td></tr>
<tr><td>O2. Mundikhulululukile ndalakwa.</td><td>O2. Forgive me, I have done wrong.</td></tr>
<tr><td>L. Koma watani pano, wagwidwa m'bele wanga.</td><td>L. But what have you been doing here? You have been convicted, my brother!</td></tr>
<tr><td>O2. Ndagwidwa zoonadi</td><td>O2. I have been convicted, it is true.</td></tr>
<tr><td>L. Ukanene kumeneko kuti ndakumana naye Paulo, uno ndi ntunda.219)</td><td>L. You go and tell people there "I have met with Paulo" , But you should also know that myself I am top (uno ndi ntunda) [219]</td></tr>
<tr><td>O2. Ayi , pepani abwana.</td><td>O2. I am very sorry, Sir!</td></tr>
<tr><td>L. Ndikugwilabetu muno, kodi nzako uja wazemba, athawa?</td><td>L. I will convict you of more things here. [startled by the sudden disappearance of the other young man]: Has your companion disappeared? Has he run away?</td></tr>
<tr><td colspan="2">At this place in my recording the sing'anga and his clients are talking a few things in Mozambiquean Portuguese which unfortunately I do not anderstand, and could not therefore transcribe. Thereafter, the conversation continued normally In Chichewa. Paulo Luka wonders why the two people of the Mozambiquan group, a man and a woman who had come with complaints about adultery (chigololo) have suddenly disappeared, and he is asking the young man (O2) who was still standing in front of him.</td></tr>
<tr><td>L. Aja anabwela zachigololo aja, alikuti anthu aja?</td><td>L. The couple which came with their reports about adultery, where are they now?</td></tr>
<tr><td>O2 .Alipo anakakhala kutali.</td><td>O2. They are present. Bu they are just sitting down at a certain distance.</td></tr>
<tr><td>L. Tsopano inva bwino bwino, umandinena muja nkuti uli pati paja?</td><td>L. Now you! Listen carefully to my words! What is the exact place you were talking bad about me?</td></tr>
<tr><td>O2. Tikuoloka pa boda ya kuMozambique, pafupi ndi kuBiriwiri.220)</td><td>O2. It was when we crossed the border from Mozambique near Biriwiri[220]</td></tr>
<tr><td>L. Ineyo ndinalipo? Nanga siunagwidwe, pita ku chipatala cha ku Ntcheu amapanaga chabe.</td><td>L. Was I there?—And yet, haven't you been caught? So go to Ntcheu hospital, there they will treat you free of charge!</td></tr>
<tr><td>O2. Iyayi, pepani apo bwana zangolakwika.</td><td>O2. Oh no! I am sorry about that, Sir, those things have just got messed up.</td></tr>
<tr><td>L. Kodi aspirin ndi kapusozi 221) zimafanana?</td><td>L. Do you think that aspirin and antibiotics[221]</td></tr>
</table>

Luka of exploitation of his clients. Paulo, as is testified by the recorded conversation reacted with bitterness.

219 *uno ndi ntunda* is a common phrase of self-praise which was apparently coined originally by a *sing'anga* and is now also used by politicians, something like saying "I cannot be surpassed by anybody".

220 Biriwiri = a border-post near Ntcheu.

	resemble each other?
O2. Sizimagwilizana ayi.	O2. No. The two cannot be associated with each other.
L. Kapusozi chifukwa ngotani?	L. Antibiotics, because of what?
O2. Wodula.	O2. Because they are expensive.
L. Aspirini?	L. And Aspirin?
O2. Amakhala wotsika mtengo	O2. The price for Aspirin is low.
L. Utamwa kapusozi ngati uli ndi zilonda za mmimba sizipola?	L. If you have stomach ulcers, will they be cured after you have taken antibiotics?
O2. Zipola	O2. They will get cured.
L. Uyende ndi mtendele, koma uli ndi thembelelo m'bele wanga, uno ndi ntunda.	L. You should then go in peace, but you are under a curse (*thembelelo*) my brother! Myself I am top!

This conversation was to demonstrate the visionary power claimed by the *sing'anga* Paulo Luka, to know what his clients are talking about him on their way to his clinic. The young man (02) admitted that on the way to Paulo from Mozambique, he did have second thoughts about going to see him, saying to his companions that this *sing'anga* exploited his clients and depleted them of their cash. Consequently, Paulo then refused to give any help to the group. In the course of their conversation he was resentful, got even angry, and he interrogated the two young men as if they were delinquents. In addition, Paulo shouted out, in front of everybody, that according to his findings, the couple of husband and wife in the same group had really come to see him because the woman had been seduced by her husband's friend. Since everbody in the audience could hear this news, it caused considerable embarrassment to the couple.

Myself, I remained with the question how the young man might have felt in his heart, after he had to return his village without receiving any help. Instead he had only been told that the trouble which motivated him to arrive at the *sing'anga*'s place, was in fact that his wife had been cheating him with another man.

About the phials (*nsupa*) and Paulo Luka's *vidiyo*

(Summary of recorded interviews with Paulo Luka on October 6, 1995, tape no. 95/4/ side I, and our participant observations)

The information following here is a summary of research data gathered during our second visit beginning October 6, 1995. On the first day of this visit, Paulo Luka took me and my companion, Donald Kachamba, to various parts of his clinic and he allowed me to photograph his activities extensively, and also the objects he had collected from people he had identified as wizards and witches (see series of photographs). While Paulo explained to us some of these objects, Donald Kachamba recorded him.

Since there was much other interaction at the same time, visible in some of the photographs, and since we eventually became participant observers, when we were allowed to

[221] He says *kapusozi* (from engl. capsules), the common term in Chichewa to refer to antibiotics, because they come in capsules.

experience his *vidiyo* (!) I will not transcribe his explanations here literally from tape no. 95/4/ side 1, but instead present our data in the form of a narrative including my own thoughts and interpretations while we were on the spot.

First, Paulo Luka took us to a place in his clinic where he used to keep the witchcraft objects he had confiscated from some of his clients. (See photographs). He was keeping them in a big bag (*chithumba*), put them out one by one, placing them on a mat, or holding them in his hand, so that I could photograph while Donald recorded his explanations. All these objects were once in the possession of *amfiti* whom he had denounced, and all were once used as magical instruments to kill. We got an overview of the *amfiti*'s "weapons", such as horns (*nyanga*) (see photos 95/2/27, 29 and 96) The term *nyanga* refers quite generally to any lengthy object that is used to keep lethal substances (*chinthu chosungila mankhwala oopsya kuti aphe*), such as original animal horns – hence the origin of the term but nowadays also lengthy plastic bottles, as shown in photo no. 95/2/29.

Next he put out some of the *nsupa* (phials), originally always a small calabash (photo no. 95/2/21), and today also plastic containers of similar shape. He also showed us *afisi* (= " hyenas") which can be various objects; sometimes an animal tail (*nchila*) can have the function of a "hyena" (*nchila umakhoza kukhala fisi*). *Fisi* (hyena) is a common transformation employed by a wizard or witch. Then he showed a remarkable example of a wizard/witch's aeroplane (*ndege*) (see photo no. 95/2/28) which is used by the *amfiti* for dislocation, when they want to fly from one place to another, in order to bewitch a person who resides far away. Paulo Luka explained that the *amfiti* also had a "hiring service" (*hayala*). If a *mfiti* lacks transport to another area where he wants to kill his brother or perhaps make him sick (*kukapha kapena kukadwalitsa m'bale wawo*) he will be assisted by other *amfiti* who are in possession of flying facilities and he can hire their plane (*ndege*). If he wants to move quickly to a remote place he then asks someone with a plane. Paulo Luka continued to explain that there are many different kinds of witchcraft aeroplanes (*zilipo zamitundu-mitundu*). But the one which we saw and photographed (photo no. 95/2/28) was made from a tortoise shell (*chigabado cha kamba*).

Paulo also pulled out from his collection in the bag, the bones of children (*timafupa taana*). The *amfiti* dig out the corpse of a child from the grave, eat the flesh, and what remains – the bones -- they keep them for various uses in further witchcraft activities. Then Paulo told us again about the *dziphaliwali* (lightning) used by some wizards/witches and he began to mention his *vidiyo* which he was keeping in a certain house and through which his clients would actually see the witchcraft activities of some others going on in their home villages.

I became very curious about this *vidiyo.* I myself and Donald Kachamba wanted to find out what that was, but when I politely requested Paulo Luka to show it to us, we saw from his facial reaction that in his heart he was not very happy about our request. I had no idea why he was so reluctant, since he had always been so generous with us. Eventually, when we continued to bring up the issue of the *vidiyo*, he said: "All right, let us go so that you see some other people who are watching it right now, and get an idea what is going on there!"

We then entered a very small house, not subdivided into rooms; it was all just one room (*kunali kopanda chipinda komwe*). Inside there were some people sitting and gazing at a large yellow-brown paper which had been fastened on a wall of that room. The people were quiet, there was no sign that they were in any state of being possessed by spirits, and yet they all were seeing something on that *vidiyo* – the large khaki-brown paper, while neither my companion nor I was seen anything at all!

The eyes of three people whom we found inside were fixed on that "screen". When we asked them what they were seeing there, everyone explained what they were seeing; one of them said he was seeing a person standing next to a coffin ready for burial; anotherone said" I am seeing a certain mother whom I know from our home village sprinkling medicines on my veranda ", and the third person told us: " I am seeing a hyena running away with a child it has kidnapped (*ndikuona fisi akuthawitsa mwana*).

To our dismay, we saw nothing at all. We found that it was hard for us to believe everything what those people were saying; but we also had doubts about our own sanity. Was it perhaps we who were stupid? (*dzitsiru*) In our hearts we were overcome by the desire to see on that *video* what sort of witchcraft activities were going on in our village in Chileka, but we noticed that Paulo Luka somehow resisted to our desire for a personal experience of his *vidiyo*. Within a short while, he left us alone with those people inside the hut.

It gave us quite bit of worries that Paulo Luka apparently did not want us to learn the truth about his *vidiyo*. When we left the hut in search of Paulo in order to approach him once again with our desire, we heard from other people that he had already left his clinic and gone home! The time had run out, but we did not want to leave his place defeated, so we went back to the Ntcheu administrative post for finding a place in the local resthouse to stay overnight, with the aim of seeing Paulo Luka early next morning.

Next morning our thoughts had not changed that we wanted to experience that *vidiyo*, and then perhaps in the afternoon of that day return to Blantyre-Chileka. This was in our thoughts. But when we went to the *sing'anga*'s house, we received the surprising news, that he had left for Blantyre in the middle of the night, after certain people had come to fetch him. This startled us indeed. When we asked about his wife, we were told, that she was here, and had already left for the clinic (*chipatala*) of her husband. We knew of course, that the wife was involved in his medical practice, and that they helped each other; so we thought perhaps she might be willing to reveal to us the secret of seeing something on that khaki-brown paper.

At that stage we did not know why Paulo Luka did not want us to experience his *vidiyo*, and that behind it there was his fear, that we as research workers (not clients) might find the experience very uncomfortable, if we actually were subjected to the rite allowing us to experience the *vidiyo* like the others (*ngati ife tichitedi nawo mwambo wowonela nawo vidiyoyo*); we might have to stay in his clinic for two full days. In fact, everything that we had been told this morning, that some people had taken Paulo Luka to Blantyre in the middle of the night, eventually turned out to be a lie. He was seriously hoping that we would get tired waiting and leave the place, without the *vidiyo* experience.

However, he did not anticipate the determination of those young men we were! (*ife anyamata amakani*). Since we had decided to find out about the secret we went again to his clinic where we found his wife together with some boys who were helping her to administer medicines to their clients. We told her that we had already reached an agreement with her husband to let us experience the *vidiyo*, but since he was absent at that moment, what about her showing it to us, we asked! Without any hesitation the wife said: " All right" and that we should enter the little hut where the *vidiyo* was. Then she told her assistant that he should go and clean two small cups and come back with them into that hut. In the meantime a woman arrived in distress crying that her child had been caught last night by a hyena, when it was going outside to urinate; she wanted to know what was really behind it, expecting witchcraft, and so she also entered the little hut. Paulo Luka's wife was inside and we saw her with a certain plastic bottle, in which there was a whitish liquid, and she began to pour some of it into my cup, then some of it into Donald Kachamba's cup, then she drank some of it herself, probably to demonstrate that it was not poison, and finally she gave some of the liquid to the woman client who now shared the *vidiyo* hut with us. The substance looked like rice water and it reminded me of what we call in Chichewa *chisunje* or *chitiwi*, i.e. the water in which pounded maize is soaked (*kubviika*) and kept for some days until it gets soft, before spreading it out for drying. This water has a characteristic smell. What Paulo's wife gave us to drink had a smell that was somewhat similar. Each of us drank about 0.11 (one deciliter).

Thereafter she said that we should just remain quiet and look at the khaki-brown paper on the wall. We followed her instruction and stayed silent. The entrance to the hut was closed in order to block the disturbing daylight; it was now dim in the little hut, and soon there was not enough air, and also it was unbearably hot, while the eyes of the three of us were just gazing at the wall where that big paper was attached. After about 25 minutes we observed that the woman next to us who was in such distress began to shake violently, and talk various things in a manner that I began to ask her: " Are you fine? " She did not reply at all, and continued to talk things of her own.

After a short time I began to experience a state that was strange (*zachilendo*) with my head working as if I was drunk. And I began to discern things that seemed to pass across the paper (*zinthu zoyenda*). But no subjects such as people or anything in relation to our village. I asked Donald: "Have you started to see anything? " He replied: "Yes, I am beginning to see this and that, but my body is not in good shape, I want some water to drink." So I shouted, calling a person outside to bring some water, but the manner I shouted was as if my head was like that of a mad person (*munthu wamisala*). We began to ask ourselves, for how long this mental state of us would continue, and the answer was: we don't know.

Before we got as far as seeing those witchcraft things we had thought we would see, we decided to get out here, but what a surprise: we could hardly stand on our feet, we didn't get out of that hut walking but crawling, moving out on hands and feet like small children. That we should stand, even for a moment, was very difficult due to dizziness. When we had reached outside in the fresh air, we were only calling for drinking water; but the water they brought us, I had no idea what kind of water that was and where it came from. I think it was mere luck that we did not catch any serious infection.

We then tried simply to remain quiet, but experiences such as these were really alien to our lives. Donald Kachamba began to raise criticism about our field methods; he said:
"But we are idiots indeed! Why did we press for this sort of experience, while our host did not want us to get involved with this so-called video. If it had ended with our death, the people in our village would not even know where we had gone!" He continued to say

that the greatest foolishness was that we both drank the liquid at the same time, without a control person, leaving our car outside and our research equipment unattended.

Our drugged state continued for a long time, and I began to realize that it was already lunch time, and hunger began to hurt us. I tried to rise up from the ground and walk a bit, at least as far as the place where we had parked our car. Thereafter, Donald also arrived and I noticed that he was in much better shape than I, with a bit more of strength. At this point we tried to say good-bye to all the onlookers who had gathered to watch what we fools had done. It was very hard for me to get our car going because my hands to grasp the steering were too weak, even for any kind of operation. Eventually we drove away very carefully. As we proceeded, Donald said that it would be impossible to arrive in Chileka the same day; he proposed we should drive to Biriwiri store near Ntcheu to his former wife, Mrs. Hanna Kaukonde, eat something and even sleep there.

This was a wise proposal; so we set off there. She received us well, gave us clean water to drink, and something to eat. At that juncture I began to vomit terribly, in contrast to my partner who seemed to have supported that drug much better than I. The same day Donald resumed our reseaech (!) and made tape-recordings of story telling in his former wife's place. I was ill and exhausted. People in that place began to tell lots of unpleasant stories about that drug which Paulo Luka used to give his patients so that they would "see" on that "video" who had bewitched them or their relatives. Apparently the substance came from Mozambique, Paulo Luka's origin. It was impossible for us to find out what it was, but in any case our research was not pharmacological. We have checked Jessie Williamson's book on plants in Malawi, and so far not discovered any description of a substance that would match with our experience.

In the evening I began to feel better and think normally, but my stomach was still in an awful condition. We then slept at Hanna's place. Next morning we felt that we would be able to drive slowly back to our research base and home in Chileka. Now we knew why our host, the *sing'anga* Paulo Luka had not wanted us to drink that particular "medicine" (*mankhwala*) and why he seemed to run away from us when we insisted upon experiencing the *vidiyo.*

Obviously, Paulo's clients were convinced that the khaki-brown paper was a special video to allow them to watch those wizards and witches who had hurt them, at work. For me, however, the credibility of anybody who would say " I was watching such and such" on Paulo Luka's *vidiyo* had ended that day. We had experienced ourselves that it was only the power of that drug which produced that hallucinatory experience in the person's brain; and that all those things were in their thoughts. The result of our experience was simply my conviction that there were powerful mind-altering drugs, and that everything Luka's clients were believing to see actually took place in their own thoughts. But I know if I gave such a statement before the *sing'anga* Paulo Luka, he would vigorously deny it and accuse me of spreading lies with the intention of denigrating the good reputation of his medical practice (*kuipitsa dzina lawo la using'anga wabwino*), while my statement is simply based on my own experience of what happens to a person after consuming that substance.

The two people in their white gowns are the *sing'anga* Paulo Luka and his wife, helping each other in their work to uncover the troubles of the people who come to see them for consultation. They wear a kind of uniform with Christian symbols, all in white, upon which the names Yosefe and Petulo are written. The young man seen next to them is a client whom they consult. The problem with which he came for consultation was that another man had seduced his wife. Here, the *sing'anga* Paulo Luka and his wife explain to him everything that had taken place between his adulterous wife and that man.
– At Chipula village, T.A. Njolomole, Ntcheu District, October 6, 1995. – Photo no. 95/2/8, author.

Consultation of a husband and his wife with conjugal problems, expecting help from the *sing'anga*. Luka is seen in a stooped attitude listening to their complaints; holding his staff in his right hand, in his left the red cloth. Speaking aloud, so that others would hear everything, he explains to the couple their problem, that the husband beats his wife all the time. Eventually she confesses that she had sexual relations (*chigololo*) with another man whose name she reveals to be Njema; this was the man, she admitted, who was all the time after her. In the background of Paulo Luka's consulting room we can see another couple waiting to be attended.

At Chipula village, T.A. Njolomole, Ntcheu District, October 6, 1995. Photo no. 95/2/12, author.

Medicine to be rubbed into scarifications are those which many *asing'anga* rejoice to prescribe. Here we see a young man in Paulo Luka's clinic who has just scarified his father's right foot (*kuchekela*) and rubbed in medicines to cure the disease that has afflicted his legs. – At Chipula village, T.A. Njolomole, Ntcheu District, October 6, 1995. Photo no. 95/2/20, author.

This photograph shows the weapons (*zida*) of the wizards or witches (*amfiti*) which they use during the witch dance (*pokatamba*). In order to destroy a person whom they want to eat, they use a phial (*nsupa*) and medicine vessels (*kontena ya mankhwala*), and there is also an axe (*nkhwangwa*) and the wizards/witches' tail (*nchila*) for doing their work.
– At Chipula village, T.A. Njolomole, Ntcheu District, October 6, 1995. Photo no. 95/2/21, author.

The phial (*nsupa*) whose original owner was considered very dangerous; his name was Ncherewatha, and he was from Ntcheu. People said that with this phial he was able to see and take aim at any person he wanted to kill. Even if the person stayed far away he could still spot him. Thereafter he would tell his horns from a koodoo (*nyanga yawo ya ngoma*) to kill that person . – At Chipula village, T.A. Njolo-mole, Ntcheu District October 6, 1995. Photo no. 95/2/23, author.

This is a tortoise shell (seen from the inside) about which the *sing'anga* told me that it is the aeroplane of the wizards or witches, which they use for traveling far, even to South Africa, for the purpose of bewitching (*kukalodza*) a person. This particular shell comes from a certain type of tortoise. To prepare it for its purpose, the wizards or witches boil the shell in water together with medicines. – At Chipula village, T.A. Njolomole, Ntcheu District, October 6, 1995. Photo no. 95/2/24, author.

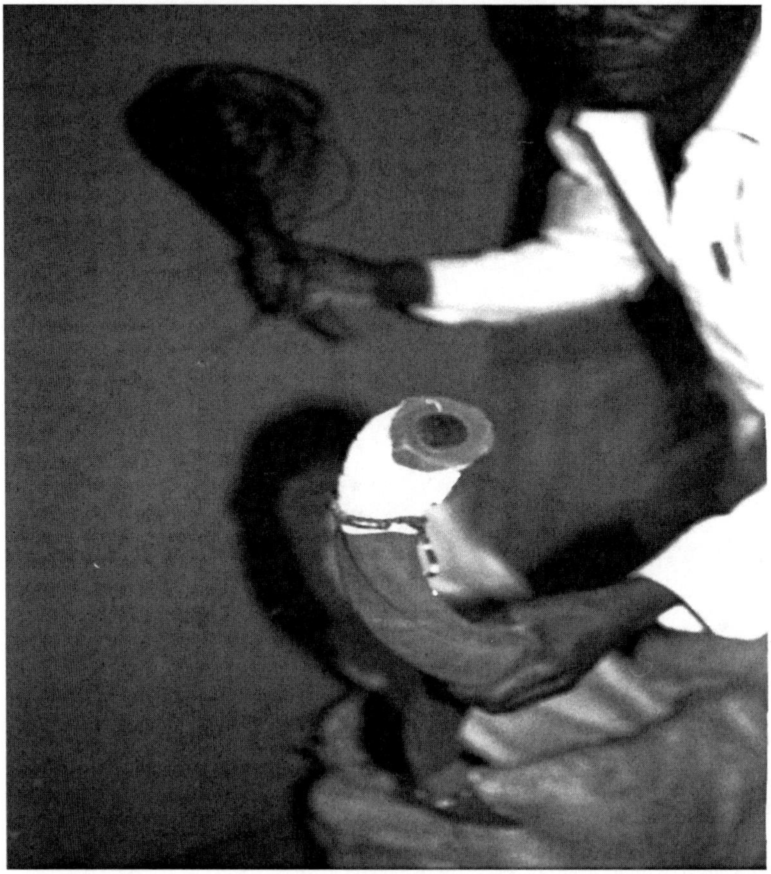

Here Paulo Luka is showing us a koodoo horn which is considered dangerous as it is used to bewitch people. The *mfiti*, he explained, stands at the wall of the house whose owner he wants to hurt, and he pierces the horn into it. He also holds the tail (*nchila*); both objects are used together for witchcraft. – At Chipula village, T.A. Njolomole, Ntcheu District, October 6, 1995. Photo no. 95/2/26, author.

This horn is dressed up like a woman with beads (*mikanda*) mixed with medicines (*kuphatika ndi mankhwala*). Inside the horn there are various types of medicines which help the wizard or witch to pierce the wall of a house and enter the house of the victim. – At Chipula village, T.A. Njolomole, Ntcheu District, October 6, 1995. Photo no. 95/2/27, author.

This is the top part of the shell with the eyes of the aeroplane painted on top of the shell. The owner of this "aeroplane" was a certain Mr. Ncherewatha, from Tsangano in the Ntcheu area. There was a real power struggle between the *sing'anga* Paulo Luka and that man, until the doctor recovered all the wizard's horns (*nyanga*) . The victor was Paulo Luka, he managed to get the culprit to the point that he submitted all his "horns" and the aeroplane. – At Chipula village, T.A. Njolomole, Ntcheu District, October 6, 1995. Photo no. 95/2/28, author.

These are yet other types of horns which were taken away fom Ncherewatha, a very dangerous wizard. In the bottle, Paulo Luka explained, there are dangerous substances such as poisons which the wizard makes his victim drink during the latter's sleep and next morning that person is dead. There is also a small object like a snake's head which the wizard puts on a woman's buttock so that she should not bear children; its work is to intercept the sperm of the man and throw it outside so that there should be no pregnancy. – Chipula village, T.A. Njolomole, Ntcheu District, October 6, 1995. – Photo no. 95/2/29, author.

Za using'anga and *ufiti* in public perception

In Malawi the incident of witchcraft practice is extremely common, but because of geographical distance between the people in different parts of the country and poor communication in rural areas most people never get to know what is happening elsewhere. Some of the most surprising and strange events therefore occur unnoticed by the wider public. And also, in most people's perception the news about witchcraft is nothing to be laughed about, but it is bad news; indeed in those places where things concerning witchcraft happen, the result may be serious social disturbance (*phokoso*) and even violence (*ndeu)* between those accusing each other. When it gets to that point, then it also touches upon the work of the police because of their task of defending law and order (*chitetezo*) and prevent the people in the country to hurt each other. Therefore, whenever it occurs in a village that someone was bewitched (*walodzedwa*) and dies, and serious disturbance results from this, then the news about it also reaches the police. It is here that the police begin to investigate the matter on their own (*kufufuza kwawo*) in order to learn what really happened. In other cases it may be that a person suspected of having practised magic (*zamatsenga*) is taken to a *sing'anga* to establish whether he or she is guilty or not.

When this happens the result is that the police would also compile a lot of information about the designs of wizards or witches, and the work of the *asing'anga* in certain places. Some of the most unusual events have therefore been recorded by the police, and some of these are printed in the *Malawi Police Magazine* which is the official magazine of the Malawi Police, appearing four times a year. Of course, it is not the purpose of this magazine only to produce articles about that particular subject; it is a magazine that covers a wide range of affairs that concern the police and the general public. And yet, because the articles on any subject are factual, and sometimes analytical, it is a formidable source of information also for the cultural anthropologist who is interested in depth analysis of people's lives, their thoughts and their emotional problems.

Cover design of the Malawi Police Magazine
(reproduction)

Fig. 4

MALAWI POLICE magazine

CONTENTS

Published under the authority of the Inspector General of Police
The Opinions expressed in this Magazine are those of the contributors and are not necessarily shared by the Editorial Board or Police Authorities
The Editor
Malaŵi Police Magazine
Private Bag 305
Capital City
Lilongwe 3

EDITORIAL

THANKS TO POMA CONTRIBUTORS AND READERS

That the Malaŵi Police Magazine was voted Number One in the Magazine category of the 1989 Entertainers of the Year was, and definitely still is, a most welcome occurrence. It is as much an encouragement, indeed, because it goads us to go on; a challenge, undoubtedly, in that it is, as it were, an acid test of our capability to again win Number One position this year (1990).

It is worth noting, not at all the less, that if the Malaŵi Police Magazine won the first place in 1989, it was, to a greater extent, because of the quality of its contents or items which, consequently, won the hearts of the readers. Those quality contents or items were contributed by many people. To those people or contributors, much is owed by the Magazine which is equally indebted to its enthusiastic readers.

May we, in conclusion, appeal to you all to continue or begin contributing to POMA as many entertaining or informative, as well as educative, articles as you possibly can in order to make the Magazine as live as ever. It is, do remember, your magazine.

Editor

COVER PICTURE:
The Malaŵi Police Orchestra in action.

Page 1 of a 1990 number of the Malaŵi Police Magazine with Editorial

The Police Magazine is one of the most popular magazines in Malawi; when a new number appears it is quickly sold out, because of strong public interest in criminal cases, including cases of witchcraft and sorcery. One reason for this enormous interest is that people in Malawi are generally apprehensive of witchcraft, and many would like to know more about what exactly wizards and witches do. Since the Police Magazine is not only sold to policemen, but is available to the general public, containing articles in English or Chichewa, it is very much liked.

Nowadays there has also come up what can be summarized as investigative journalism. There are many reporters employed these days by the great number of Malawian newspapers which have appeared since 1992, trying to find out about things of public importance, and uncover secrets. They also have interest in knowing something about witchcraft and healing practices in the country. I have already given some examples in this book how journalists have published news about certain witchcraft events in the press. It also happens that an investigative journalist actually meets someone who admits having been a wizard or witch and asks the person what he or she was doing at that time and how he or she was feeling about it.

All this has led to an explosion of the popular literature about the subject of witchcraft, sorcery and healing practice. It is very much in the mind of the public, and there is now a vast amount of reports on *asing'anga* and particularly witchcraft cases found in local publications in Malawi, such as newspapers, magazines etc., and also there are archival sources. A particularly important source is the various reports about legal cases involving witchcraft, and investigations carried out by the police.

I have been able to probe a good deal into the literature written in Malawi, found in the National Library and in private collections. Here I would like to express my special gratitude to Mr. Waliko Makhala, Producer at Television Malawi, who gave me worthwhile contacts to archives of newspaper companies, and also to the Malawi Information Department. In 1998 during a sojourn at home I have been able to photocopy many of those materials. But the material is so copious that its evaluation would constitute a book within this book!

Since the emphasis of the present book is on the results of my personal work in the field, I will therefore throw only a few highlights into the discussion selected from those reports in the media about witchcraft cases. These examples may serve as a preliminary account of the newspaper and magazine coverage of the subject in Malawi, supplementing the results of my own fieldwork.

(1) Comment on Oliver A.Z. Soko: "Agwidwa ufiti atapezeka ndi malemu" Police Magazine, Second Quarter, 1989: 36

In 1989 the Police Magazine in the section called *Nkhani zakumudzi* (News from the village) published the story of a youngster, aged 18, Moffat Benson Banda, from Kamonga village, T.A. Kaphuka, in Dedza District, who was caught because of practising witchcraft. On March 29, 1989 he admitted to the investigating reporter that he was a *mfiti* and that in 1986 he had killed (by witchcraft) his biological mother Nalitchowa Gosito, and on January 23, 1989 the young sister of his mother, Filinesi Gosito. He told the police reporter that he had started witchcraft practice when he was nine years old, and that his teachers in witchcraft had been his maternal uncle (*malume*), Mr. Barley Gosito together with his grandfather in the female lineage, Mr. Pearson Banda.

The report says that the boy was taught witchcraft by those two through coercion; and that they threatened him that if he did not carry out their wishes or revealed the secret of their witchcraft, he would die. Eventually the two men instigated Moffat to kill his mother because she had denied them *thobwa* (a drink of refreshment) which was for sale, and not for free, and which she used to sell at the roadside.

- 217 -

NKHANI ZAKUMUDZI

AGWIDWA UFITI ATAPEZEKA NDI MALEMU

Wolemba: Oliver A. Z. Soko

Mnyamata wogwidwa ufiti ndi ameneyu

Moffat Benson Banda ndi mnyamata wa zaka khumi ndi zisanu ndi zitatu (18) zakubadwa, ndipo amachokera pa mudzi wa Kamonga, mfumu yaikulu Kaphuka m'boma la Dedza pafupi ndi pa Tete ndipo popita kwaoko amadzera njira yopita kwa Lobi.

Pa 29 Marichi, chaka chonchino, Moffat adatsimikizira mtolankhani wathu zoti iye ndi mfiti ndipo adapha mayi wake omubereka, mayi Nalitchowa Gosito m'chaka cha 1986 pamodzi ndi mayi ake ang'ono mayi Filinesi Gosito pa 23 January, 1989.

Ufiti adayamba ali zaka zisanu ndi zinayi zakubadwa, ndipo amene adam'phunzitsa ufitiwo ndi amalume ake bambo Barley Gosito ndi agogo ake akuchikazi a Pearson Banda omwe amatchuka ndi dzina Loti a Ntchona m'mudzi wa Kamonga mboma la Dedza. Moffat adaphunzitsidwa ufiti ndi anthu aŵiriŵa mokakamizidwa ndipo adamuopsyeza kuti ngati iye sadzapanga zofuna za anthu aŵiriŵo kapena ngati adzaulula chizimba chaufiti wao, nthaŵi yomweyo Moffat adzafa.

Kenaka azibambo aŵiriŵa adaumiliza Moffat kuti aphe mayi wake chifukwa adawamana thobwa logulitsa. Mayi Nalitchowa, ankagulitsa thobwa pa msewu wopita kwa Nkhwewu, pomwe ankatolapo logulira sopo ndi mchere. Ndipo mayi Filinesi anali odzipereka pa ntchito ya ulimi wa chimanga ndi ndiwo zaku dimba zomwe zinkaŵapatitsa ndalama zokwanira ndinso chakudya chokwanira pakhomo pawo.

M'chaka cha 1986 Moffat adaphadi mayi wake omubereka mayi Nalitchowa kupyolera ku matenda a mutu wa litsipa.

Chodabwitsa chinali choti, tsiku loyika maliro litakwana, kudapezeka kuti mayiwo ankakodzabe mikodzo ngakhale anali atafa ndipo pamene adagonaponso panali chithaphwi cha mikodzo.

Amalume a Moffat bambo Manyondola Gosito adapita kwa sing'anga Magombo wa mudzi mwa Nyankhwi yemwe ndi otchuka kwambiri pa ntchito yake. Sing'angayo adaulula kuti amene adapanga zimenezo ndi anthu atatu aja; a Barley, a Pearson ndi Moffat. Iwo adaonekera pa galasi atavala ziguduli m'chiuno ali maliseke ndikumazungulira nyumba ya mayi Nalitchowa.

Moffat ataona zoti waululidwa ndi sing'angayo adathawira ku Ntchisi kwa Chisonga komwe adakalowa ntchito yolima fodya kwa bambo Sulamoyo. Adagwira ntchitoyi kwa zaka ziŵiri. Kenaka pamalopo padagwa matenda a kaodzera, Moffat adawauza bambo Sulamoyo kuti iye ankadziwa mankhwala anthendayo ndipo adatemera anthu onse apa mudzipo. Chizimba chake chinali choti; ngati wina afuna kutuluka ali maliseke, ankati adzaona chomwe chidameta nkhanga mpala. Poona kuti adawanamiza anthuwo adaganiza zothawa.

Kumayambiliro a chaka cha 1988. Moffat adabwerera kwao ndipo anthu atamufunsa za kafedwe ka mayi wake kaja, iye adakanitsitsa kwantu wa galu kuti sindiye amene adapha a mayi ake.

Moffat sanasiyebe ufiti pamodzi ndi azimalume ake aŵiri aja, (Barley ndi Pearson). Iwowa ankayenda pa ndege usiku popita kukatamba ndipo zonsezi Moffat sanaulure, ngakhale mapangidwe a ndege yawoyo kudzanso mmene ankatambila.

A Barley ndi a Pearson adauza Moffat kuti aphenso mayi ake aang'ono a Filinesi Gosito m'matsenga, chifukwa choti mayiwo sankawagawira zokolola zawo. Ankati akawapha m'matsenga mayiwo adzakhalabe moyo koma m'matsenga momwemo. Izi zidachitikadi pa 24 January,

Aphunzitsi a mnyamatayu ndi omwe muku ŵawonaŵa

36 Police Magazine, Second Quarter, 1989

Moffat then killed his mother, Nalitchowa, by transmitting to her a disease of serious headache at the side of the skull called *mutu wa litsipa. Litsipa* is translated by Scott and Hetherwick (1929 (1970): 243) as " swelling of the temple vein".

But the startling thing which happened was at the end of the day of her death. When the corpse was kept in the mortuary, people noticed that she was still urinating, though she was supposed to be dead. There was a pool of urine at the place where the body was on display.

After this had happened, another maternal uncle of Moffat went to a famous *sing'anga* in the area, Magombo who uncovered through divination that those guilty of witchcraft practice were three people, Barley, Pearson and Moffat (see also the photograph of them taken by the reporter, in the article, page 36). The *sing'anga* discovered them when they appeared in his mirror (*galasi*) as they were circling the house of their victim, all of them naked, only wearing a loincloth (*ziguduli*) round their hips. When Moffat realized what had been discovered by the medical practitioner he ran away to the area of Chisonga in Ntchisi District, where he began to work on the tobacco farm of a certain person called Sulamoyo. He stayed there for two years. When there was an outbreak of sleeping sickness (*matenda a kaodzera*) in the area, Moffat told his boss that he knew medicines to treat that disease, and he scarified everybody there. He told those workers whom he scarified, rubbing in medicine, that one condition (*chizimba*) that his medicines would work was this: never in their lives should any of them step out of their houses naked during the night (if for example they wanted to urinate). If they did so they would see for themselves "what shaved off the feathers of a guinea-fowl" (*chomwe chidameta nkhanga mpala*). With this metaphor the boy wanted to warn them that they would encounter bad things if they did not observe his interdiction. However, when it turned out that he had only deceived the people, and in view of the fact that his boss had paid him for the whole operation, he had no choice but run away.

At the beginning of 1988 he then returned to his village where he was instantly asked by the villagers about the circumstances of the mysterious death of his mother. He denied any involvement "like a dog's head" (*kwantu wa galu*), but secretly he had not stopped witchcraft at all. The story then goes on how his witchcraft teachers, Barley and Pearson, had told him, also to kill the young sister of his mother, Mrs. Filinesi Gosito, by magic, because she had not shared with them her harvest.

These extracts of the story which I have translated, will suffice to give the reader an impression of the manner in which the subject is treated in a popular magazine like that, in fact, in very great detail, giving names and dates of observations. Successful police investigators seem to work like trained anthropologists doing field-work. This particular writer, Oliver A.Z.Soko, whom I know personally and who is now a spokesman of the Malawi Police also often uses metaphors (*miyambi*). Thus, these reports do not only give Chichewa-speaking readers interesting and thrilling stories, but quite often they also constitute fascinating Chichewa literature, hardly known outside the country.

(2) Comment on Anon. :"Gogo aphunzitsa zidzukulu zake ufiti", Police Mgazine, Third Quarter, 1990: 39

GOGO APHUNZITSA ZIDZUKULU ZAKE UFITI

Izi ndi zidzukulu zomwe zimaphunzitsidwa ufiti. (Pix. C.I.D. Chikwawa)

Awa ndi womwe amaphunzitsa anao ufiti. (Pix. C.I.D. Chikwawa)

Masiku apitawa a bambo Alick Chona adakadandaula ku polisi yaku Chikwawa chifukwa choti mayi awo adaphunzitsa ufiti ana awo.

Bambo Alick Chona a zaka 45 zakubadwa omwe amachokera m'mudzi mwa Msomo kwa Ngabu ku Chikwawa adakwatira kufupi ndi kwawo komweko koma amakhala ndi banja lawo ku mudzi kwawo komweko osati kuchikamwini.

A Chona adayamba kudandaula chaka chatha cha 1989. Zidafika poipa penipeni pamene adayamba kuona malodza osiyanasiyana pa nyumba pawo. Mwana wawo wang'ono adamwalira pa 1 Januare chaka chomwe chino. Mwambo wa maliro utatha anadabwa kumva mwana wawo wamkulu Maria wazaka 13 akuseŵera ndi anzake akunena kuti amalephera kudya nyama ya mwana amene adafayo. Bambo akewo atamufunsa mwanayo pa zomwe ankayankhulazo sadanene kanthu ayi adangozolika mutu pansi.

Patapita masiku ambiri mkazi wa bambo Chona adayamba kudwala. Usiku atagona bambo Chona adalota ana awo onse asanu akuseŵera panja pa nyumba yawo uku kunali kuseŵera koopsa chifukwa anawo ankaulukauluka mozungulira nyumba yawoyo. Komanso anawo ankapangana zoti aphe mayi wawo kapena kumupundula maso kuti asamapenye.

M'mawa kutacha matenda a mkazi wa bambo Chona adakula. Tsono poganizira za maloto aja bambo Chona adasonkhanitsa ana ake onse aja ndi kuwafunsa mmodzimmodzi ngati ankadziwapo kanthu za matenda a mayi awowo. Wanawo adakana ponena kuti sakudziwapo kanthu. Koma patapita nthaŵi wanawo adayamba mmodzimmodzi kuulula zoti anali mfiti ndipo mayi wawowo amafuna kumupha potumidwa ndi gogo wawo mayi awo a bambo Chona (mayi Liviness Benard).

A Chona omwe amakhulupirira Chauta kupyolera mpingo wa Zioni akuti kuyambira nthaŵi imeneyo adayamba kuwapempherera anawo kuti asiye ufitiwo koma ayi sizinatheke. Mmalo mwake anawo sankasamala mayi wawoyo ngakhale akamadwala. Akuti nthaŵi zina ankawalonjeza bambo wawowo kuti asiya kulodza mayiyo koma akuti ankangochira tsiku limodzi lokha tsiku lina kuyambanso kudwala.

Bambo Chona adayesa kukamba ndi mayi wawo (mayi Liviness) kuti achotse zidzukulu zawo ufiti koma mayiyo ankalonjeza kuti awachotsa koma ayi ndithu sizinatheke.

Malinga ndi momwe anawo ankalongosolera akuti usiku kukada gogoyo amawatenga ulendo wopita nawo kokatamba. Potambapo akuti amayamba asanduka zirombo zosiyanasiyana. Mariya mwana wa zaka 13 ndipo woyamba m'banja la bambo Chona akuti ankasanduka galu, Lute ng'ono wake ankasanduka mbalame ya mtundu wa kadzidzi. Rozina amasanduka buluzi. Zefania amasanduka mphaka ndipo Ezara amasanduka nyani.

Mayi Liviness adauza a polisi kuti iwo pophunzitsa wanawo amakhala ndi chidzukulu chawo china Bichi Chona mwana wa akulu awo a bambo Alick Chona. Iwo adati adaphunzitsa anawo kutamba, kulodza wanthu khaya kuti afe kapena kuti angodwala chabe amauluka ndi ndege ya ufiti usiku kumapita ku manda ndi malo ena alionse.

Bambo Chona adafotokozera apolisiwo kuti iwo adayesetsa kupita kwa asing'anga osiyanasiyana kuti akachotsetse anawo ufiti koma amati akawachotsa lero pakatha masiku pang'ono mayi wawowo amawabwezeretsanso ufitiwo. Ichi ndi chifukwa chake adaganiza zoti apite ku polisi kuti awathandize powalangiza mayi wawowo kuti asiye khalidwe lake lophunzitsa ana awo ufiti.

Pongowathandiza chabe bambo Chona, a Polisi adauza mfitizo (mayi Liviness Benard ndi Bichi Chona) kuti akabwerera kunyumba akachotse anawo ufitiwo ndipo ngati adzabwerezanso kuchita za ufitiwo adzaona chomwe chidameta nkhanga mpala. Apolisiwo adalangiza wanthu aŵiriwo kuti nawonso asiye ufitiwo.

This report, by an unidentified investigator of the C.I.D. (Chikwawa Criminal Investigation Department, Chikwawa) is about the case of two grandmothers who were convicted teaching their grandchildren witchcraft. A certain man, Alick Chona, about 45 years old from Msomo village near Ngabu in Chikwawa District had married close to his village, but then the couple had opted for a virilocal marital residence avoiding that the man would be under the rule of his wife's family (*osati kuchikamwini*).

One day in 1990 Alick Chona went to the police in Chikwawa to file a complaint that his mother was teaching witchcraft to his children. He reported that already in 1989 he had witnessed several incidents of witchcraft; his small child had died on January 1 of that year. But when the funeral ceremony was over he was very surprised to hear his elder child Maria, aged 13, while she was playing with her peers, saying that she "had failed to eat the meat of the child which had died." He then asked his daughter for an explanation, but she did not give any reply, and only hung her head downwards. Many days thereafter, the wife of Mr. Chona began to fall ill. In the night Chona was dreaming that all his five remaining children were playing outside their house, but they were playing a frightening game, because they were flying (!) round their house. And also, those children were acting out a game of killing their mother, maiming her eyes so that she should not be able to watch them.

When the man woke up in the morning he found that the sickness of his wife had increased. Thinking of his dream, he summoned his children and asked them one by one what they knew about the illness of his wife. They declined, saying that they knew nothing. But after some time they began to confess one by one that they were *amfiti* and intended to kill their mother by order of their grandmother, Mrs. Liviness Bernard, mother of their father, Alick Chona.

Chona was a member of the Zionist church (*mpingo wa Zioni*). At first he tried to pray for his children, so that they would leave witchcraft. But it did not work. They did not help their mother, and though they promised their father to renounce witchcraft, they continued even a day after their promise. Mr. Chona also tried to talk to his mother that she should remove the witchcraft from his children, but his mother also only promised to do so, never keeping her promise. According to what the children related, their grandmother used to take them on a trip during the night in order to dance the witches' dance (*kokatamba*). At the dance there they would transform into various animals. Maria, aged 13, who was the first-born, said that she would turn into a dog, Lute her smaller sister would turn into an owl (*kadzidzi*), Rozina would turn into a lizard, Zefania into a cat and Ezara into a baboon.

The grandmother, Mrs. Liviness Bernard, eventually told the police that when she taught those children witchcraft she was assisted by another grandchild of hers, a daughter named Bibi Chona of the elder brother of Alick Chona. They both taught the smaller children the dance of *kutamba* and how to bewitch people so that they would either die or just get sick. They used to fly with their "witchcraft aeroplane "(*ndege ya ufiti*) in the night, proceeding to the graveyard and to other places where they wanted to go.

Mr. Alick Chona explained to the police that he had tried to consult various *asing'anga* to remove the witchcraft power from his children, but whenever that was done his mother restored their witchcraft. It was because of that he had thought of contacting the police. The police then issued a warning to Mrs. Liviness Benard and Mrs. Bichi Chona.

****

****

What is particularly interesting in the two cases I have cited from the Malawi Police Magazine is the consanguine relationship between the people involved in the aggressive practice of witchcraft.The examples demonstrate where tensions are found in that particulars society with a matrilineal social organization. In both cases teenagers, even children had been taught to carry out witchcraft designs by adults. In the case reported by Oliver A.Z.Soko (1989:36) a boy aged eighteen had been coerced by his maternal uncle to kill his own mother which of course, was that uncle's sister. A second uncle then appears as a savior helping to uncover his brother's viciousness. But one more person in the family was involved: the biological father of both women who were killed by the boy, the boy's mother and her sister.

The situation can be shown in a diagram (fig. 5)

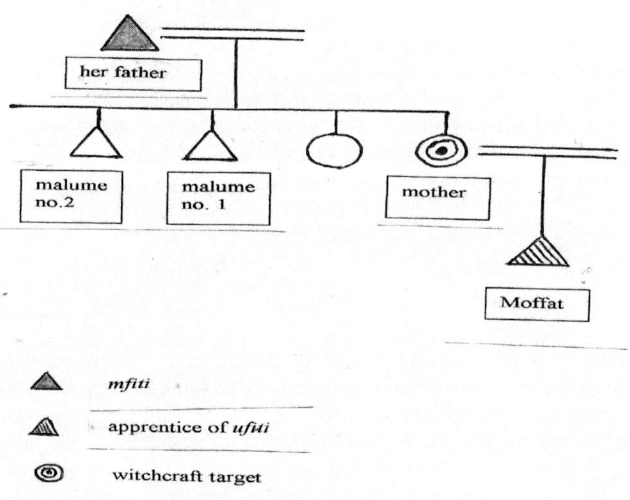

The question arising from this is why did those wizards, the woman's father and her brother not kill her directly, why did they train an intermediary to do so?

I can only offer a guess, but perhaps I am right. First, we have to know that wizards also have their own laws and rules (*lamulo lawo*). For example, they cannot kill without any provocation, i.e. some kind of disagreeable behaviour towards them by their victim; in this particular case both women had denied them drinks or food. And certain forms of behaviour may be prohibited to do, also for a wizard, such as coming physically too close to a relative who for one of them was a daughter, for the other a sister. It could also be that she was much protected by medicines against her father and her brothers. So, when they tried to enter her house as wizards, or come close to her, they failed (*ana-lephera*). By contrast, a child is close to his mother. The boy was free to enter his mother's house and it was easy for him to deposit the witchcraft medicine. So the wizards trained him as a proxy.

In the second case, that about Alick Chona (reported in Malawi Police Magazine 1990:39) we are introduced to another potential area of social conflict. Here it is the man's biological mother who – in cooperation with a daughter of the man's elder brother conspires to kill her son's wife. Once again the evil design is to be carried out indirectly, through intermediaries, by involving her grandchildren. Two key facts illustrate the suble relationships which probably developed between those involved, leading to aggressive designs: (a) that the man, contrary to usual custom, did not opt for uxorilocal marital residence, but undertook what is called *chitengwa,* i.e. taking the wife to his village (cf. Kubik/Malamusi1987:8 and (b) that the possibly close relationship by the man and his mother was leading to jealousy between the *apongozi* (mother-in-law versus daughter-in-law) reinforced by a tense relationship between his wife, as a stranger in the village, and the daughter of his elder brother.

(3) Comment on Times Reporter: "No social class at Chisupe's clinic" Daily Times, Monday, March 20, 1995

This is a report about a *sing'anga*, Billy Chisupe, who in 1995, managed to attract scores of people to the village where he practised, Chikamana, in Machinga District. He claimed that he was able to cure AIDS (Acquired Immune Deficiency Syndrome). The reporter describes the circumstances in the *sing'anga*'s clinic as "filthy"and states that Chisupe seems to have united behind him the people of Malawi more than the country's president ever managed. Chisupe also claimed that his concoction was able to strengthen the "immune system against the virus."

The English-Language report cited is rather superficial. There are many more reports in the press in Chichewa, and some that are quite instructive, also showing Chisupe's picture (cf. for example Mphuthu 1995, and an anonymous report in *Tikambe*, March 24-31, 1995) . I myself visited the place in February 1995. I was unable, however, to get access to the *sing'anga*, due to the crowds of people who were trying to obtain his medicines. Although the story about Billy Chisupe had only begun to be heard in Malawi at the end of 1994, by February 1995 everyone in the country knew about him, even in neighbouring countries. The news was that Chisupe gave his patients a liquid medicine that would cure AIDS and also make the virus disappear from the bloodstream of those who had tested seropositive. This news was stirring a lot of excitement across the country. People, even from far, began to flock to that place, until Chisupe was simply unable to attend to all of them. The liquid was given orally. The local administration intervened in order to control those crowds, providing them with basic needs, such as sending containers (*migolo*) to store hectoliters of the medicine, guaranteeing an orderly distribution. Social workers were sent and even road workers were employed to improve the track leading to the *sing'anga*'s place, so that motor vehicles could pass more easily. Among many organizations involved was the Malawi Red Cross providing tents especially for many sick people who arrived every day. Some commercial companies brought their employees in their own vehicles to drink the miracle medicine for their future protection against infection with the virus. The famous medicine began to be known under the name *Nchape,* a word that comes from verb *kuchapa* = to wash, to clean up. The psychologically interesting idea behind the choice of this term was that the body of those who drank the medicine would be "washed up" and full-fledged AIDS or just the virus (*kachirombo*, literally: the little animal) removed.

But the name *Nchape* is old. It was already heard in the 1930s in a different context. In 1930 a *sing'anga* appeared in the country who distributed medicine to those whom he identified as wizards or witches, and they died thereafter (see also S.A. Paliani 1971).

About his anti-AIDS medicines, the *sing'anga* Chisupe says that he discovered it all in a dream. He was dreaming that such and such a tree had substances that were able to cure AIDS. Then he gave those medicines experimentally to people to drink. However, there was no hard evidence, that people would get cured because of that medicine. At the time it was not known what really pushed so many people to go there; but soon thereafter the crowds began to diminish, and not much later, the *sing'anga* Chisupe died.

LOCAL

No social class at Chisupe's 'clinic'

Times Reporter

HE IS ABOUT six feet tall lanky. He has no shoes on his feet and in temperatures above 30 degrees celcius he is wearing a grey cardigan on top of a light-blue shirt. As he goes round the meandering queues of human souls his clients nod and whisper to each other "That's him".

This is Billy Chisupe, the man who will no doubt replace his home district man and the country's first citizen Bakili Muluzi as 'man of the year' for 1995.

An estimated 100,000 people are believed to have visited him at his Chikamana Village, Machinga,since August last year, to partake of what is believed to be the answer to the people's health problems, Aids in particular.

Everyday vehicles of all makes and sizes rush to Chikamana ferrying anxious souls. At Chisupe's 'clinic' both the poor and the rich are treated equally as each clutch their plastic cups from which they drink the concoction.

At Chisupe's 'clinic' there is no social class as all clients have to stand on the queue in sweltering heat. They have no choice but to inhale lungfuls of dust and air pregnant with urine and feaces, as they patiently wait on the queue for their turn.

Honourables,(even some from neighbouring countries?) too, are believed to have found themselves in this filthy environment.

If there is one man who has truly united the people of this land in these days of political turbulence it is no other than Billy Chisupe. At Chisupe's clinic people forget who or what they are in society. They forget their poverty and riches; they forget about hygiene and sanitation. Chisupe has become so important to people's lives such that even unbelieving company chief executives have been forced to release their employees, in some cases give them and their families transport or bus fares, to enable them to travel to Chikamana village.

No chief executive would dare refuse people from going to Chikamana village, not if he wants his job.

The crowds that flock to Chikamana village is enough evidence of how scared people are of Aids because only about less than five per cent of Chisupe's clients go to his 'clinic' because they are ill. The majority who flock to the 'clinic' are plysically strong people. But they go there just in case.

Chisupe claims that his drug not only cures Aids but that it also forms an immune system against the virus.

So far government has not yet recognised Chisupe's drug as an effective Aids cure.

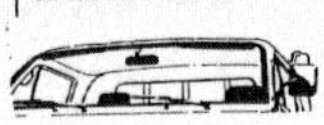

MAP warns of 'poverty alleviators'

THE MALAWI Against Polio says thats it recently handed over to Limbe Police a man who was found soliciting funds for a sponsored walk "purpotedly organised by the organisation (MAP)."

A press release from MAP says that the organisation is not at the moment organising any sponsored walk. It further says should MAP organise one or any event, the public will be advised through the media.

"Any person trying to get money in the name of MAP is therefore cheating and should be reported to the nearest police," the release says.

The man whom MAP handed over to police was found soliciting funds in offices. His identity was not disclosed.

As it has happened in the past (see the popularity of the *sing'anga* Chikanga Chunda in Rumphi District, Northern Malawi in 1962, Kubik in: Soko 2002; field–notes Moya A. Malamusi/Lidiya Malamusi/ Boston Soko/Gerhard Kubik in 1987) there are, from time to time epidemics of mass movements following a traditional healer who comes up with promises of a miraculous cure. Many historical examples could be cited from south-east Africa alone. The tumultuous events around Billy Chisupe are an instructive recent example.

(4) Comment on: Pilirani Kachinziri: "Sowa – the witchcraft apprentice", Malawi News, December 20-26, 1997: 9

The story of the twelve-year old Sowa Kabango, from Mizenje village, T.A. Kapeni, about 10 km west of Blantyre (in direction of Lunzu) created much feelings of sympathy in the general public. After his maternal uncle, Mr. Dominic Kabango, a businessman, had died mysteriously in December 1997, the news spread that the boy had been coerced into witchcraft apprenticeship by his grand-mother. The uncle was the sixth person in the family to die within a short time.

At the funeral of the uncle, Sowa confessed in front of journalists that he and five other witches and wizards were responsible for his death and that of several other relatives. However, he insisted that he had refused to kill his uncle. As a result, he was expelled from the club of *amfiti*. Now he wanted to quit witchcraft and lead a normal life. But he was in danger, he said, because both the witches and the relatives (mourning their losses), were threatening him.

He assured the journalists that what the people had just buried was merely a banana chunk instead of the corpse of his uncle! And that his uncle was still alive, but as a captive of those wizards and witches. He said, that through the power of his own witchcraft which was still in him, he could actually see his uncle as he was being forced by the witches to eat *nsima* (hard porridge) with human flesh as relish (*ndiwo*). Whenever his uncle refused to eat he was beaten. Sowa said that his uncle was wearing the same clothes into which the mourners had dressed him, putting the body into the mortuary. But his uncle was surprised that everybody was mourning. He was talking to Sowa asking him to tell his wife to cook for him *nsima* together with cassava leaves so that he could eat something secretly. When Sowa told his uncle that people were thinking he had died, the uncle laughed.

It was at that point that I got involved into the matter as a participant researcher (see also the reference in the last three paragraphs of Kachinziri's article, 1997:9). This is a long story – my field notes in Chichewa are eight typed pages – so I will only give a summary here, without touching on the complex relationships within the family of the businessman Kabango and his nephew Sowa. An important motif of the witches and wizards was jealousy. Dominic Kabango's own uncle, of course, was his biological mother's brother. Jealousy arose when Dominic's maternal uncle died and left a lot of property behind which his nephew inherited. Dominic's own mother decided to kill her son; but apparently there was no way, so here again as in other cases an innocent proxy, Sowa, Dominic's nephew, was used.

Sowa was a child staying with his maternal uncle whom he addressed *bambo* (father). The reason was that his mother had died long ago, and his biological father was never seen. Witchcraft was implanted into his body by his grandmother (the mother of his *malume*, maternal uncle) when he was very small. He remained totally unaware of the fact that he had witchcraft power and that someone else, the mother of his father, used him for her aims. She taught *ufiti* to her grandson (*nzukulu*) without the latter knowing about it (*sanadziwe*).

MALAWI NEWS DEC.20 –26,1997 9

Sowa – the witchcraft apprentice

By
Pilirani Kachinziri

SOWA Kabango 12 is regretting. He was taught witchcraft by his grandmother at a tender age a couple of years ago and now he wants to finally quit after bewitching a lot of people in his village.

The Standard 3 child who failed the final term exam has bewitched a lot of people including his relations at Mizenje Village, Traditional Authority Kapeni which lies 10 kilometres from the commercial city Blantyre .

Sporting unkempt hair, the soft spoken and light-skinned Sowa confessed before a team of journalists at his uncle's funeral that together with other five witches and wizards they were responsible for the mysterious death of some of his relations. But he refused to participate in bewitching his uncle, a businessman Dominic Kabango, who mysteriously died last week after a short illness.

Sowa has therefore been stricken off from the witches list in that area. Malawi News learnt that Kabango is the sixth person to die in his family of eight.

Three of the people two men and one elder woman, who were implicated by Sowa in the death of Kabango were locked in a separate room for interrogation by village elders but they all denied the charges. As the body was awaiting burial the trio was put in the same house with the mourners but it was difficult to mete on them any punishment since there was no evidence that they really bewitched Kabango.

"My relatives are sour with these witches for revealing their names that they killed uncle and that people are mourning a banana chunk. They came last night threatening to kill me with panga knives and other blunt objects," said Sowa.

He further revealed that wherever he was he could see his uncle who was being forced by the coven of witches to eat nsima with human flesh.

"If uncle refuses to eat the human flesh he is being beaten badly. Right now he is wearing the clothes he was dressed in at the mortuary. Recently, he asked me to tell his wife that she should cook him Nsima with cassava leaves. But he has warned that she should cook the nsima in hiding. He doesn't want anybody to see her cooking," said Sowa.

He said the uncle was even surprised to see women weeping and singing religious hymns when paying the last respect to the late Kabango as they were awaiting to take the dead body to the graveyard which is about 500 metres from the house.

He asked me why these people are weeping. I told him that they [people] say you are dead and he was laughing, he said.

Sowa's allegations have triggered fear in Mizenje Village. The relatives of Sowa and other villagers are afraid of being the next victims of witchcraft.

Sowa Kabango

One of the relatives commented that if Sowa will not be exorcised of witchcraft most of them will be bewitched.

"We are afraid. We have to ask Luka to exorcise Sowa of witchcraft. The boy is dangerous," said a close relative to Sowa.

The deceased's relations went to consult the well-known traditional medicine man in Ntcheu Paul Luka to ressurect the dead man and to exorcise witchcraft in Sowi.

Reports said Luka confirmed the child's allegation that Kabango is not dead and people were weeping for a banana chunk. He asked the people to go ahead with the burial ceremony claiming he will come and resurrect the man at a fee of K3,000.

He is also believed to have warned the relations that Sowa is a dangerous wizard and if he is not exorcised ofwitchcraft, the entire family will perish.

The director of Literature Research Centre in Blantyre Moya Malamusi who worked together with the deceased relatives for preparations of the burial ceremony said Paul Luka screened everything from Ntcheu and confirmed that the man is not dead and that people were indeed weeping for a banana chunk.

He, however, said it was difficult to believe in the allegations until Luka ressurrects the dead man but promised to continue following the issue until it ends.

Malamusidisclosed that when he took the deceased's relatives to Paul Luka in Ntcheu the wipers of his car jammed amid heavy rainfall. " We tried to identfy the fault but we failed until they started again on their own. I was surprised with that," he said.

The relationships and interaction can be shown with much more clarity in a diagram (fig.7)

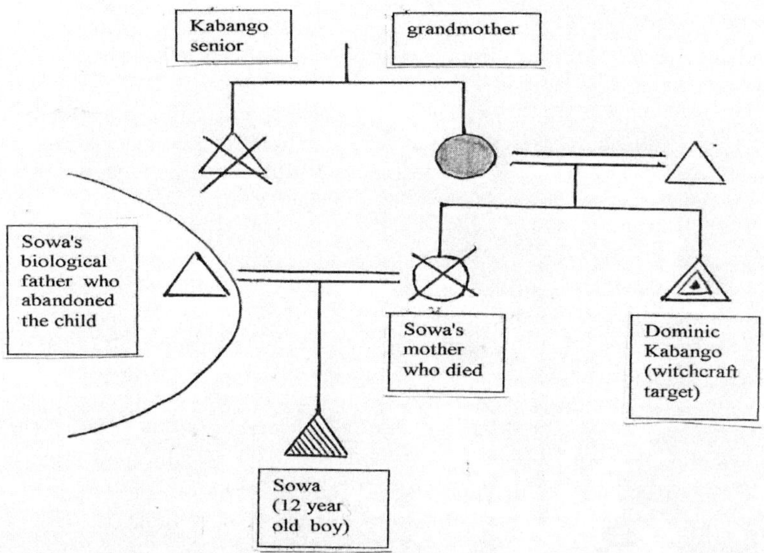

fig. 6

Eventually the grandmother sent out (*kumutuma*) her grandson, Sowa, or at least tried to do so, to kill her own son, Dominic Kabango. She sent the child to be the executioner. Someone sent to kill a person through witchcraft can do so without knowing it; only later he discovers what he has done. The grandmother's motif of killing her son was to get back the estate of her brother which her son had inherited.

I gained access to this case, because Dominic Kabango – who was called Dominiko by everybody – had been a personal friend before he died. In November 1997 he told me about strange things that were happening in the place where he stayed. Often when he had stepped outside in the night to watch out for thieves, or go and urinate, to his surprise he found his adopted son Sowa sitting outside alone. After some time the boy confessed to his uncle that he was *mfiti* who was taught by the uncle's mother. He continued to tell me, that thereafter he had gone with the boy to a *sing'anga* in Thyolo, but without any result, so he left it at that.

I became a witness of Dominiko's deteriorating health, in the course of which we visited both a *sing'anga* (the one called Eliya, no. 13 in the list) and a private hospital. The news about his death came one day at midnight. Next morning I went to their house, only to find the boy Sowa crying that his uncle had not died at all, what had died was only a banana stalk… and that the grandmother had paralyzed him with medicines she had obtained from a certain man in a night club in Nkhumbe. Thereafter, the boy and other people, including the police of Lunzu went to call upon a *sing'anga* to try and resurrect the man, while the body was still warm. The *sing'anga* was not successful, but said that it was necessary that the person who was in possession of poisonous medicines should be identified.

This is where I stepped in, and indicated that if I was accompanied by a policeman I would volunteer to fetch that man from the bar. We got the man, driving back to Mizenje village where Domniiko's body was kept, but the *sing'anga* was still unable to resurrect him. The people blamed the *sing'anga* as incompetent, and their thoughts were now upon Paulo Luka of Ntcheu, that he alone might be able to bring their relative back to life. Because of the words of the boy Sowa, people were extremely afraid that if they buried the body of Dominiko, perhaps they would bury a person who was alive.

I myself became extremely curious about what would happen next, and what Paulo Luka might do, so I volunteered to drive some of the relatives to Ntcheu, if they paid for the petrol. We started the journey, five people in the car, the boy Sowa and other relatives. It was only me who knew the place where Paulo Luka could be found. By luck we met Paulo already upon arrival in his car, and we explained the matter. He then asked the boy many questions. Unfortunately at that time, Paulo had problems with the administration, and a possible lawsuit because of inciting violence. We then proposed that Paulo should go to the local police to get special permission. The family would offer an amount Mk 3.000.- if he brought back to life their relative. The superior of the police agreed reluctantly, but indicated that he would not be responsible for what would happen to Paulo Luka thereafter. Paulo then was afraid to go.

On our return journey strange things happened; and I began to have an impression as if we had been under constant surveillance by the *amfiti*. On the road between Ntcheu and Blantyre, all of a sudden a heavy thunderstorm started, so that it became difficult to drive in the heavy rain. I intended to drive very slowly, but suddenly the windscreen wipers stopped to work. I had no choice but stop and wait at the roadside for the end of the rain. One of the men inside my car began to accuse the boy Sowa of being the wizard who caused all the trouble (!) and that if he did not stop it we would all spend the night on the road and be eaten by a hyena. He said, the boy should stay outside the car as a punishment to be soaked by the rain! Shortly thereafter, the rain stopped, I tried to start the car, the wipers resumed their work and we continued our journey.

At that time it was already half past 9 p.m. and I was driving very carefully, because it was still raining a bit, until we reached Lilangwe. What did I suddenly see? Two very big owls (*akadzidzi*) were sitting just in the middle of the road. Now I also began to be affected psychologically. My body was gripped by fear, but the owls cleared the place and I passed. Now it was already about 11 p.m. When we arrived at the village where the body of Dominiko was kept we found a crowd of people waiting for us, to know what would happen. They became very sad when they saw that we were arriving without Paulo Luka. The situation now became tense. Despaired that nothing could be done to bring Dominiko back to life, the crowd began to be enraged about the person from Nkhumbe who was accused of producing poisonous medicines to kill people. Some people began to propose that we should buy petrol and burn that person, so that he should also die, and that the boy Sowa and his grandmother should also be killed. Fortunately, the police was still there, so the worst did not happen.

I began to be scared fearing that a very unpleasant, if not dangerous situation might arise from this, and I decided to return to my home in Chileka, rather than stay on , and come back next morning for the burial ceremony. However, many people tried to prevent burial, because the body did not look as if the man was dead. Sowa continued to say words such as "my father wants something to eat" and that he was hidden (by) the wizards and witches in a place nearby in a hill. Eventually, the relatives agreed that the body should be buried, and if there was something left to be done, it should be done afterwards. But Sowa was never seen again. It is believed that he ran away to Thyolo to stay with someone else, for fear of being killed at Mizenje village.

(5) Comment on: Deguzman Kaminjolo: "Baston George: The wizard who killed his mother", *Malawi News*, July 17- 23, 1999: 2

This is one more witchcraft report I came across during my research in the 1990s. I collected it during a stay at home in June/July 1999. It is about a man in his thirties who was "cleansed" of witchcraft and thereby was able to talk to the repoter about his past activities. The article is in the form of a dialogue between the reporter and the wizard, and the wizard's photograph (Baston George's) is printed twice, once inclined by 45°, across the printed text, apparently to communicate to the reader something about the man's strange double personality.

This is another case of a grandmother teaching her grandson witchcraft when he was very young, while staying in Mangochi. The text is very clear, and can be taken literally. It gives an intimate look at the world of witchcraft, reconfirming many of the things I have observed during my fieldwork.

The report is an example of independent, investigative journalism which has come up in Malawi during the 1990s in newspapers not controlled by the government. Malawi News is one of these weekly papers. Some of the journalists are interested in things that concern life in the rural areas, and witchcraft is a subject that comes up from time to time. The background to the story presented by Deguzman Kaminjolo was that the village headman of a certain place in Zomba District felt threatened by too many cases of witchcraft reported in his area. He called a *sing'anga* to clean it all up. The man who came was apparently an expert and he confiscated several "horns" (*nyanga*) from various individuals in that village. Among those persons was Baston George. After his *nyanga* had been taken, and his witchcraft removed by the *sing'anga* he began to reveal many details about his earlier condition as a wizard, such as how wizards and witches are initiated through anthropophagy, and how they even offer credit to one another, in the form of human flesh. Such talk came to the attention of newspapers and a journalist (*ntolankhani*) was dispatched to conduct an interview with the man.

2 — WEEKENDER MALAWI NEWS JULY 17—23, 1999 — PROFIL

Face to face

With host Deguzman Kaminjolo

Baston George:

The wizard who killed his mothe

THE mystery of witchcraft remains an enigma to normal people the whole world. It's fascinating, and there are plenty stories which are said about sorcery. So when someone took me to Sunuzu in Zomba to neet a man who would reveal to me what sorcery was all about, I did not hesitate. But what I was to hear when I finally came face to face with Baston George made my stomach turn. Weird in all sense. Baston is a man in his mid thirties was cleansed of witchcraft and that's why he is able to share his wizardly experiences. This is how he shared his experiences with Face to Face now read on:

Q: How did you get involved in witchcraft?

A: I cannot remember the exact date, but it was when I was very young. I was staying in Mangochi with my parents and my grand parents. My grandmother, Lozalio is the one who turned me into a wizard.

Q: But how exactly did you know that you were now a wizard?

A: One day, I just woke up from my sleep and found myself at a graveyard. There were several elderly people who I remembered as being from the same village. They were all naked, and body the parts looked strange. For example the lips were sort of out stretched, the fingers very long and the stomachs big. I got scared, then I noticed my grandmother (Lozalio). Nobody was saying anything, but there was a big clay pot on the ground, in which something was boiling. Everybody drank, and my grandmother forced me to drink as well. Then suddenly I was home again.

Q: Did you tell your parents about your experience?

A: No, I thought it was a dream. But the following evening, I had another experience. Late at night my grandmother came to me and grabbed me by my hand. We went out of the house and started to run very fast to an extent where even the legs weren't touching down. We were flying. We went to a very strange place, where I was left alone under a tree. My grandmother came back with a woman holding a baby who I guessed was dead. The strange woman took a few charms from her bag, made some tattoos on [illegible] some black powder. She also made a big cut on my thigh where she inserted a human finger. After forcing me to drink a bitter concoction, we all ate the meat of the dead baby and then we left the same way we came: My grandmother holding my hand and running really fast.

Q: But you still didn't tell your parents?

A: This particular day I almost told my mother, but what was happening was that every time I was about to start, my grandmother would appear and stare at me angrily. But when I got so involved it was impossible for me to quit since I was one of them.

Q: What do you mean when you say one of them?

A: You see, there are several phases you are made to undergo. Charms are administered into your body in phases.. Eventually I became my grandmothers pal and we were always together.

Q: We hear there are 'planes' involved in witchcraft. Just what are these planes?

A: Planes are some sort of transport. When we want to go to the mountains or even to far away areas, we would use the planes. Basically, it is some sort of *'Lichero'* (bamboo plate) which has once been used at a funeral. The plane would accommodate over 100 people.

Q: Sometimes we have heard of these planes crashing. What happens?

A: Normally, it is when the procedure has not been properly followed, or simply when you pass a protected area.

Q: What do you mean by protected area?

A: This is an area which has been treated by a witch doctor.

Q: How were you meeting your fellow wizards?

A: Usually there is a sort of a leader. So at night, he would blow a whistle which is made from a reed stem. Ordinary people would not hear the call.

Q: Again we hear that in witchcraft, people can engineer a person's death. How is this done?

A: It can be done in many ways. There are times when one can use a magic hammer. You just go to the house of the person you want dead at night, and hit him hard on the head with the hammer. The following morning that person will start complain of a headache and then dies. Then there are times when you can install several objects like knives, nails and several such objects in people's body. These things make them sick, and eventually they die.

Q: Did you ever kill anyone in the time you were a wizard?

A: I killed many people. I killed even my mother. But it was after I was forced to do that.

Q: How were you forced?

A: It was the time my grandmother had died, and there was really noone to defend me. Someone made me eat some meat, and then they told me I had to pay back. They forced me until I succumbed.

Q: How were you managing to get inside people's houses, while all doors were securely locked?

A: Normally we us drop a charm at one c corners of the house. then use another corn enter. If by bad luck charm changes position you won't be able to con of the house, until i morning when people find you.

Q: So what made quit witchcraft?

A: Our Village Hea had invited a famous doctor from Mozambic get rid of all who pra witchcraft.

Q: How did this know that you were a ard?

A: This witch docto the magic whistle exacti what we used at night. went at a corner of the v and blew the whistle. So of us went there think was our friend calling. arrival, I got beaten wi stick, and then I collaps my unconsciousness treated me and remove the charms which we my body. I st unconscience for two and when I woke up, he me porridge, which ma vomit a lot. Then I w longer a wizard.

Q: What did you low villagers say realising you were a ard?

A: They came to bu house, and I fled and why I am found here.

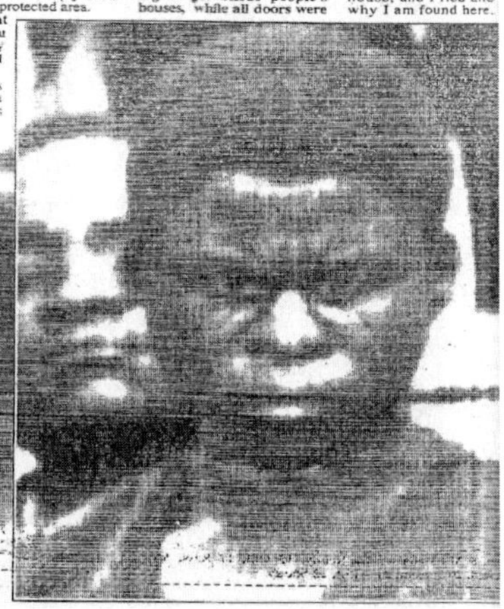

Concluding remarks and outlook

In this book I have tried to give an overview of the related subject areas of *using'anga* (medical practice) and *ufiti* (witchcraft) in southern Malawi on the basis of the results of my personal experiences, systematic field-work carried out during the 1990s and archival work in Malawi. In the central part of this book I have laid out in detail the results of my work with four *asing'anga* out of a database of thirteen and tried to throw light on characteristics of their personalities, the kinds of clients they receive, and the socio-cultural context of their medical practices, by allowing them to articulate their ideas themselves in recorded interviews which I have transcribed from my fieldwork and annotated. This was followed by an account – though selective – of my archival findings, including newspaper articles etc. which reflect public opinion about witchcraft and the practice of local healing, as well as the status of the various *asing'anga* .

Although this book is not meant to be a general, comparative study of healing practice across Africa, it is evident from the material I have presented that there are many concepts and themes that are analogues across different cultures. The reader will be able to follow up those analogies by studying the vast literature relating to various African societies such as summarized, for example, by Barbara Multhaupt (1990); in particular, some classics such as Edward E. Evans-Pritchard's *Witchcraft, Oracles and Magic among the Azande* (1973) and more recent studies in that ethnic group by Armin Prinz (1986), Sabine Haller and Manfred Kremser (1975) and others. Specific motifs which I have documented in southern Malawi, such as the imaginary anthropophagy by wizards and witches, or the fact that they "fly" in the night, have been researched cross-culturally by Manfred Kremser (1988, 1994). A summary of witchcraft practices in Europe, useful for comparisons on a wider scale, can be found in a book by Christa Tuczay (1992) on magic and magicians in the (Europan) Middle Ages.

From the database of my own fieldwork I arrived at the conclusion that *sing'anga* (pl. *asing'anga*) is really a blanket term. Even if we restrict the meaning of the abstract noun *using'anga* only to cover local African medical practice, excluding imported medicine as in foreign-established hospitals, the terms include many different approaches and methods for curing people. Already during the early stages of my research I arrived at a typology of the *asing'anga* as persons on the basis of folk classification, according to the accents of their practice and the sources of their knowledge. This typology can be condensed and summarized in the form of a chart.

Typology of *asing'anga* in southern Malawi
– according to dominant ways of medical intervention
and the origins of their knowledge

I. *Asing'anga* with exclusive expertise in herbal medicines (*mankhwala amitengo*). They do not get inspiration through spirit possession, nor do they practise divination (*kuombeza ula*). Their knowledge is obtained through apprenticeship with older herbalist.

II. *Asing'anga* who are middlemen/women and virtually only traders in herbal medicines of all kinds. They obtain their knowledge from eclectic information which they extract from experts (the real *asing'anga)* where they buy those medicines for retail distribution. They do not undergo any formal apprenticeship.

III. *Asing'anga* who get regularly possessed by spirits and obtain their knowledge about medicines in dreams and states of possession. This group practises divination (*kuombeza ula*) to identify wizards and witches, as well as evil spirits which may haunt their patients, and they prescribe both psychological and herbal treatments.

Within this group there are several subgroups according to the type of spirits, often regional, from which they obtain their knowledge:

(a) personal ancestral spirits (*makolo*)
(b) *amambo* spirits which appear as wild animals
(c) spirits such as *mazooka*, *mfukula* etc.
(d) spirits taken from the Bible, referred to as *aneneli* (apostles, prophets)

In a sense a classification is always subjective, and I do not claim that mine is perfect. In addition, I realized during my fieldwork that many other factors of subjectivity come into play. One is the effect it has on one's perceptions and approach, if one is a believer or a non-believer in the existence of witchcraft and magic. This determines very basically how one conceptualizes about the ways a *sing'anga* intervenes to control these forces.

Let me therefore relate a few personal experiences concerning this matter, talking about the implications and the effects of people's disbelief in things witchcraft and magic (*kusakhulupirira kwa anthu za ufiti ndi matsenga*).

These days, many people in Malawi simply declare that they do not believe that anything like witchcraft or magic exists. This is due to the fact that such people in the first place have never experienced extremely frightening events (*sanaone zinthu zina zazikuluzikulu zoopsya*) such as feeling bewitched (*monga kulodzedwa*) and starting to fall ill; or otherwise that someone in their environment died without any rational explanation.

Many people who spread the news that witchcraft and magic do not exist, often belong to Christian congregations and they pray in churches of one or another kind. For example, those who are in the religious sect of the Zionists (*kumipingo ya ziyoni*), or the Seventh-Day-Adventists, among other Christian religious groups, do not accept that there may be people on earth who are able to inflict evil upon others by bewitching them so that their victims die, or cause them to become ill. Whenever we bring up the subject in front of people who belong to any of these religious groups, they deny vehemently (*kunena motsutsa*) that something like witchcraft exists anywhere on earth and that it is possible to kill someone through witchcraft or magic.

These are the thoughts of people who also reject everything connected with *using'anga* (traditional medicine) and particularly divination (*zamaula*) which is carried out by *asing'anga* in their quest for a cure of their patients' hidden troubles, how he or she became ill, or otherwise, under which circumstances someone died. Those observers simply say that this is without substance, and that there could also be nobody with the power seeing in a dream what has just happened to someone in another place, or what will happen in the future. In fact even the possibility of phenomena described and studied in parapsychology (cf. Bonin, 1981:49-51, 168,172) i.e. any ESP (extrasensory perception) phenomenon, is categorically denied.

Indeed, dreams can turn out to be true or not true, and there may be no evidence (*palibedi umboni*) that predictions are accurate or merely coincidental, but what is known is that many people accept the work of the *asing'anga*. They believe in the abilities of *asing'anga* who search for the hidden causes of a patient's complaints and they acknowledge that *asing'anga* try hard to find ways of solving their problems. On many occasions I have noticed that someone who failed to find a cure through foreign medicinal practice in local government hospitals or private clinics, gets a cure from *asing'anga*. Before giving any help to the patient, the *sing'anga* begins by carrying out divination (*kuombeza*) in order to get hints about what happened to that person; only thereafter does he know what kind of treatment should be given.

The people who do not agree with the idea that there could be witchcraft, when they eventually go to consult a *sing'anga* they ask him or her: "Please give me medicine only, but do not examine me through divination (*koma kuti muombeze ndiye ai*), because if you subject me to the oracle, and perhaps identify the person who has made me sick, I might begin to quarrel with him or her after hearing this news. Making noise (*phokoso*) is not needed at all, and therefore, you only give me medicines!"

Taking this issue a little further, I would like to make some concluding remarks about a personal problem that made me embark on the study of witchcraft and healing practice. As to what I had experienced in the past I was trying to obtain an opinion from many different people in that matter. On December 14, 1993, I visited the headman (*nyakwawa*) Majola in his residence near Kunthembwe, Blantyre District, and recorded *nthano* (stories) from him (cf. orig. tape no. 93/12, side 2, archived at the Institute für Ethnologie und Afrika-Studien, University of Mainz). Majola is also engaged in the work of *using'anga.* I wanted to know from him what he thought was behind the deaths of my young brother, Fulaye Aliya, in January 1982, and that of my sister Lidiya Malamusi in November 1989, both of whom had died under mysterious circumstances. My brother was only 16 years old when he fell ill with what appeared to be a trivial matter. Then all of a sudden a bird entered our house and began to play around inside. When the village people noticed the bird they killed it, and that very day, after they had killed the playful bird, the condition of my young brother (*mphwanga)* deteriorated to the point that I decided to take him to a public hospital. There he died within a day. The second similar incident, a few years later, was when my younger sister, 26 years old, had caught malaria (*malungo*). While she was ill, a rat (*khoswe*) was seen running away from some other place in our village into our house, and there it entered the suitcase of my sister. My father came and tried to find the rat inside the suitcase, and when he discovered it, he killed it. In the evening of the same day, my sister demanded that I take her to a hospital, although she did not appear to be seriously ill. There she died the same evening.

Those events are puzzling (*zododometsa*) and I have remained with the tormenting question in my mind, how it happened that both of them died under comparable circumstances, after something else had entered our house and was killed. That was the question I posed Majola and he said to me:

Mwanawe usadabwe awo ndiwo
matsenga, ndiye kuti alipo
anthu ena pa banja lanu kapena
pa ntundu wanu amachita za
matsenga kuti munthu afe, ndipo
izi zili chonchi: choyamba
amakhala ali amfiti ndipo
alephela kuchita chili chonse
pa ufiti wawowo, ndiye amayesa
njila ngati imeneyi kuchoka
mu ufiti ndikuchita matsenga
ndi cholinga chakuti ngati
apha kanthu aka ndiye kuti
wapha m'bale wake. awo ndiwo
mau omwe amanena potumiza
chinthu chaocho. Ndiye inu
anthu wamba pomwe muona
chinthu chodabwitsa mumaganiza
kuti tiphe mbalame kapena
tiphe khoswe, pomwe ameneyo
samakhala khoswe konse,
amakhala ali mankhwala awo
omwe aponya kwainu kuti inu
ngati mupha kanthu kameneka
ndiye kuti mwapha m'bale
wanu. Amenewa timati matsenga
odzela muufiti.

My son! You should not be surprised,
(but) it is magic. This is to say
that there are certain people in
your family, or perhaps your
extended family, who practice
things of magic, so that someone
should die. What happens is this: first
they act as wizards/witches, but when
they fail to be successful through their
witchcraft, they try another way like
the one (you have experienced).
They proceed from witchcraft to work
through magic with the aim that if
someone kills a small thing, at
that moment he or she has killed a relative.
These are the words they pronounce when
they actually send their thing.
And you uniformed people, when you see a
stunning thing, then the idea occurs to you:
"Let us kill that bird!" or "Let us kill that rat"
while that creature is not a rat at all, it
incorporates medicines they have thrown
at you, so that if you kill that little creature
you have killed your relative!
We call such a design "magic that grows
out of witchcraft".

Since I have lived through the circumstances of the death of my two relatives I can also reconstruct what happened in the village prior to their deaths, when they were still healthy. Concerning my sister, what happened was that three days before she fell ill, she was quarreling with a certain woman in our village, and in the course of their dispute, my sister mentioned the subject of witchcraft accusing that woman of being a witch who "exterminated" people (*anali amfiti akupha anthu*). Within three days after that statement, my sister began to fall ill. Then other things happened, and the rat which had entered her suitcase was killed. We believe that the rat was sent by the witch.

In the same manner in which I had taken my brother to the hospital seven years earlier, leaving him there, only to find him dead shortly thereafter, I now took my sister to the same hospital. She had 38.3° fever upon arrival, but was talking normally, walking to her bed and signing the paper of admittance by herself. After I had left her there in a condition that looked like a minor problem, most likely of malaria terciana, a type of malaria that is endemic in our area, but not very dangerous, she died an hour later. According to her mother who had stayed with her at her bedside that evening, she was attended only by nurses, because it was Sunday and the only doctor had gone home. The nurses came and gave her an injection. Thirty minutes later, in the middle of a conversation with her mother, she suddenly sat up in her bed, complained about convulsions and died – less than two hours after she had been admitted. In the report which we received several weeks later, the hospital authorities claimed that she had died of "cerebral malaria".

For me this painful event was the trigger to make me decide to study how witchcraft may be effectuated. Because I had seen how my sister began to fall ill, and witnessed her quarrel, there is nobody who can convince me that the cause of her death was any physical ailment; I believe that she was bewitched.

There is also another example which I can give. In 1995, a funeral took place in our village, all of a sudden, after a stray cat had arrived and had been killed by one in a group of boys staying in that place. Within a day the sister (*mulongo wake*) of the boy who had killed that cat, died. This was now the third analogous case. It has reinforced my conviction that such a chain of events could not be coincidental. In this particular case, I am unable to give any names for verification, because the people involved would not want to be identified.

When news such as this is spread it often happens that relatives begin an argument about who in the group could be the wizard or witch. As a result of social pressure it can happen that the accused yells out: "Yes, I am the wizard/witch who bewitches people in our consanguine group (*inedi, ndine mfiti yomwe ndimalodza anthu pantundu wathu uno*). Such incidences happen particularly when many people die in a village without an apparent cause. When witchcraft is taught to small children the latter might even declare openly: "We are wizards / witches, and as concerns such and such a person it is we who killed him/ her; and also that person there we 'fixed' him/her (*ife ndife amfiti ndipo munthu wakuti wakuti tinamupha ndife, ndiponso wakuti wakuti tinakonza ndife*)". Even in their statements those children use the special jargon of wizards and witches, such as for example saying *tinakonza* (we have arranged, repaired, fixed, cleansed, put right such and such a person), which is an euphemism for saying " we have killed him or her".

It also happens in my home area in Chileka that children would declare that they had "eaten" people or killed such and such a person by witchcraft, and that they committed these deeds jointly with their adult relatives who had taught them witchcraft. Such reports came out at Chief Chinkango's place, for example, that a group of four children had been instructed in witchcraft techniques by their maternal uncle (*malume*) and that those children knew everything that can be activated for killing people, and that they were regularly sent on a mission to kill a person whose flesh was wanted by their family (*banja lawolo*). But later when it had become clear that this was not a game (*kuti sanali masewela*) but real killing, it happened that one in the group of children who had been told to kill his mother, began to reveal the facts when yet another funeral took place for someone in their compound (*malilo ena panyumba pomwepo*). At the time the boy began to reveal the truth, his mother was already very ill. After the boy realized that he had already prepared everything for people to find his mother dead when they came back from the graveyard where they had gone for the other funeral, he began to reveal their witchcraft designs. He was saying these words: "Our mother, when we return from the graveyard, we will not find her again, because we have already arranged everything" (*amayi wathu tikamachoka kumandako sikuti tiwapeza, pakuti zonse tinakonza kale*). The people around, upon hearing these words, were startled and they wondered what the boy wanted to say. So they took him to the side, where he began to confess, mentioning the names of all the people whom he and his companions had killed in the past. The people realized that those deceased had been victims of witchcraft.

They also realized that if they did not act quickly the mother of the boy would die and they tried to search for medicines (*anayesa kufufuza za mankhwala*) to prevent that woman from dying. That day there was a violent verbal exchange with the uncle, who had taught witchcraft to those children. Some people in the village were thinking of killing those children by cutting their throats and also their witchcraft teacher by the same method. But eventually they did not do that, but hired a *sing'anga* that he should remove the witchcraft power from the culprits (*kuti awachotse ufitiwo*).

All this happened in September 1996 in the village of Chinkango, T.A. Kuntaja in Blantyre District. The family where the funeral was taking place was that of Mr. Mitembo Gilibati. The report about this incident was heard everywhere in the area, and more and more names came up of persons who were involved in the same secret ring of wizards controlled by that uncle (*malume*). Not all the members, as it turned out, belonged to the family, but others were involved because of their expertise in witchcraft (*ukatswiri wa ufiti*). Mr. Mitembo Gilibati was not personally accused, but many people thought that he was also involved. The reports also implicated an old-timer musician (*wa make dzana*) Mr. Deko Asani Sato, about whom I have written in another conext (cf. Malamusi 1994:17-18). Deko was also knowledgable in *using'anga* (medical practice).

The *sing'anga* who had been called ended the quarrels by submitting the four children to receive scarifications with anti-witchcraft medicines rubbed in (*kuwatemera mankhwala*). But their maternal uncle refused to be treated, and in fact he eventually left the village to settle somewhere else. The young boy who had revealed the secret, and thereby saved his mother, died a few months later. It is thought that he was "put right" by his maternal uncle, because of the insolence (*chipongwe*) he had committed "betraying" him. At the time when the *sing'anga* had arrived at that place he predicted that "all those who are involved in bewitching people here shall be removed one by one!" (*Onse amene akukhudzidwa ndi kulodzedwa kwa anthu amenewa pano, adzichoka mmodzi-mmodzi).* This curse became engraved in the mind of everybody in the area.

Epilogue

When I went for a brief sojourn to my home in Malawi in June/July 1999, I heard rumours that Deko Asani Sato had died. But one day I walked to the shops near my house and suddenly saw him standing in front of the shop of Mr. Masimbe! I felt embarrassed, because I had thought he was dead. I did not know what to say to him. Should I have said: " *Kodi simunamwalire*? (Oh, didn't you die?)"

But the last strange "coincidence" in this matter happened on the 12th September 1999 in Vienna. I was doing the final revisions of this book and had arrived at the story of the four children. In the afternoon the text of the story was read to my two youngsters who are going to school in Vienna, and they were highly amused and found these witchcraft reports thrilling, especially the section about the throat-cutting. There was a lot of laughter and enjoyment about my writings.

Later in the evening the three of us went out for a walk and at about 7 p.m. we phoned my wife in Malawi to discuss another matter. Among other things she told me that Deko Asani Sato had just died the same day and would be buried on Monday, September 13.

Bibliography

Abdallah, Yohanna B.

1919 *Chiikala cha Wayao*. Zomba: Government Printing Office. New edition, arranged, edited and translated by Meredith Sanderson 1973, London: Frank Cass

Anon.

1990 "Gogo aphunzitsa zidzukulu zake ufiti " *Police Magazine*, Third Quarter 1990, p. 39

Anon. (Times Reporter)

1995 "No social class at Chisupe's clinic" *Daily Times*, Monday, March 20

Anon. (Reporter of the Nation)

1995 "Red Cross Shelters Chisupe's Patients" *The Nation,* Vol. 2(177), March 22, p. 2

Anon.

1995 "Chisupe, G. Bille Mankhwalawa ali ndi mwambo wake", *Tikambe* Supplement to Malawi News. March 24-31 1995. p. 3

Anon.

1997 "Simbazako alowa Chikhristu", *Moni*, 34 (388), February, p. 15

Bock, Philip K.

1980 *Rethinking Psychological Anthropology*. Continuity and Change in Psychological Anthropology. New York: W.H Freeman

1969 *Modern Anthropology. An Introduction*. New York: (1974) Alfred A. Knopf

Bonin, Werner F.

1981 *Lexikon der Parapsychologie und ihrer Grenzgebiete*. Frankfurt an Main: Fischer Taschenbuch Verlag

Chafulumira, E. W.

1948 *Mbiri ya Amang'anja*. Zomba: Nyasaland Education Department

Chikokola, Kasalika

1989 "Athakati Agonja kwa Sing'anga" *Police Magazine*, First Quarter, p. 31

Chilivumbo A.B.

1972 "Vimbuza or Mashawe: A mystic therapy" *Journal of the African Music Society* 5 (2): 6-8

Chingwaru, Willie

1987 "Msungwana Aphunzitsidwa Kutamba" *Police Magazine*, Fourth Quarter, Vol. 16, Issue 4 p. 38

Crosby, Cynthia A.

1980 *Historical Dictionary of Malawi.* African Historical Dictionaries, No. 25, Metuchen, N.J. & London The Scarecrow Press, Inc.

Editors of the American Heritage Dictionaries
1998 *Compact American Medical Dictionary. A concise and up-to-date guide to medical terms.* Boston/New York: Houghton Mifflin Company

Evans-Pritchard, Edward E.
1937 *Witchcraft, Oracles and Magic among the Azande*. Oxford: Clarendon Press

Guthrie, Malcolm
1948 *The Classification of the Bantu Languages*. London: International African Institute

Gwengwe, John W.
1965 *Kukula ndi mwambo.* Limbe: Malawi Publications and Literature Bureau

Hetherwick, Alexander & David Clement Scott
1929 *Dictionary of the Chichewa Language*. Blantyre: C.L.A.I.M. (1970 edition)

Kachinziri, Pilirani
1997 "Sowa – the witchcraft apprentice", *Malawi News*, December 20 - 26: 9

Kajombo, Innocent
1993 "Msungwana awoneka patapita zaka makumi awiri pachimwalilile", *Police Magazine*. Vol. 22, p. 38

Kalunga, L.B.
1989 "Sing'anga athandiza aPolice" *Police Magazine*. First quarter 1989

Kaminjolo, Deguzman
1999 "Baston George: The wizard who killed his mother", *Malawi News*, July 17-23: 2

Kazombo, Mackson
1995 "The power of herbs: 5000 people daily flock to the medicine man". *Malawi News*, March 18-24, p. 5

Kosko, Bart and Satoru Isaka
1993 "Fuzzy Logic", *Scientific American*, 269 (1), July, pp. 62-67

Kremser, Manfred
1988 "Psychische Menschenfresser – Reflexionen über historische Quellen und eigene Feldforschungsaufzeichnungen betreffend Hexerei und Kannibalismus in Zentralafrika", in: *Methodische Probleme bei der Auswertung von Primärquellen: Magische Vorstellungen und Praktiken vom Mittelalter bis zur Gegenwart im überregionalen Vergleich.* Heide Dienst, Hrsg.

1994 "Avule – Zande Ritual Therapy" in: *For Gerhard Kubik. Festschrift* ... August Schmidhofer and Dietrich Schüller, eds. Frankfurt a. Main: Peter Lang, pp. 161-178

1997 „Nächtliche Flüge afrikanischer Hexer und ihre Bewertung bei den Azande.“ In *Fliegen und Schweben: Annäherung an eine menschliche Sensation*, hg. Dieter R. Bauer & Wolfgang Behringer. München: dtv. Pp.189–222

Kremser, Manfred & Sabine Haller

1975 "Danse et Thérapeutique chez les Azande", *Bulletin of the International Committee on Urgent Anthropological and Ethnological Research*, 17: 65-78

Kubik, Gerhard

1994 "Nchimi Chikanga Chunda in 1962 – three eyewitness accounts of the man and his impact". Article written for a volume edited by Dr. Boston Soko, University of Malawi, Zomba. Manuscript 28 pages (deposited at Oral Literature Research Programme, Chileka, Malawi).

1999 *Mahamba* – Konzeptualisierung transzendenter Kräfte im Ostangola-Kulturraum. Feldforschungen 1965 - 1987. Mit Bild- und Tondokumenten. – Vortrag gehalten am 17. Mai 1999, Österreichische Gesellschaft für Parapsychologie und Grenzbereiche der Wissenschaften, Wien. - Manuskript (unveröffentlicht)

Kubik, Gerhard (in cooperation with Moya Aliya Malamusi)

1987 *Nyau. Maskenbünde im südlichen Malawi.* Wien: Verlag der Österreichischen Akademie der Wissenschaften

Kubik, Gerhard (assisted by Moya Aliya Malamusi, Lidiya Malamusi and Donald Kachamba)

1987 *Malawian Music: a framework for analysis.* Zomba: Department of Fine and Performing Arts, and Centre for Social Research (University of Malawi)

Kubik, Gerhard (in cooperation with Moya Aliya Malamusi)

1989 *Opeka Nyimbo - Musician-composers from Southern Malawi.* 2 LP stereo, with commentary in English and German. Museum Collection MC 15 (editor: Artur Simon), Berlin: Museum für Völkerkunde

Kubik, Gerhard, Lidiya Malamusi und Moya Aliya Malamusi

1990 "Typen der Oralliteratur im Chichewa/Cinyanja", in: *Die Vielfalt der Kultur. Ethnologische Aspekte von Verwandschaft, Kunst und Weltauffassung. Ernst Wilhelm Müller zum 65. Geburtstag.* Karl-Heinz Kohl, Heinzarnold Muszinski und Ivo Strecker, eds., Mainzer Ethnologica, Bd.4, Berlin: Dietrich Reimer, pp. 357-379

Mabry, Marcus

1997 "Traditional Healer, M.D. Does your medical plan cover bone throwing?" *Newsweek*, Vol. CXXIX, No. 10, p. 21

Makumbi, Archibald J.,

1955 *Maliro ndi miyambo ya Acewa.* London: Longman Group Ltd. (Fourth edition 1970)

Malamusi, Moya Aliya

1990 "Nthano chantefables and songs performed by *bangwe* player Chitenje Tambala", *Contributions in Honour of David Kenneth Rycroft*, special number of the *South African Journal of African Languages*, 10 (4): 222-238

1992 "Thunga la ngororombe – the panpipe dance group of Sakha Bulaundi", *African Music*, Vol. 7, No. 2: 85-107

1993 "Kambazithe Makolekole Valimba Band", *Perkussionale '93* Programmheft, Berlin: Museum für Völkerkunde und Haus der Kulturen der Welt

1994 "Rise and Development of a Chileka Guitar Style in the 1950s" in: *For Gerhard Kubik.Festschrift*…August Schmidhofer and Dietrich Schüller, eds. Frankfurt a. Main: Peter Lang, pp. 7-72

1997 "Two panpipe ensemble traditions" *Kalinda. The Newsletter of Afro-Caribbean and U.S. Black Music Interconnections* (published by CBMR Chicago) Fall 1997 pp. 22-24

Mandala, E.C.

1978 "Nature and substance of Mang'anja and Kololo oral traditions", *The Society of Malawi Journal*, 31 (1), January

Moore, Burness E. and Bernard D. Fine

1990 *Psychoanalytic Terms and Concepts*. New Haven and London: The American Psychoanalytic Association and Yale University Press

Mphuthu, Jemusan

1995 "Boma lithandiza sing'anga wa kuLiwonde", *The Daily Monitor 3* (48), Friday 10th March, page 11

Multhaupt, Tamara

1990 *Hexerei und Antihexerei in Afrika*. München: Trickster

Mwale, E.

1952 *Za Achewa*. London: Macmillan & Co. Ltd.

Nkhalamba, Felix

1993 "Ufiti Ulipodi" ,*Police Magazine*, Vol. 22 p. 36

Ntara, S. J.

1969 *Mbiri ya Acewa*. Blantyre: Malawi Publications and Literature Bureau

Ntonya, George

1995 "Herbalist Chisupe challenges health authorities" *Daily Monitor*, March 24,1995

Nurse, George T.

1967 "The name 'akafula'", *The Society of Malawi Journal*, 20(2): 1-6

1978 *Clanship in Central Malawi.* Acta Ethnologica et Linguistica Nr. 41, Series Africana 12, Vienna: E. Stiglmayr

Nurse, George T., Joseph S. Weiner, and Trefor Jenkins
1985 *The Peoples of Southern Africa and their Affinities.* Oxford: Oxford University Press

Pachai, Bridglal (ed.):
1972 *The Early History of Malawi.* London: Longman

1973 *Malawi: The History of the Nation.* London: Longman Group Ltd.

Paliani, S .A.
1971 *1930 Kunadza Mchape.* Lilongwe: Likuni Press and Publishing House

Pampalk, Josef
1982 *Sprichwörter der Asena.* Grundlagen für die Kenntnis und für die Erneuerung ihrer Kultur. (Bibliothek des Institutes für Afrikanistik der Universität Wien), Wien

Phiri, Kings M.
1979 "Northern Zambezi From 1500 to 1800", *The Society of Malawi Journal*, 32 (1), January

1982 "The historiography of Nyau", *Kalulu* (Bulletin of Oral Literature), University of Malawi, 3: 55-58

1983 "Some changes in the matrilineal family system among the Chewa of Malawi since the nineteenth century", *Journal of African History*, 24: 257-274

Prinz, Armin
1978 "Azande" (Äquatorialafrika, Nordost-Zaire). Films and notes, Encyclopaedia Cinematographica: E 2321, 2326, 2379-2380. Göttingen: Institut für den Wissenschaftlichen Film.

1986 "Die traditionelle Heilkunde der Azande Nordost-Zaires. Ethnomedizinische Forschungsergebnisse aus Zentralafrika", *Mitteilungen der Österreichischen Gesellschaft für tropenmedizinische Parasitologie*, 6: 143-155

Quirk, Sir Randolph, ed
1990 *Longman Dictionary of Contemporary English.* New Edition. Burnt Mill, Harlow: Longman Group UK Limited.

Reichmayr, Johannes
2003 *Ethonopsychoanalyse. Geschichte, Konzepte, Anwendungen.* Gießen: Psychosozial-Verlag.

Rita-Ferreira, Antonio
1968 "The Nyau brotherhood among the Mozambique Cewa", *South African Journal of Science*, 64 pp. 20-24

Salaun, N.
1969 *Chichewa Intensive Course*, Lilongwe: Likuni Press. – Reprinted 1978, Lusaka: Teresianum Press

Sanderson, G. Meredith
1954 *A Dictionary of the Yao Language*. Zomba: The Government Printer

Simbazako, M. K. M. (Dr.)
1997 "A Simbazako atsutsa bodza", *Moni*, April, 34 (390): 22

Soko, A.Z. Oliver
1989 "Agwidwa Ufiti Atapezeka ndi Malemu" *Police Magazine*, Second Quarter, p. 36

1990 "Munthu asanduka fisi", *Police Magazine*, First Quarter, p. 45

1993 "Lufanesi asowetsedwa m'matsenga "*Police Magazine*Vol. 22, p. 39

Soko, Boston
2002 *Nchimi Chikanga* The Battle against Witchcraft in Malawi. Kachere Text no. 10 CLAIM

Tracey, Andrew
1991 "Kambazithe Makolekole and his *valimba* group: a glimpse of the technique of the Sena xylophone", *African Music*, 7 (1): 82-104

Tuczay, Christa
1992 *Magie und Magier im Mittelalter*. München: Diederichs

Williamson, Jessie
1975 *Useful Plants of Malawi*. Published by the University of Malawi Limbe: Montfort Press

Yoshida, Kenji
1993 "Masks and secrecy among the Chewa", *African Arts*, April, pp. 34-45, notes p. 92

Studien zur Ethnopsychologie und Ethnopsychoanalyse

hrsg. von Werner Egli, Gerhard Kubik, Maya Nadig, Johannes Reichmayr und Vera Saller

Brigitta Hug
Babyjahre anderswo
Theorie und transkultureller Vergleich der frühen Kindheiten bei den Gusii, den !Kung San und den Iatmül

Babys überleben anderswo wie in westlichen Gesellschaften nur dann, wenn sie mit innerer Anteilnahme ins Leben getragen werden. Aber nicht überall übernehmen Mütter und/oder Kleinfamilien diese faszinierende und arbeitsintensive Aufgabe. Die erste Lebenszeit wird – so die These der Ethnologin und Psychoanalytikerin Brigitta Hug – sozial organisiert. Je nach wirtschaftlichen und politischen Bedingungen werden Kleinkinder verschieden gepflegt und werden ihnen besondere Eigenschaften und Bedürfnisse zugeschrieben. Der transkulturelle Vergleich der frühen Kindheiten bei den Gusii, den !Kung San und den Iatmül veranschaulicht dies und analysiert gleichzeitig westliches Denken über Babys.

Bd. 8, 2007, 280 S., 24,90 €, br., ISBN 978-3-8258-0127-4

Gerhard Kubik
Tabu
Erkundungen transkultureller Psychoanalyse in Afrika, Europa und anderen Kulturgebieten

Sigmund Freud, der Begründer der Psychoanalyse, war auch der erste, der Tabus quer durch die Kulturen psychoanalytisch auflöste. Inzwischen ist von uns viel weiteres Terrain erschlossen worden, u.a. in den Initiationsriten, im Spiel und in relgiösen Bereichen. Die im Prinzip dreiteilige Struktur der Tabu-Formeln wurde erkannt. Durch Verinnerlichung der Tabu-Inhalte hilft eine Kultur dem Individuum, mit sozial nicht akzeptierten unbewußten Tendenzen fertig zu werden. Aus diesem Grunde sind Tabus auch eine Neurose-Prophylaxe.

Der vorliegende Band gibt einen Überblick heutiger Tabu-Forschung zum Verständnis der Tiefenpsychologie des Menschen. Er gründet sich auf jahrzehntenlange Feldforschungen des Verfassers und seiner Mitarbeiter in Afrika, Europa und anderen Kulturgebieten.

Umschlagbild: Tabu-Bereiche. Zeichnung des Verfassers.

Bd. 7, 2007, 104 S., 19,90 €, br., ISBN 978-3-8258-9799-4

Gerhard Kubik
Tusona – Luchazi Ideographs
A graphic tradition practised by a people of West-Central Africa

Various graphic systems designed to express and transmit ideas or to convey messages were known in sub-Saharan Africa in pre-colonial times, ideographic and pictographic systems. One of the most intriguing of these traditions, known across eastern Angola into northwestern Zambia, among speakers of Luchazi, Chokwe, Lwena and related languages is the *tusona* ideographs.

This work is a fascinating excursion into symbolism, the remote history of eastern Angola, Luchazi oral literature, mathematics, graphic art and communication.

Bd. 6, 2. enlarged edition 2006, 376 S., 29,80 €, br., ISBN 3-8258-7601-2

Werner M. Egli; Uwe Krebs (Hg.)
Beiträge zur Ethnologie der Kindheit
Erziehungswissenschaftliche und kulturvergleichende Aspekte

Das Leben, das Aufwachsen und das Erziehen von Kindern in aussereuropäischen Kulturen bilden das Generalthema dieses Sammelbandes. Beiträge aus Ethnologie, Erziehungswissenschaft und Humanethologie bieten einen interdisziplinären und vielseitigen Zugang. Eine erste Gruppe von Beiträgen behandelt kulturübergreifende allgemeine Themen wie Generationen- konflikte oder Prozesse Impliziter Erziehung; eine zweite Gruppe widmet sich jeweils einem speziellen Thema in einem spezifischen kulturellen Kontext, z. B. mathematischen Rätseln in Afrika, den Folgen des Erbrechts auf den Lebenslauf in Nepal oder den Kastenunterschieden und gemeinsamem Schulbesuch in Indien. Der einleitende Beitrag von Pierre Erny liefert einen weiteren Rahmen und erleichtert die Zuordnung der Beiträge.

Bd. 5, 2003, 192 S., 19,90 €, br., ISBN 3-8258-7247-5

LIT Verlag Berlin – Münster – Wien – Zürich – London

Auslieferung Deutschland / Österreich / Schweiz: siehe Impressumsseite

Relindis Dzeaye Yovsi
Ethnotheories about breastfeeding and mother-infant interaction
The case of sedentary Nso farmers and nomadic Fulani pastorals and their infants 3-6 months of age in Mbven sub Division of the Northwest province of Cameroon
Parenting styles and predominantly the breastfeeding of infants among the sedentary Nso farmers and nomadic Fulani pastorals of Cameroon have been appraised in this book. Breastfeeding is not only a process of infant feeding, but also a parenting system which is practiced differently in diverse cultures depending on the eco-cultural challenges. The primary socialization goal of the two groups is the health and survival of the child in a hazardous environment with high infant mortality rate. Yet, their ideas about self construal differ with the Nso following a more interdependent developmental pathway and the Fulani following a more individualistic pathway. The results are discussed with respect to their applicability for supporting breastfeeding in rural Africa, and also highlight how parenting strategies carve out the different psychological orientation profiles.
Bd. 4, 2003, 240 S., 25,90 €, br., ISBN 3-8258-6547-9

Gerhard Kubik
Zur ontogenetischen Basis der Inzestscheu
Ein kulturvergleichender Ansatz
Psychoanalyse und Ethnologie, afrikanische Feldforschung und Mythenanalyse verbinden sich in diesem Rundgang durch die Kulturen zu einer integrativen Reinterpretation verschiedenster Inzesttheorien. Dabei geht es nicht um den realen Inzest, sondern um Inzestverbote als gesellschaftspolitische Strategien und Inzestscheu als komplexe Abwehrreaktion des Individuums gegen seine Rückkehr zu den primären Objektbindungen, an denen es so schmerzhaft enttäuscht wurde.
Bd. 3, 2003, 96 S., 15,90 €, br., ISBN 3-8258-6024-8

Gerhard Kubik
Totemismus
Ethnopsychologische Forschungsmaterialien und Interpretationen aus Ost- und Zentralafrika, 1962 – 2002
Afrika war aus der Totemismus-Diskussion in der Ethnologie des frühen 20. Jahrhunderts so gut wie ausgeklammert. Aber gerade im subsaharanischen Afrika finden sich vielfach Systeme postulierter Verwandtschaft mit Tier/Pflanzen-Symbolen und Tabus, die heute ethnopsychoanalytisch auflösbar sind. Unbelastet von den evolutionistischen und religionshistorischen Interpretationen von einst gehen der Autor Gerhard Kubik und seine Mitarbeiter – Maurice Djenda (Z.A.R.), Charles Sekintu (Buganda) und andere – an dieses Thema auf der Basis lokaler Terminologie und zeichnerischer Darstellungen heran. Schwerpunkte sind u.a. die Phänomene tumbi oder ajeõ der Mpyɛmɔ̃ im äquatorialen Waldland der Z.A.R. und die Doppeltotems omuziro und akabbiro eines jeden Menschen im Königreich Buganda, dargestellt aus intrakultureller und psychoanalytischer Sicht.
Bd. 2, 2003, 144 S., 20,90 €, br., ISBN 3-8258-6023-x

Werner Egli; Vera Saller; David Signer (Hg.)
Neuere Entwicklungen der Ethnopsychoanalyse
Beiträge zu einer Tagung im Dezember 2001 in Zürich
„Die Ethnopsychoanalyse auf akademischem Boden ist zwar geschrumpft, in der lokalen Szene hat sie sich aber einen Überlebensraum in der psychosozialen Beratungsarbeit mit Flüchtlingen und Migranten geschaffen und damit gleichzeitig ein neues Berufsfeld für Ethnologen und Psychologen abgesteckt. In dieser Beratungsarbeit gingen in den letzten Jahren Professionalisierungs- und Spezialisierungsprozesse vor sich, bei denen auch ethnopsychoanalytische Denktraditionen eine Rolle spielen. Ähnliche Prozesse lassen sich an verschiedenen Orten beobachten; ihre Protagonistinnen und Protagonisten kämpfen auf vorgeschobenen Posten auf psychosozialem Neuland.“
(Aus der Einleitung von Johannes Reichmayr)
Bd. 1, 2002, 208 S., 20,90 €, br., ISBN 3-8258-6070-1

LIT Verlag Berlin – Münster – Wien – Zürich – London
Auslieferung Deutschland / Österreich / Schweiz: siehe Impressumsseite